- Note from the Publisher -

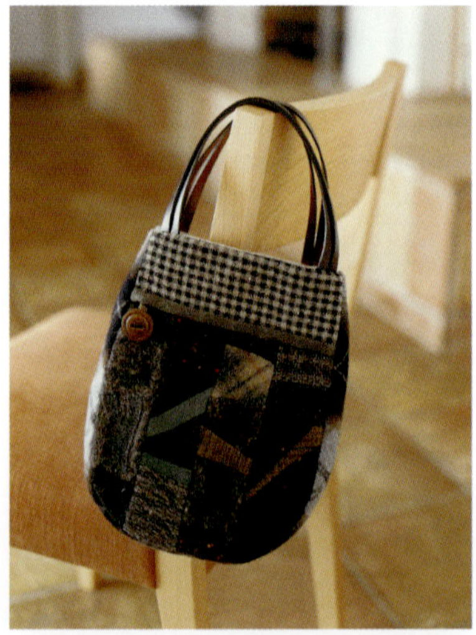

Welcome to a glimpse into the world of international quilting. At Stitch Publications our wish is for you to be able to explore beyond the boundaries of the country you live in to experience and see what other fiber artists are doing.

In many countries, rather than learning from various books, quilters study under a single master, spending years progressing from simple techniques to the extremely difficult. Intricate designs are celebrated and sewing and quilting by hand is honored and as such, hand-quilting is the typical method used to quilt.

This book was written in its original language, Japanese, by a master quilter, Yoko Saito. We have done our best to make the directions for each project easy to understand if you have some level of quilting experience, while maintaining the appearance and intent of the original author and publisher.

We hope the beautifully designed handmade items in this book inspire and encourage you to make them for yourself.

- Important Tips Before You Begin -

The following facts might suggest that intermediate or advanced quilters will be more comfortable working on these projects.

- Techniques -

Certain detailed descriptions of specific techniques are located in the first half of the book, however, the author assumes that the creator is familiar with sewing, quilting and bag-making techniques to some degree. It is advisable to read through and understand each project's direction page from the beginning to end, including finding the corresponding pattern on the included pattern sheet pages.

- Measurements -

The original designs were created using the metric system for dimensions. In order to assist you, we have included the imperial system measurements in brackets. However, please note that samples that appear in the book were created and tested using the metric system. Thus, you will find that if you use the imperial measurements to make the projects, the items you make will not be exactly the same size as when using the metric measurements.

- Patterns/Templates -

Full pattern information for each project appears in several different ways: a) in the materials list b) in the illustrations and captions c) in the pattern sheet inserts. One must read through all the instructions carefully to understand what size to cut the fabric and related materials including instructions for each project relating to seam allowances.

Stitch Publications, 2013

This book, more than some of her others, have less step-by-step detailed instructions and relies heavily on the illustrations for each project. Although the numbers in squares or circles give you the order in which to work, they will often make you jump from one page to another as details are given for specific sub-steps. Read through the instructions and study the illustrations carefully for understanding before beginning any of the projects for the best result.

Legend

1. - Black squares with numbers in them indicate the main steps in a project.

1a - White squares with numbers and letters in them indicate further details in a step.

❶ - Black circles with numbers in them indicate the sub-steps in a given step.

Yoko Saito's

Woolwork

Bags, Pouches and Quilts that Add Color to our Lives

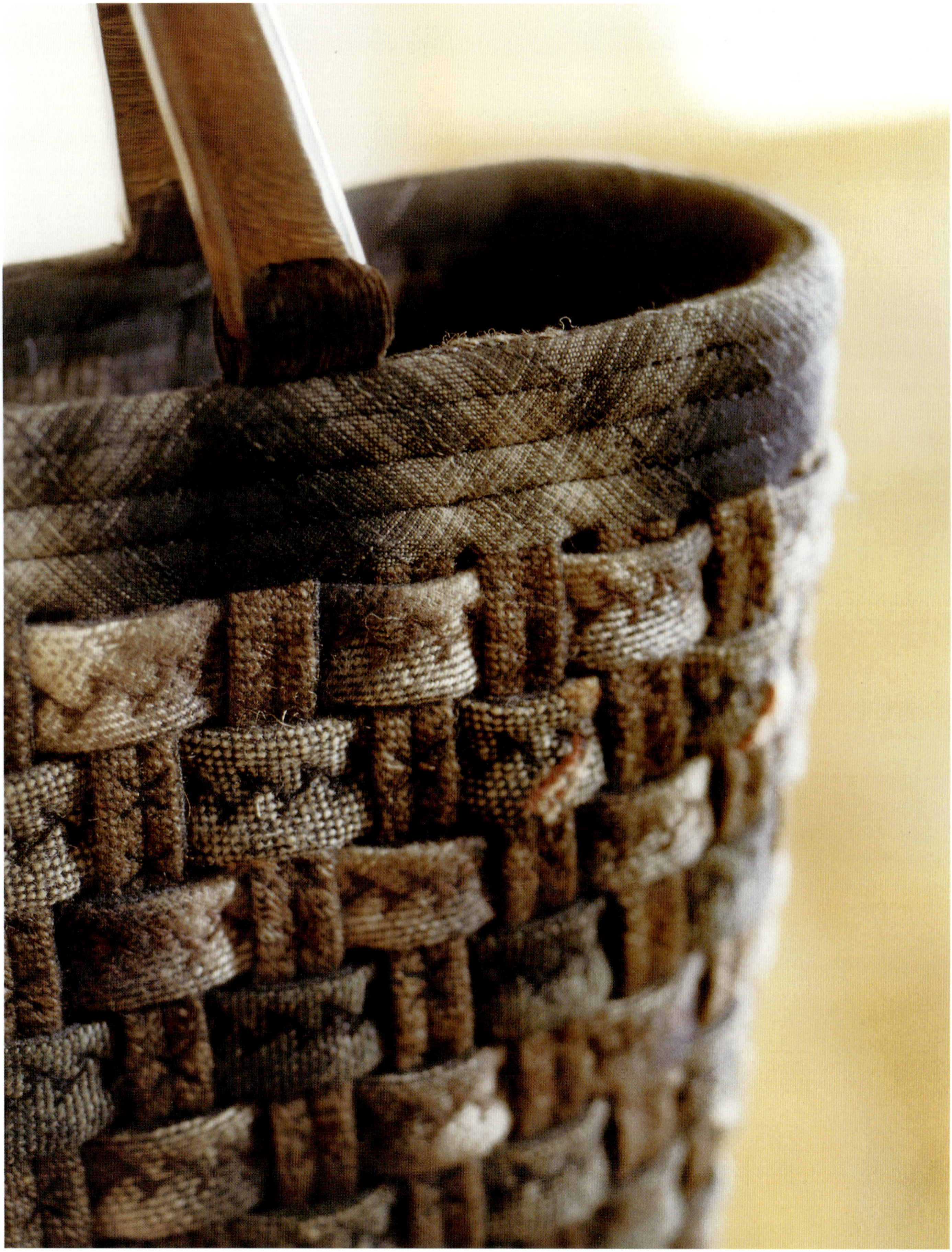

Around the same time that I became interested in patchwork and quilting, I also learned of the art of rug hooking, but had only seen it made into rugs for the floor. Although I had used wool for other purposes, when it came to patchwork, I only worked with printed cottons or homespuns. It had not occurred to me that the use of wool would create such visually fresh and wonderful projects.

In the era long past when quilting and hooked rugs became prominent in many households, every last bit of available material was used toward making useful items for the family and home; nothing went to waste. Compared to cotton, wool would've been equally, if not more so, treasured as a material to create usable items as it was warmer and more durable. Thus, it made sense that hooked rugs were embraced not only for their usefulness, but beauty of the designs.

Some years ago, on a trip to America, I began to notice that wool was being used more and more in quilts and other projects. So interested was I, that I began to collect wool clothing and items that were out of style, too small or ready for donation to use in my own projects.

Due to the thickness of wool in comparison to cottons and other fabric, the finished projects are rarely made up of many intricate pieces. Rather, they tend to be of a more rustic nature and give a warm and relaxed feel. Even those sewers and quilters who feel they are not skilled at traditional appliqué on cottons or other materials should find it less challenging when using wool. I hope you enjoy exploring the wonders of using wool as I have done in the projects in this book.

Yoko Saito

Contents

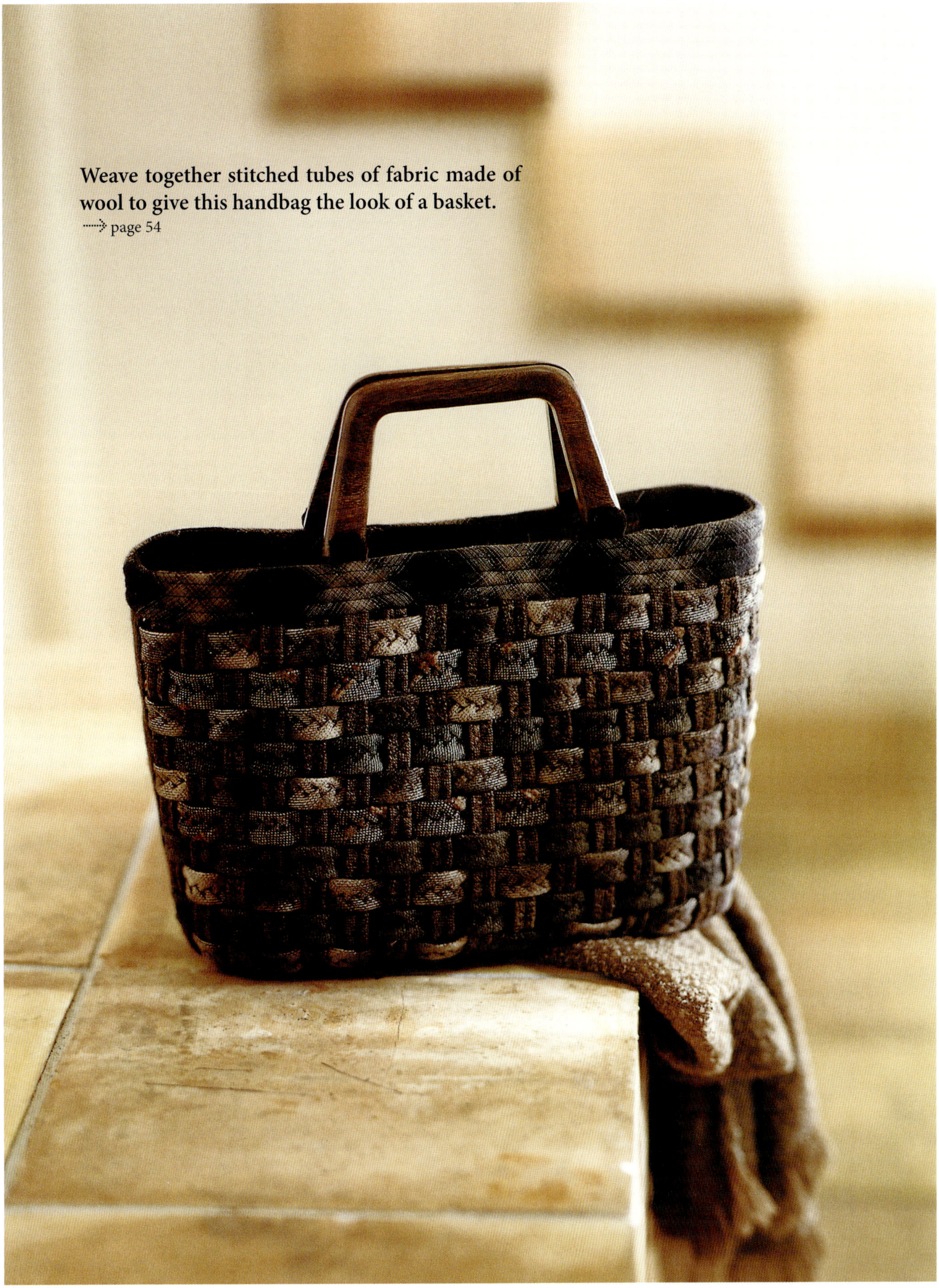

Weave together stitched tubes of fabric made of wool to give this handbag the look of a basket.

⇢ page 54

Basketweave Handbag 1

2 Semi-Circle Handbag

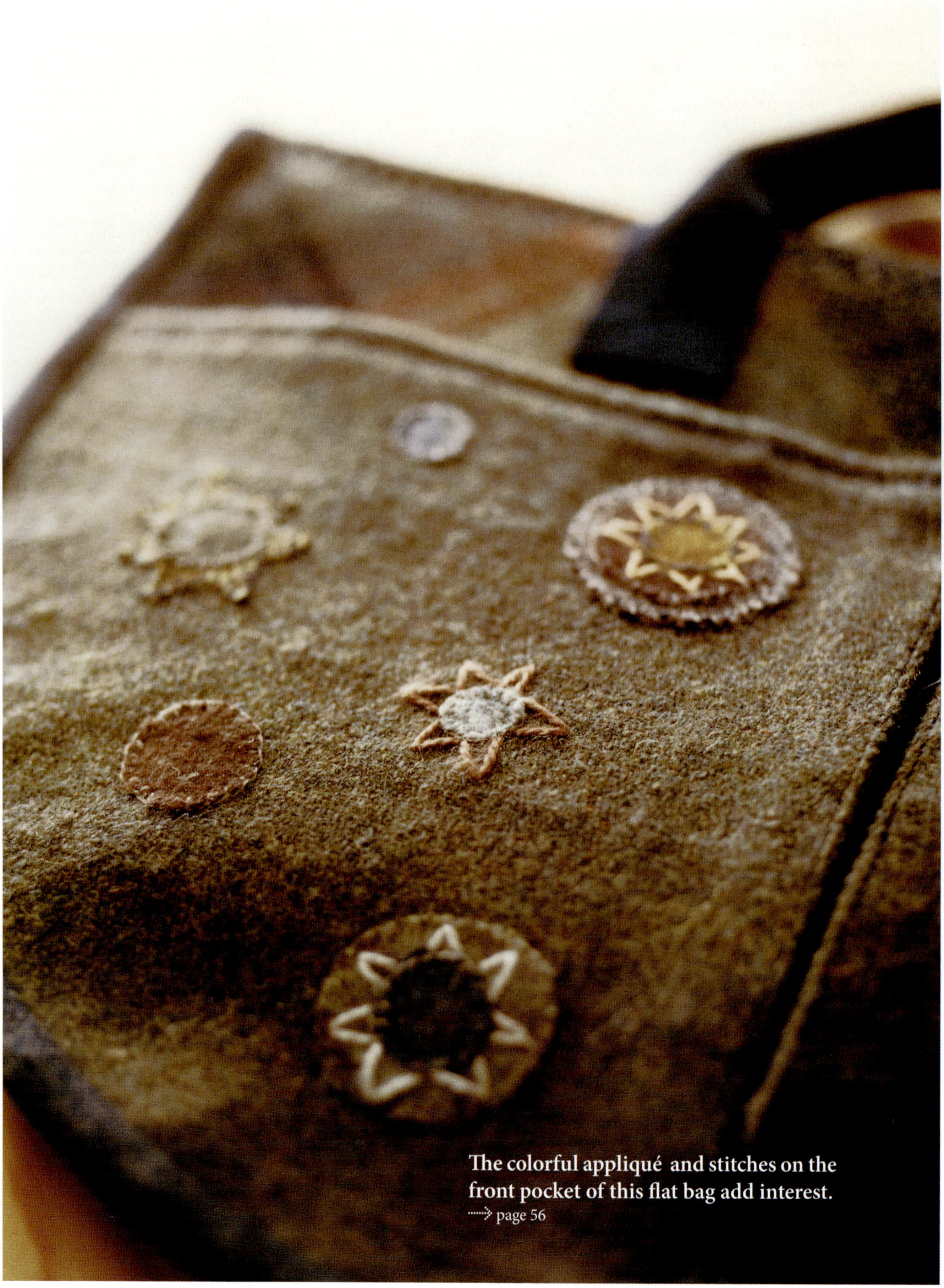

The colorful appliqué and stitches on the front pocket of this flat bag add interest.

⇢ page 56

◆ Appliqué

When it comes to working with small pieces of wool, it is often better to appliqué them onto a background piece rather than trying to piece them together. See the next two pages for an introduction to appliquéing wool.

1 Choose either 2 strands of embroidery thread or 1 strand of perle cotton for your appliqués depending on usage. Use the 2-strand embroidery thread when dealing with intricate or small shapes. Use the perle cotton when you want the design to stand out.

1

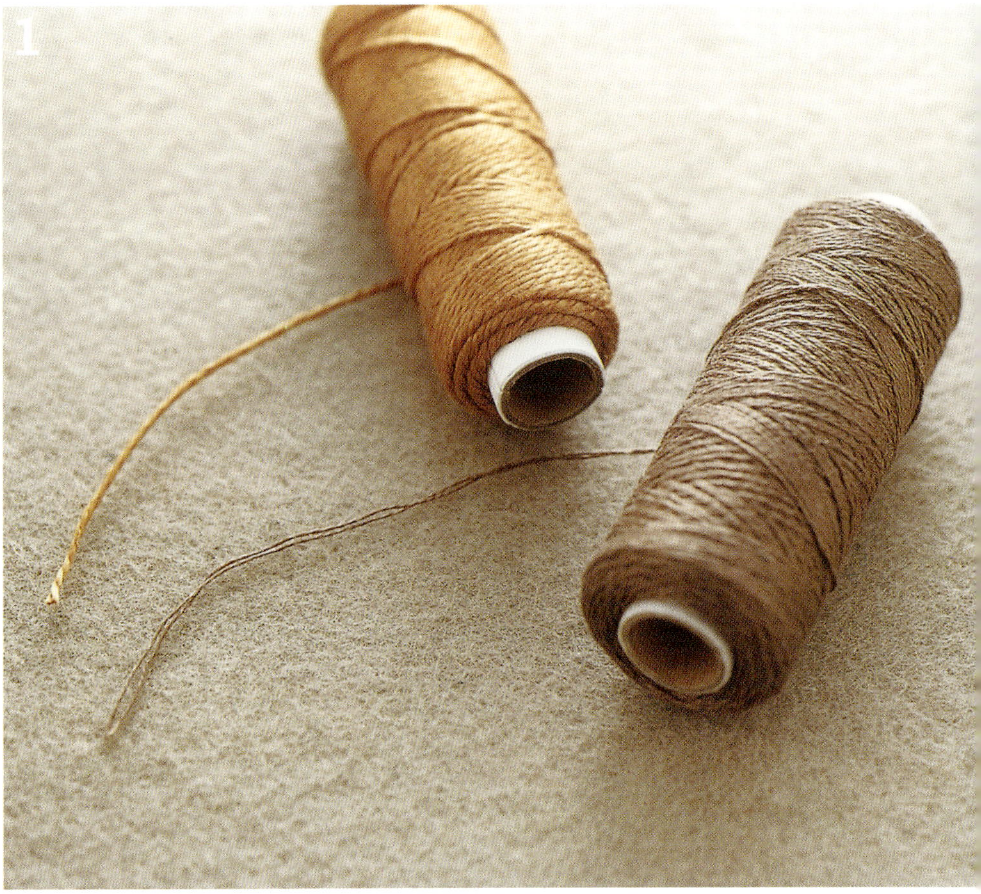

2

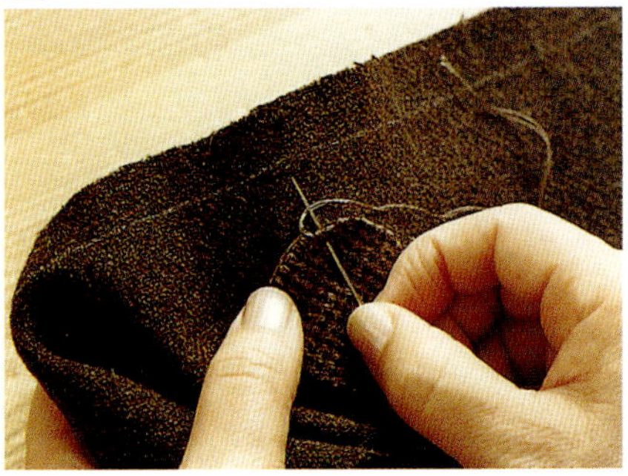

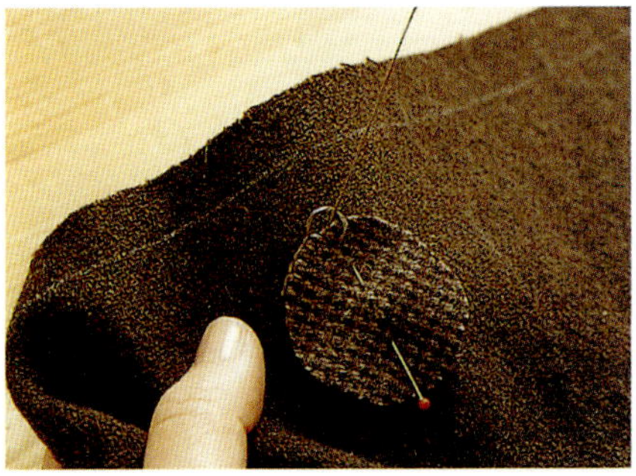

3

2 Cut out each appliqué shape to the exact size. Don't worry if the edges of the pieces fray somewhat as the stitching will keep the fraying to a minimum. Using a blanket stitch, stitch the appliqués to the background fabric.

3 Using 2 strands and coming up from underneath, bring the needle out at the edge. From the top, insert the needle 0.3~0.5 cm [⅛" or ¼"] down and over to catch the edge, bringing the needle back out at the edge equidistant to the first stitch. Loop the thread behind the needle and pull through. Repeat this as you work your way to the right all the way around.

4 The bottom layer stitched down.

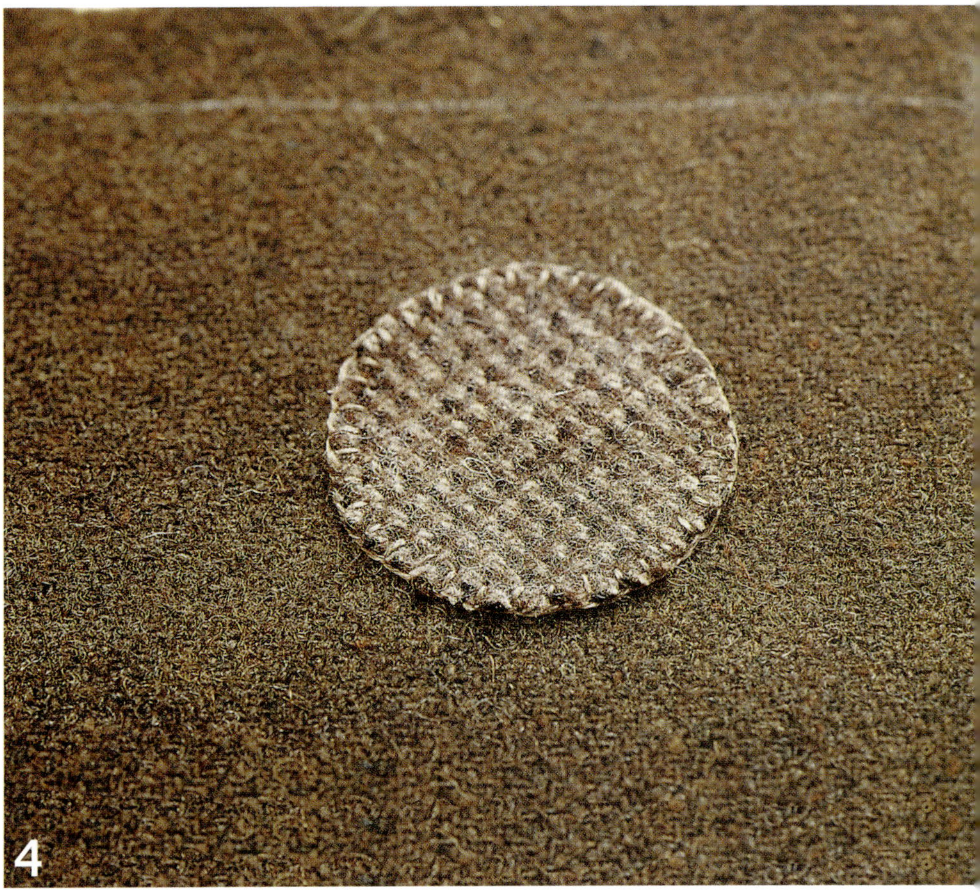

4

5 Center and attach the smaller circle on top of the bottom layer. Using tiny stitches, blanket stitch it down. Use perle cotton and a straight stitch for the star.
6 The completed second layer.

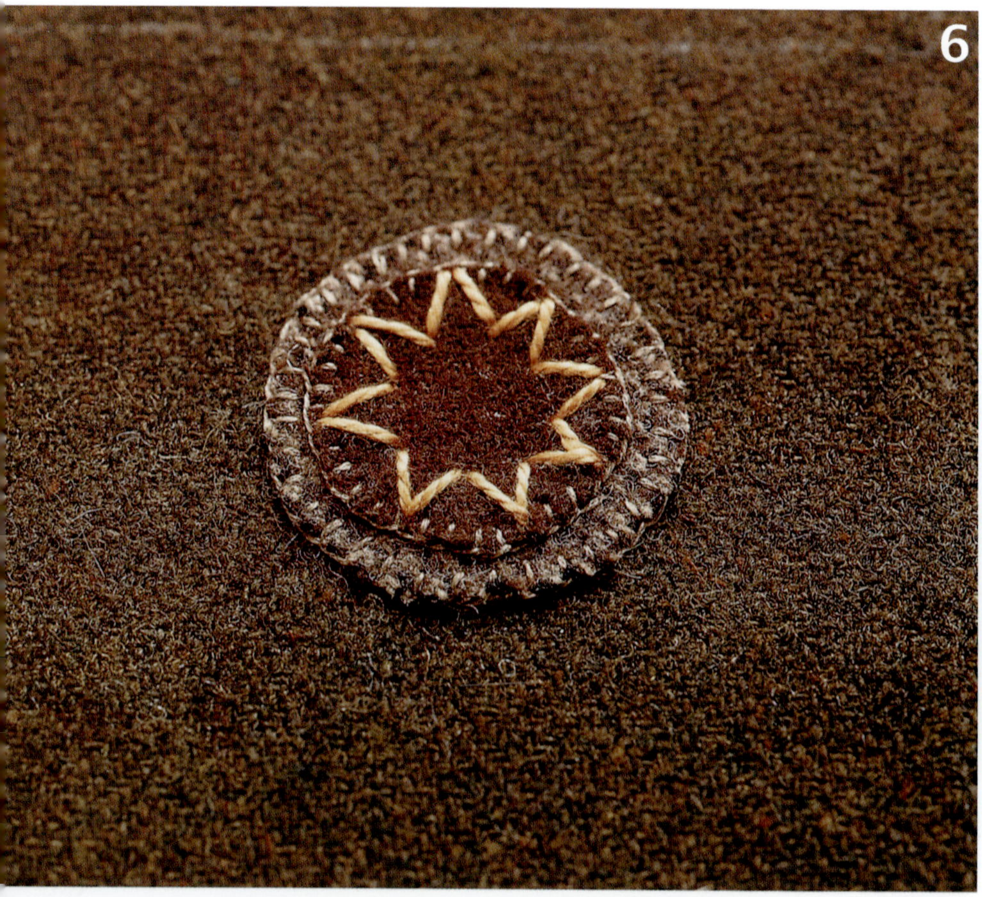
6

5

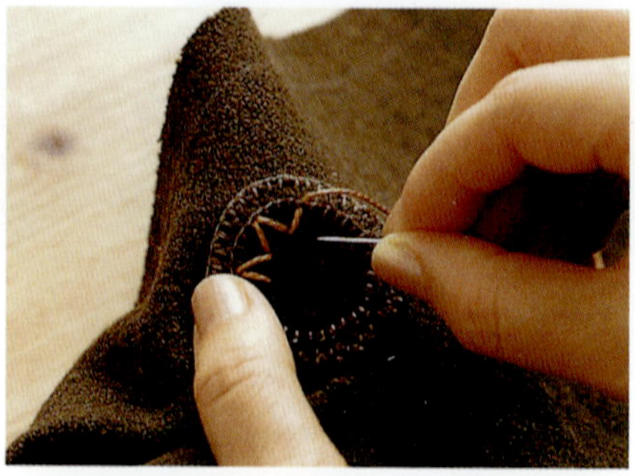

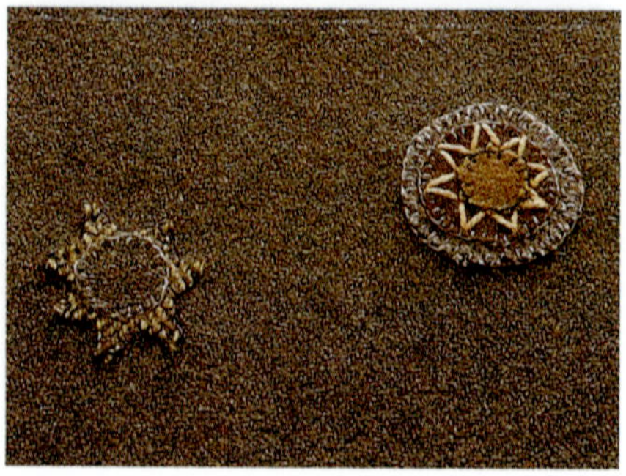

8

7 Layer the smallest circle in the middle of the star and stitch down using the blanket stitch.
8 You can layer as many pieces on top of each other as you like and blanket stitch down. Layering can add extra depth and interest to your designs.

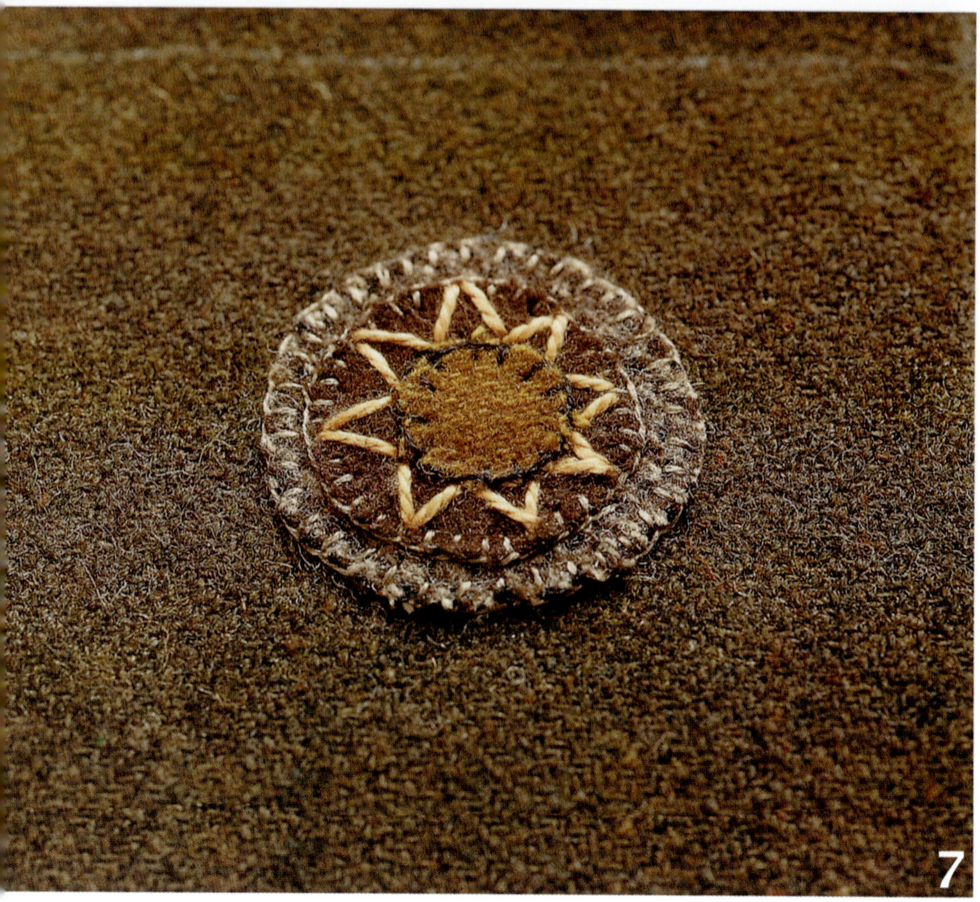
7

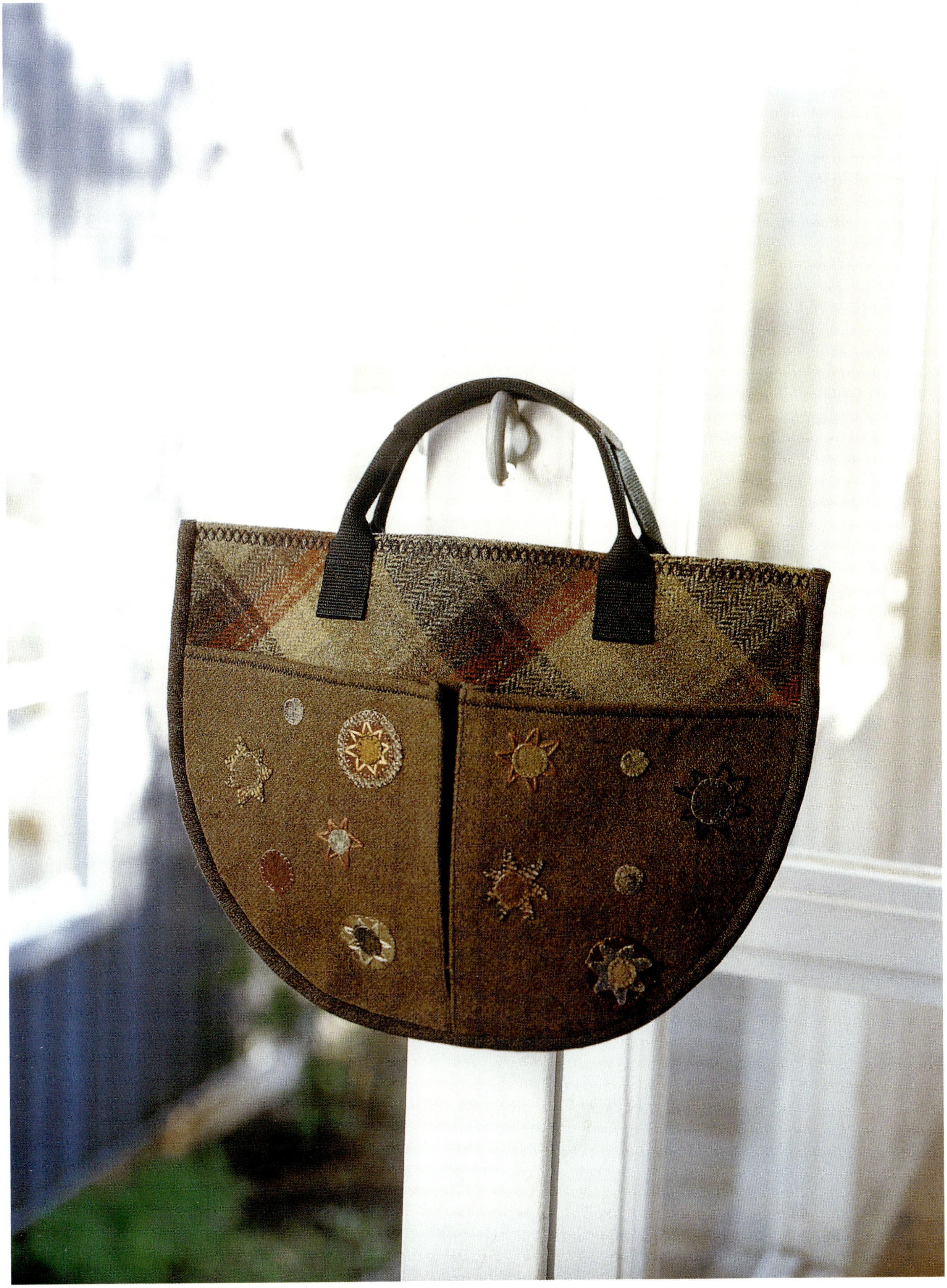

2

3 City Skyline Pouch

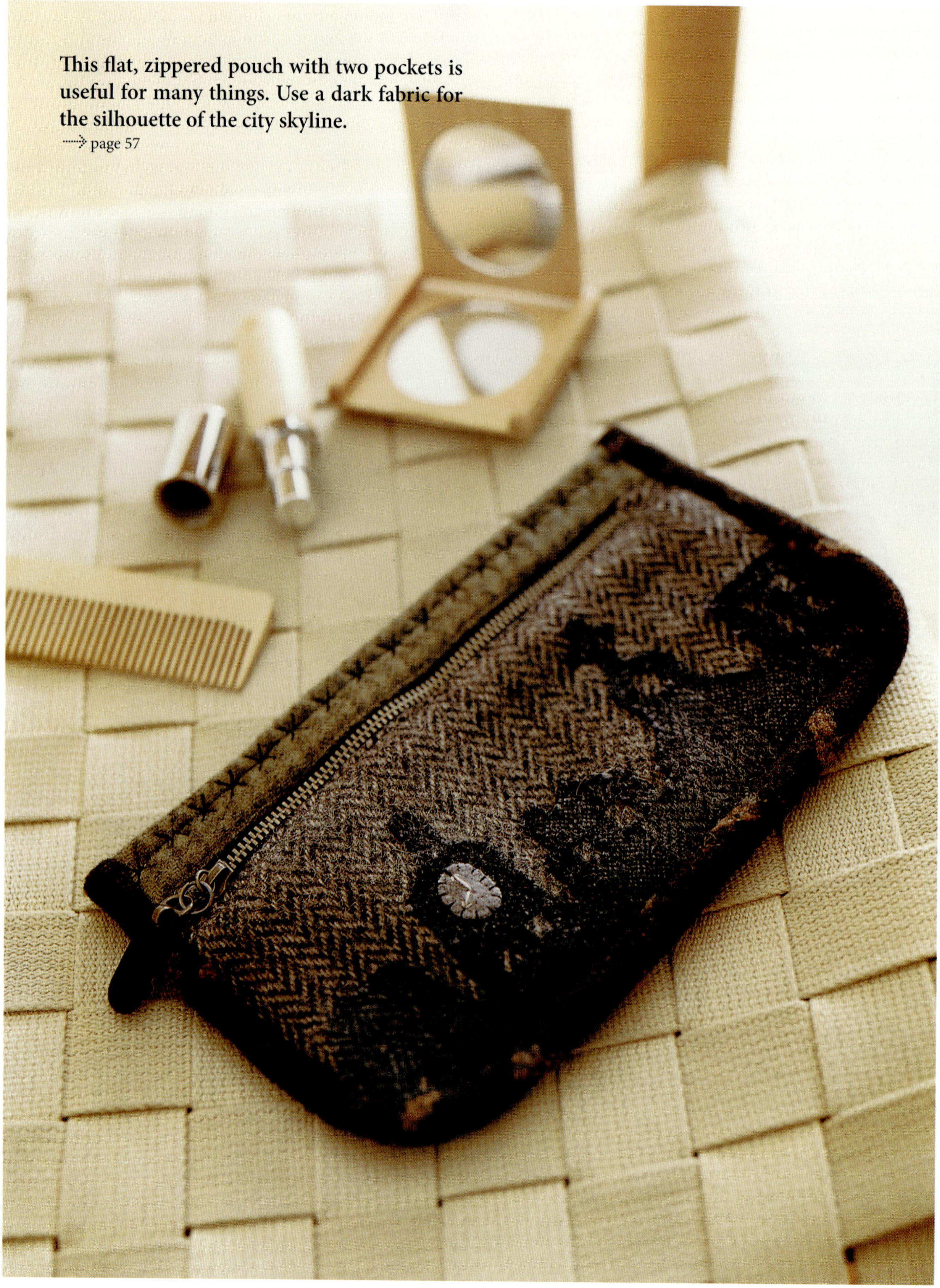

This flat, zippered pouch with two pockets is useful for many things. Use a dark fabric for the silhouette of the city skyline.

→ page 57

It is easy to keep small things organized in this little drawstring bag. Use matching embroidery thread for the stitches along the vertical seams so that they blend into the background.

→ page 58

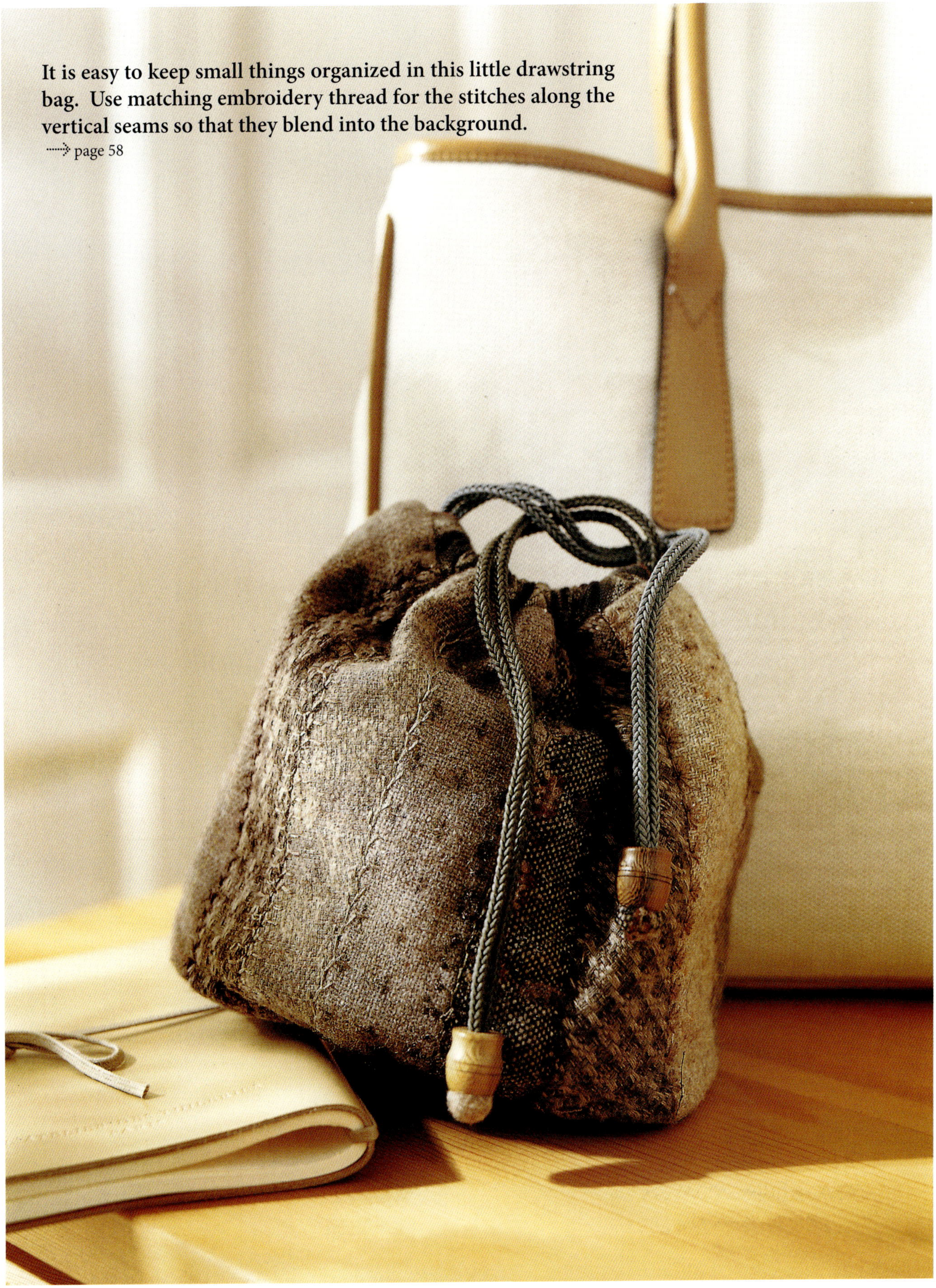

5 Crazy Quilt Boston Bag

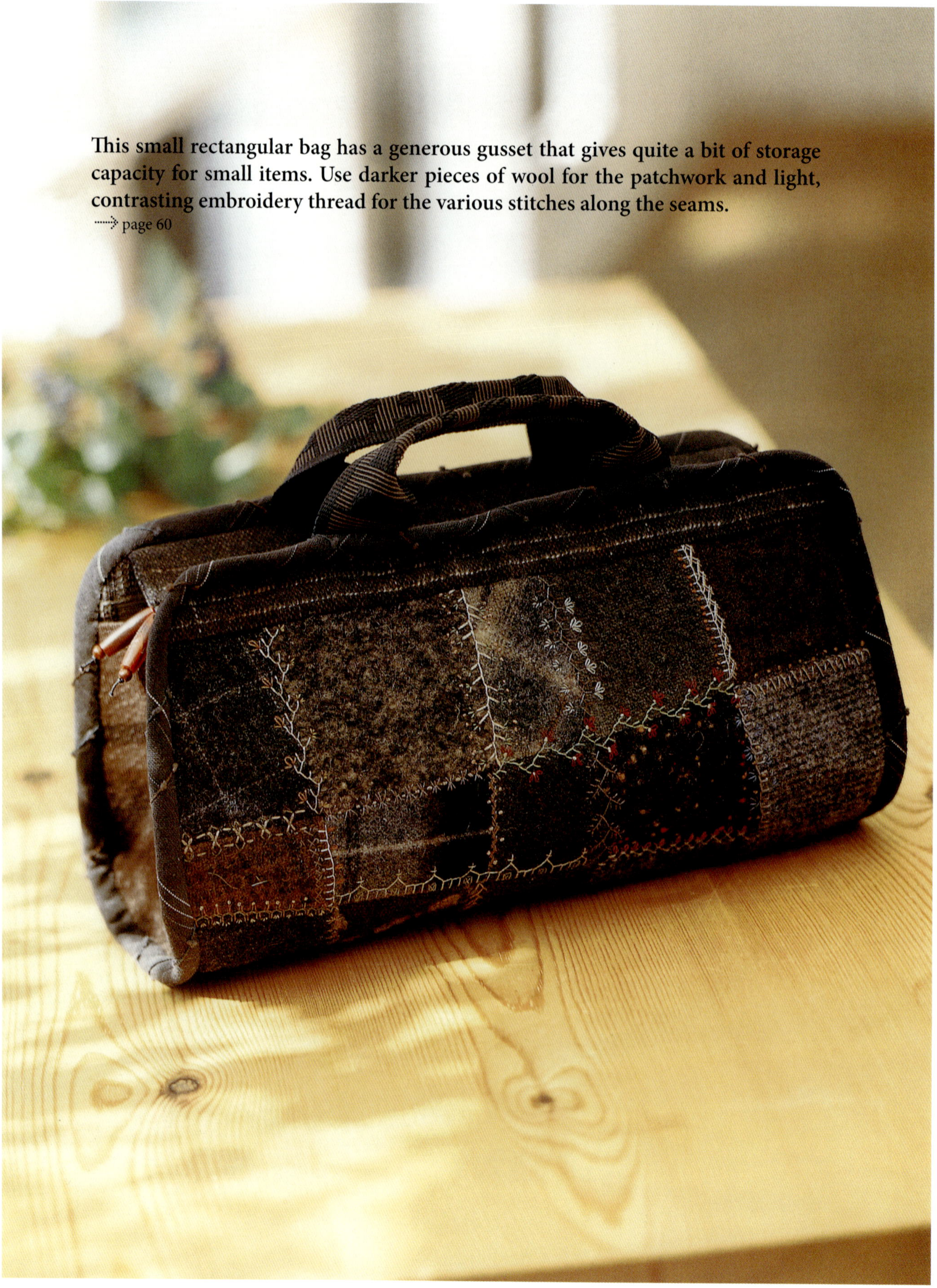

This small rectangular bag has a generous gusset that gives quite a bit of storage capacity for small items. Use darker pieces of wool for the patchwork and light, contrasting embroidery thread for the various stitches along the seams.

⋯⋯> page 60

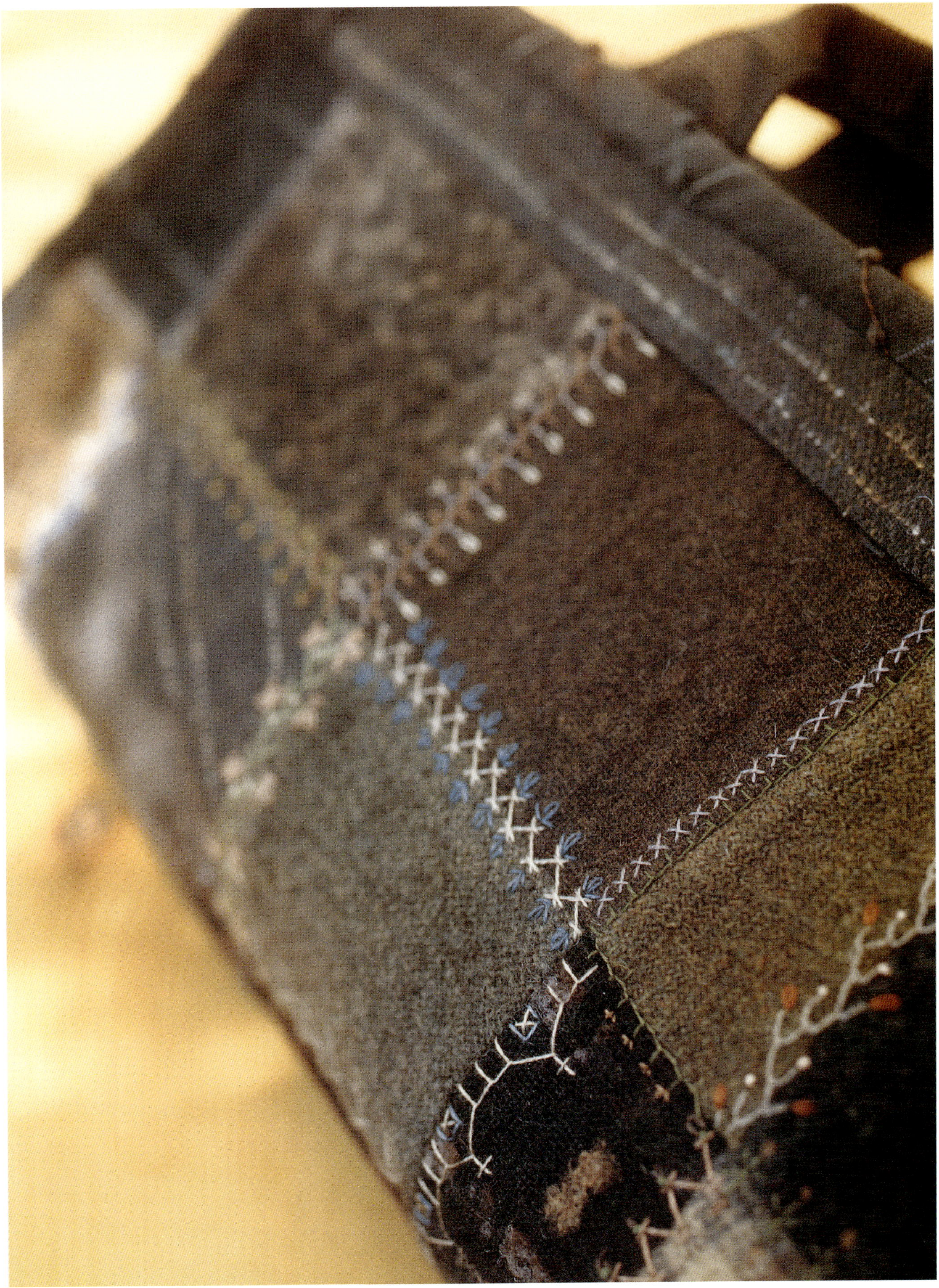

5

For the body of this chic and stylish handbag, take advantage of a checkerboard patterned wool and quilt it. The handbag flap is made by piecing together small squares of wool.

⇢ page 62

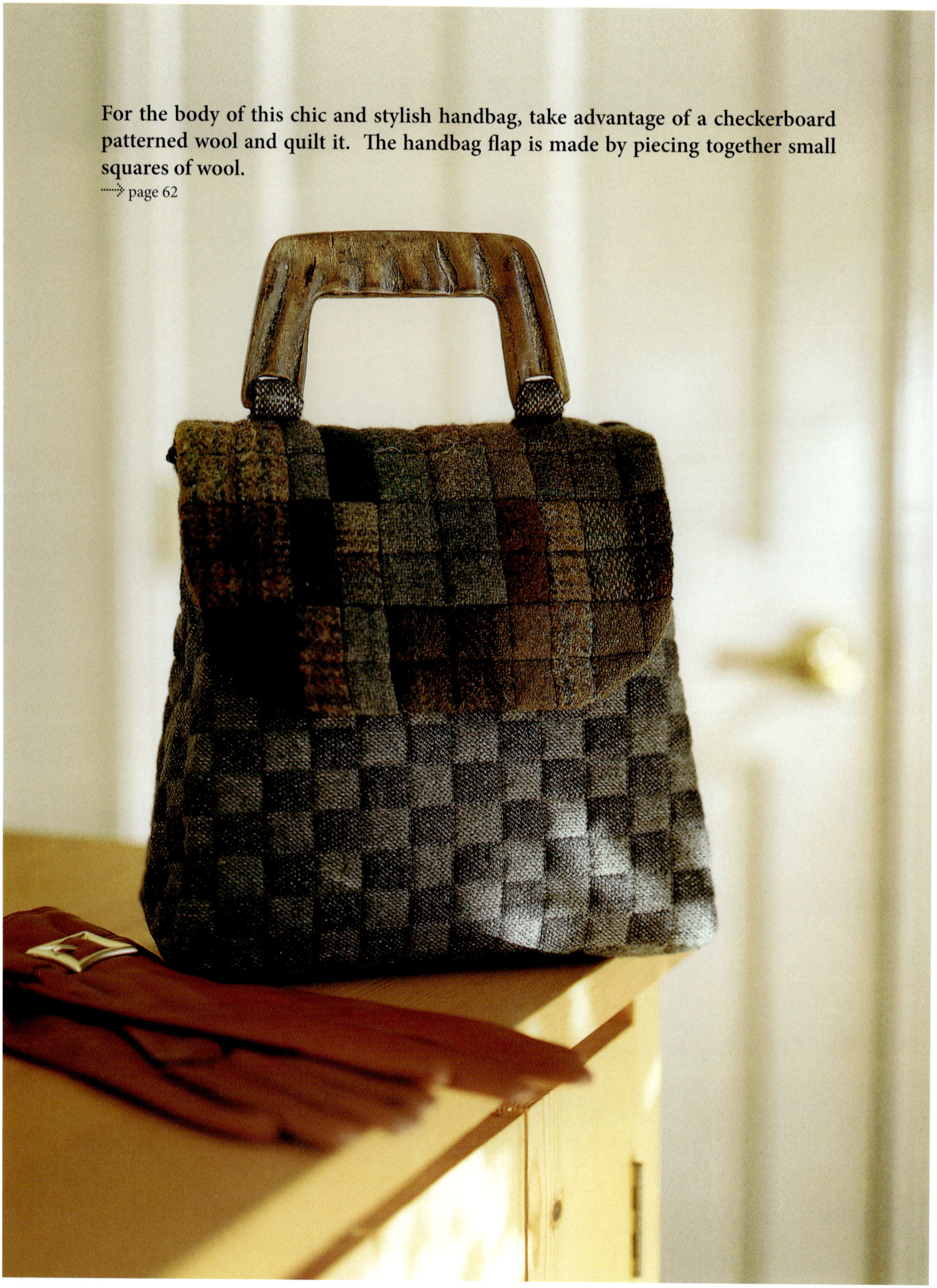

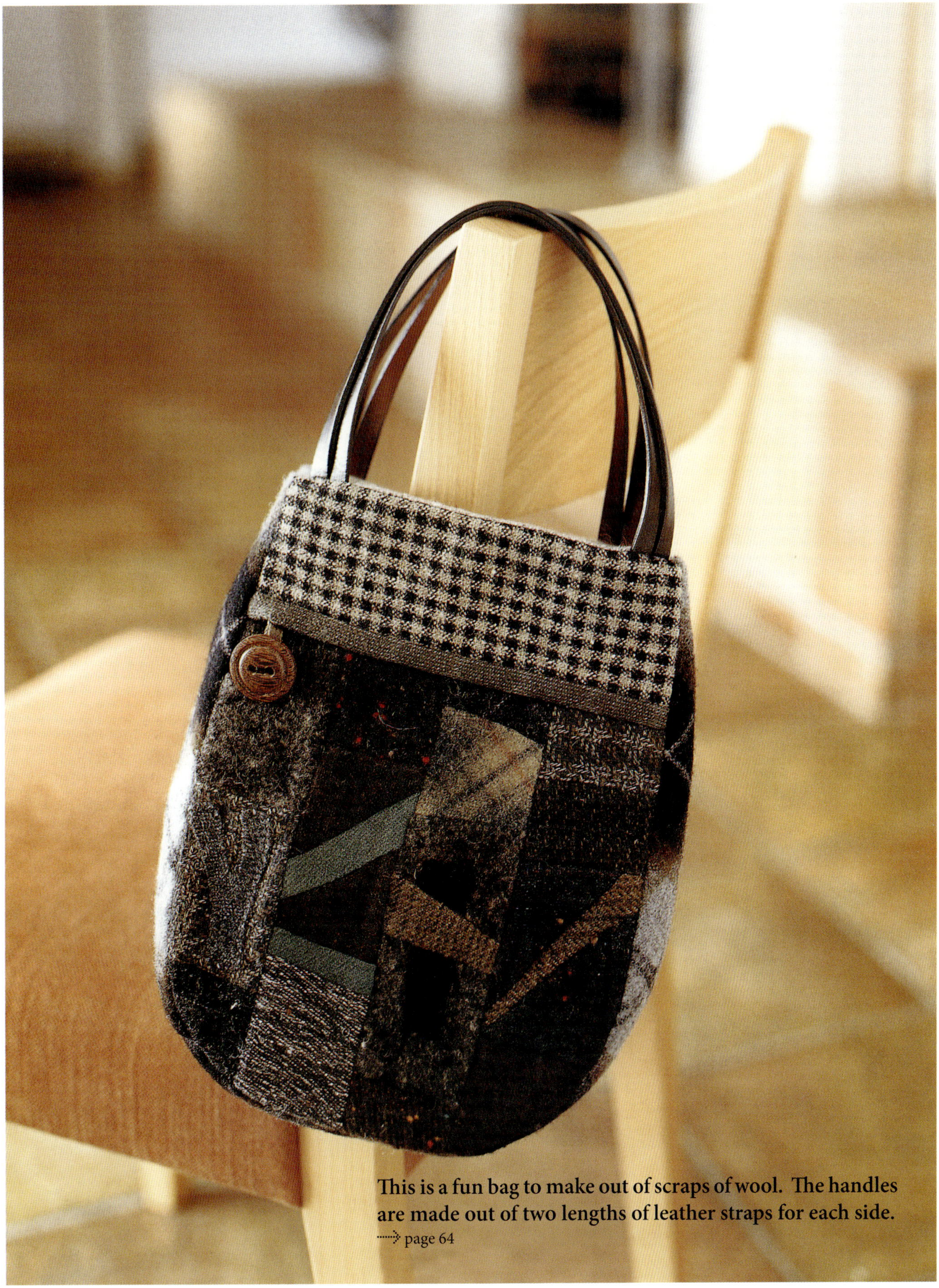

This is a fun bag to make out of scraps of wool. The handles are made out of two lengths of leather straps for each side.

⇢ page 64

8 Linus' Wall Quilt

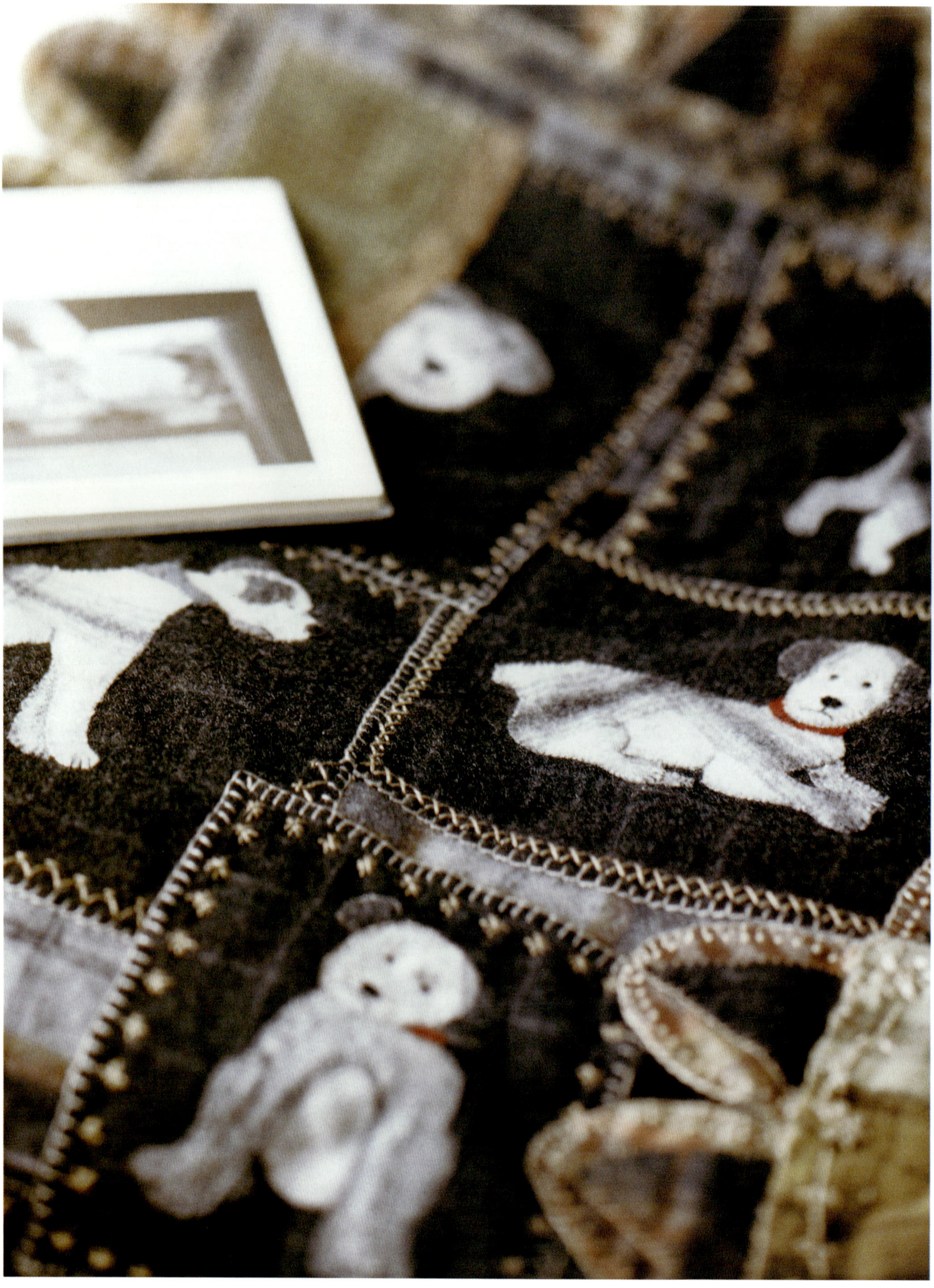

Linus, our miniature Schnauzer, is a beloved member of our family. Each block depicts him in a variety of cute poses with many of his funny facial expressions. The outer border is made up of individual wool appliqués that are then stitched to the borders with a blanket stitch.

⇢ page 66

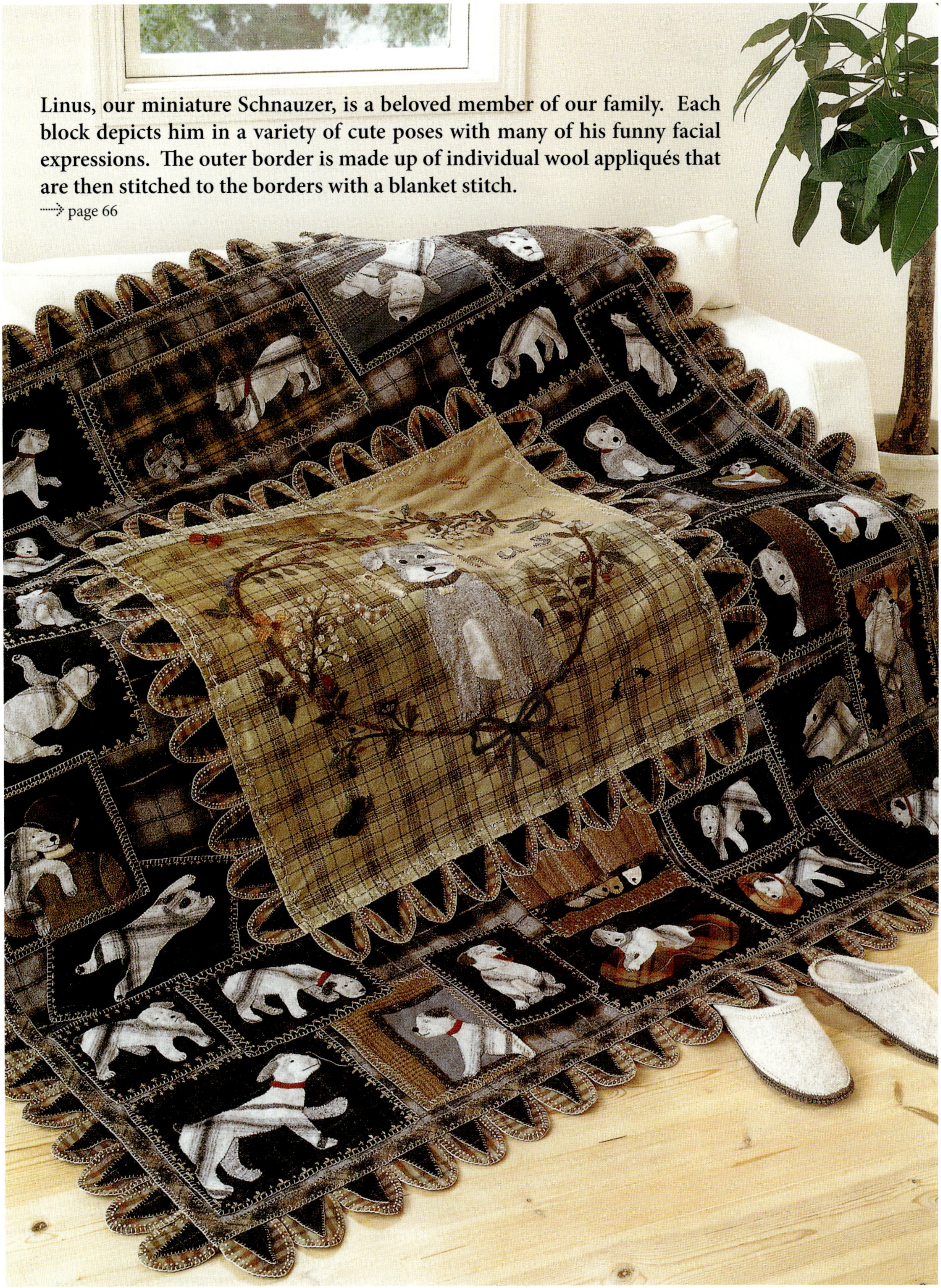

8

Fluffy looking snowflakes are needle-felted onto the wool in this fun winter project that includes a small pouch and a warm woolen scarf.

⇢ page 68

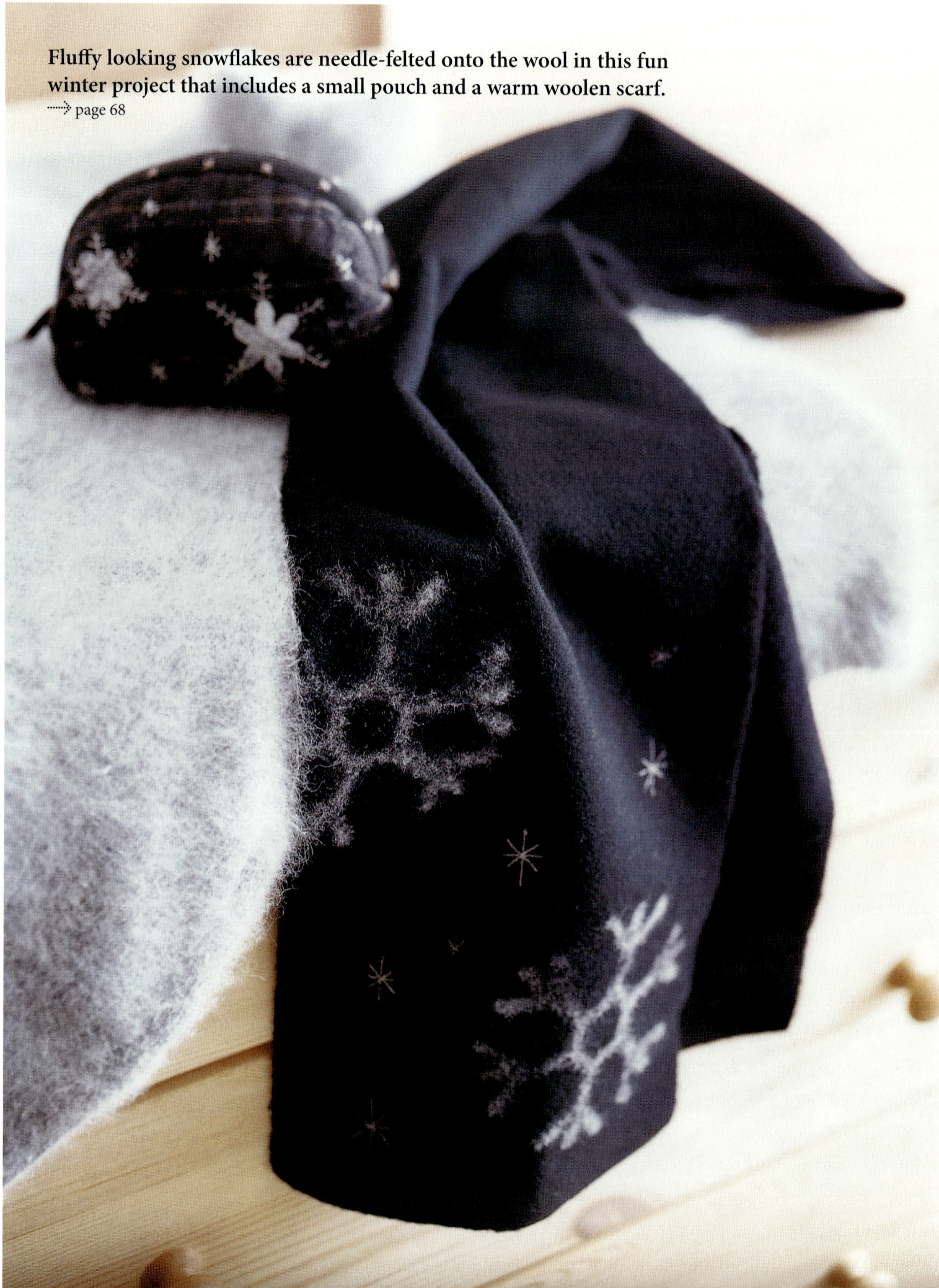

◆ Needle Felting Appliqués

In this project I use not only appliqués and embroidery, but introduce needle felting wool pieces onto background fabrics for a softer look.

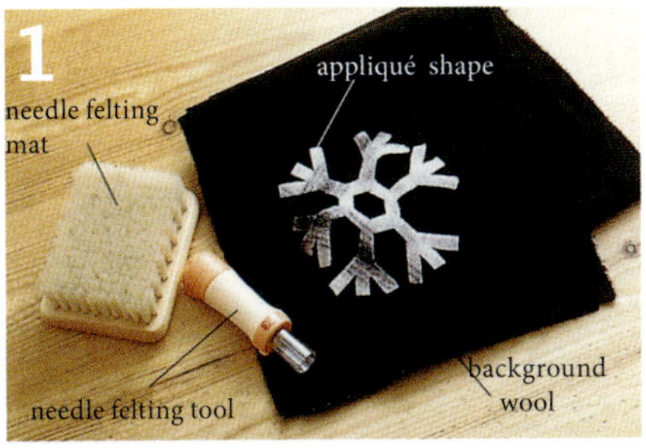

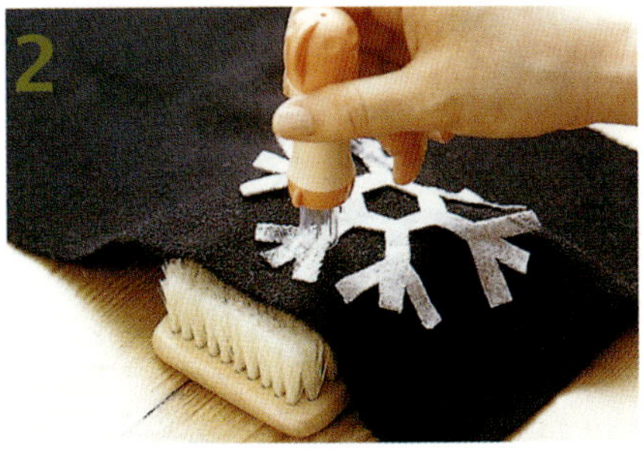

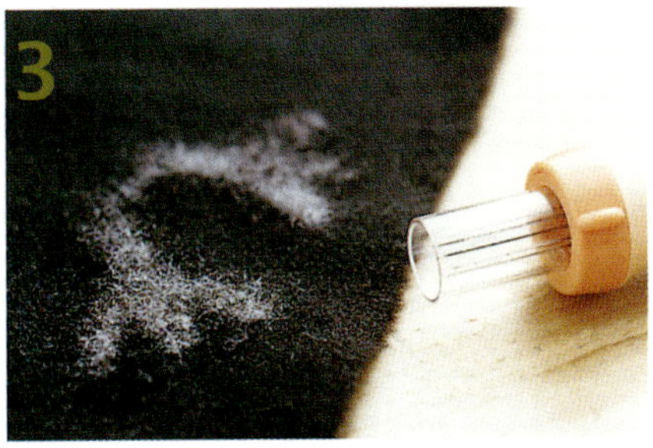

1 The tools necessary for needle felting include the needle felting mat, the punching tool, your background wool fabric and a contrasting wool appliqué.
2 Place the background wool, wrong side facing up, on the mat with the appliqué on top.
3 Using the tool, punch the needles through the appliqué into the background.
4 The appliqué shape will bloom on the right side of the background fabric.
5 Once completed, on the wrong side, the appliqué shape is firmly embedded into the background fabric, allowing for two distinct looks, depending on how you choose to wear it.

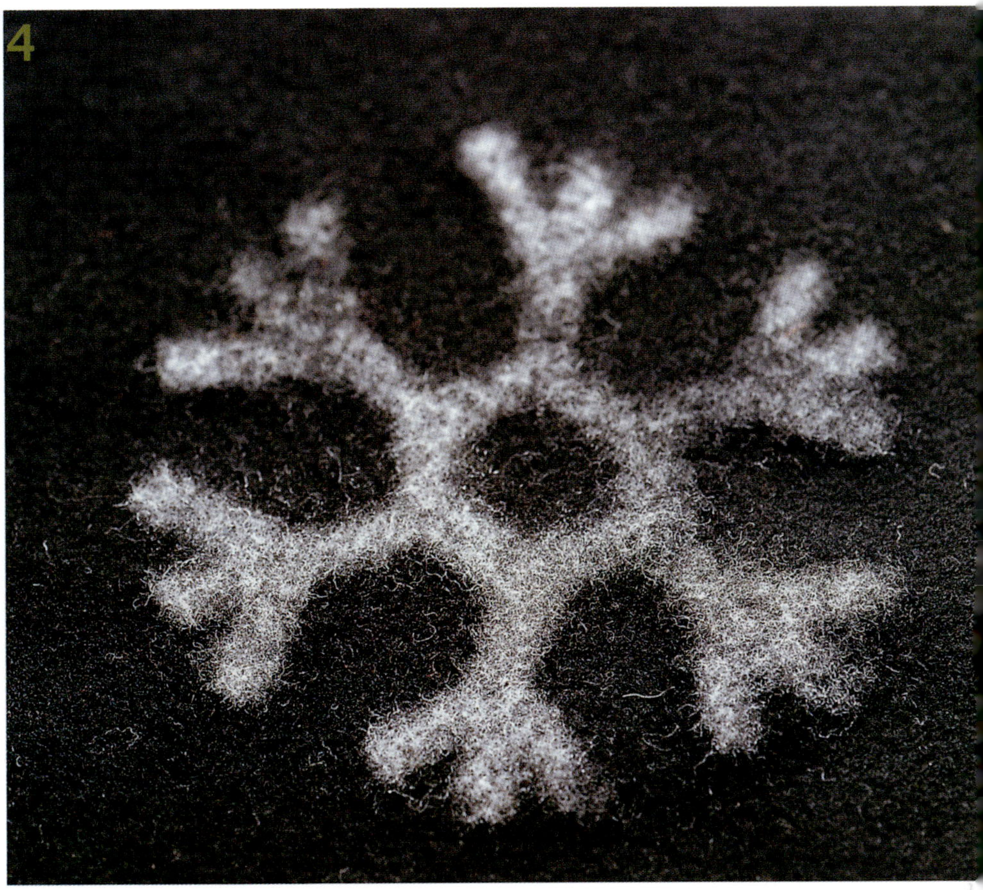

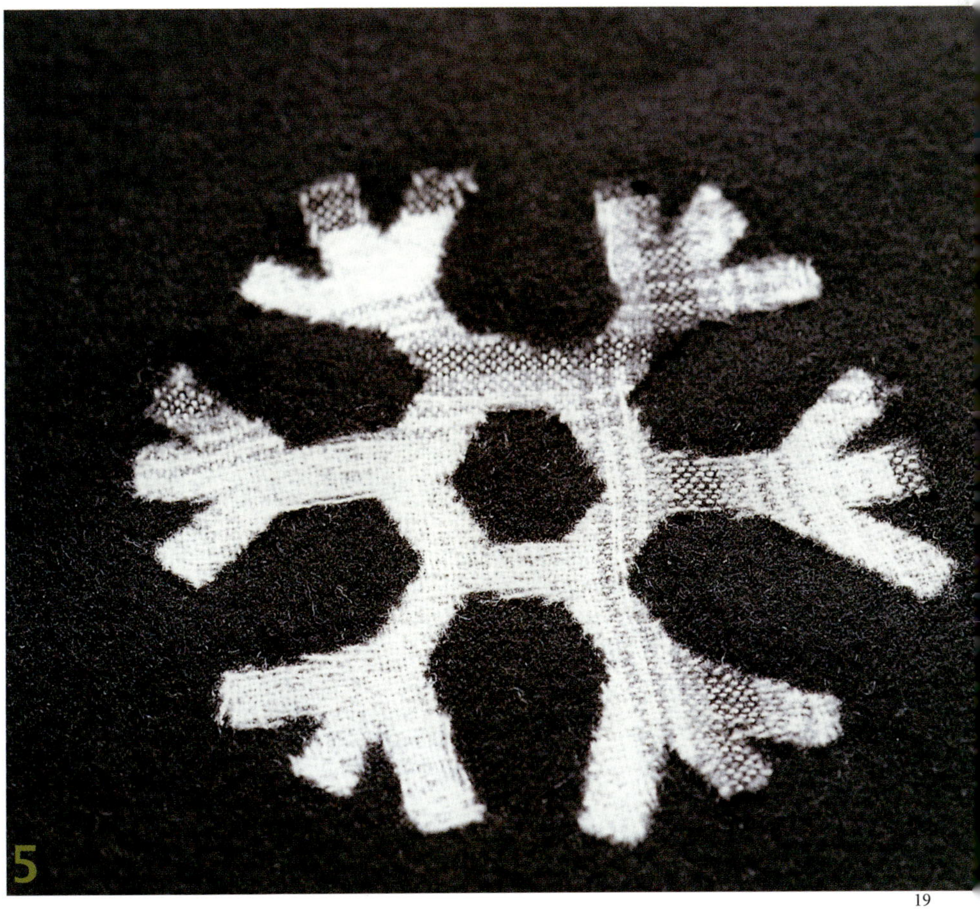

10

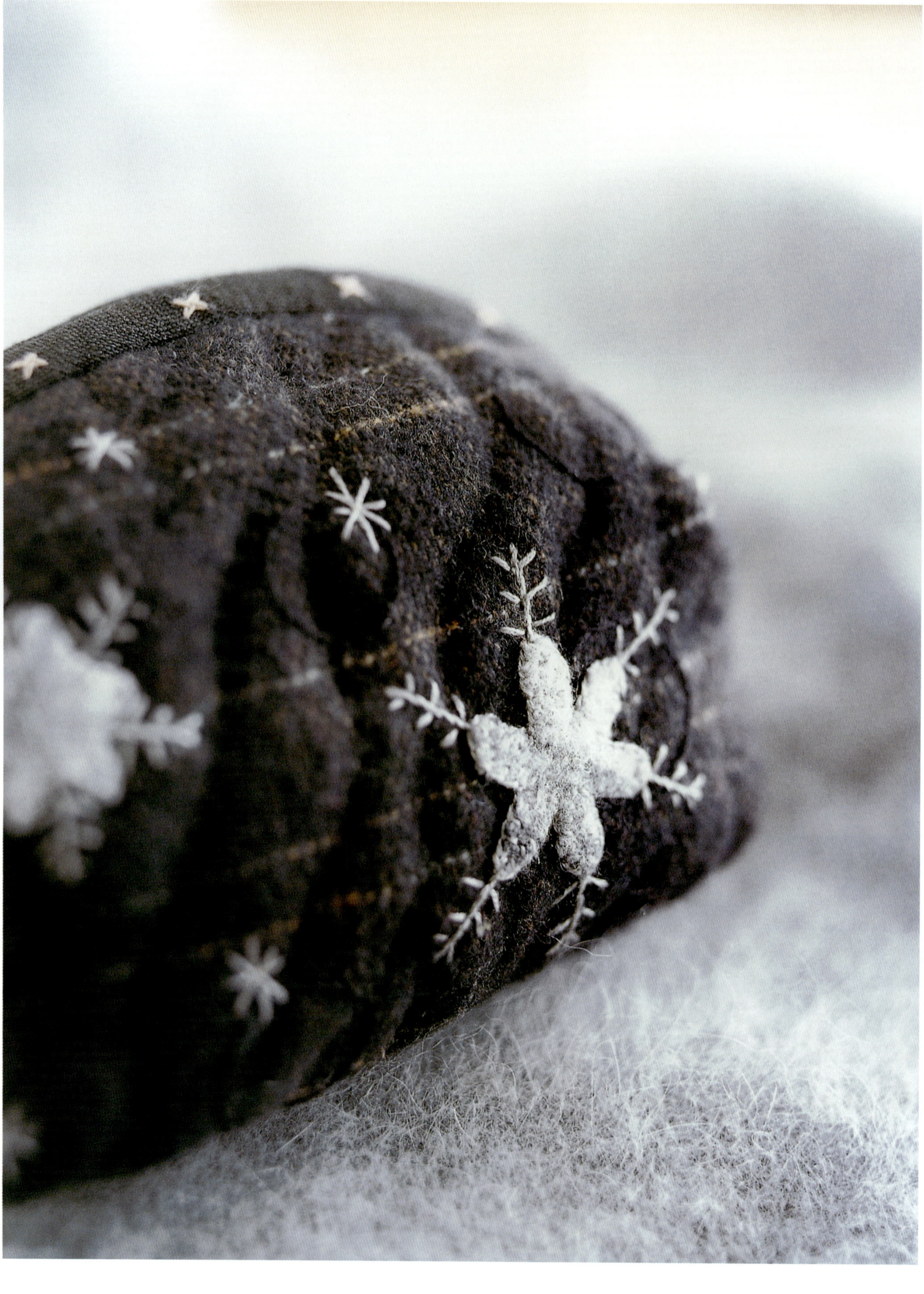

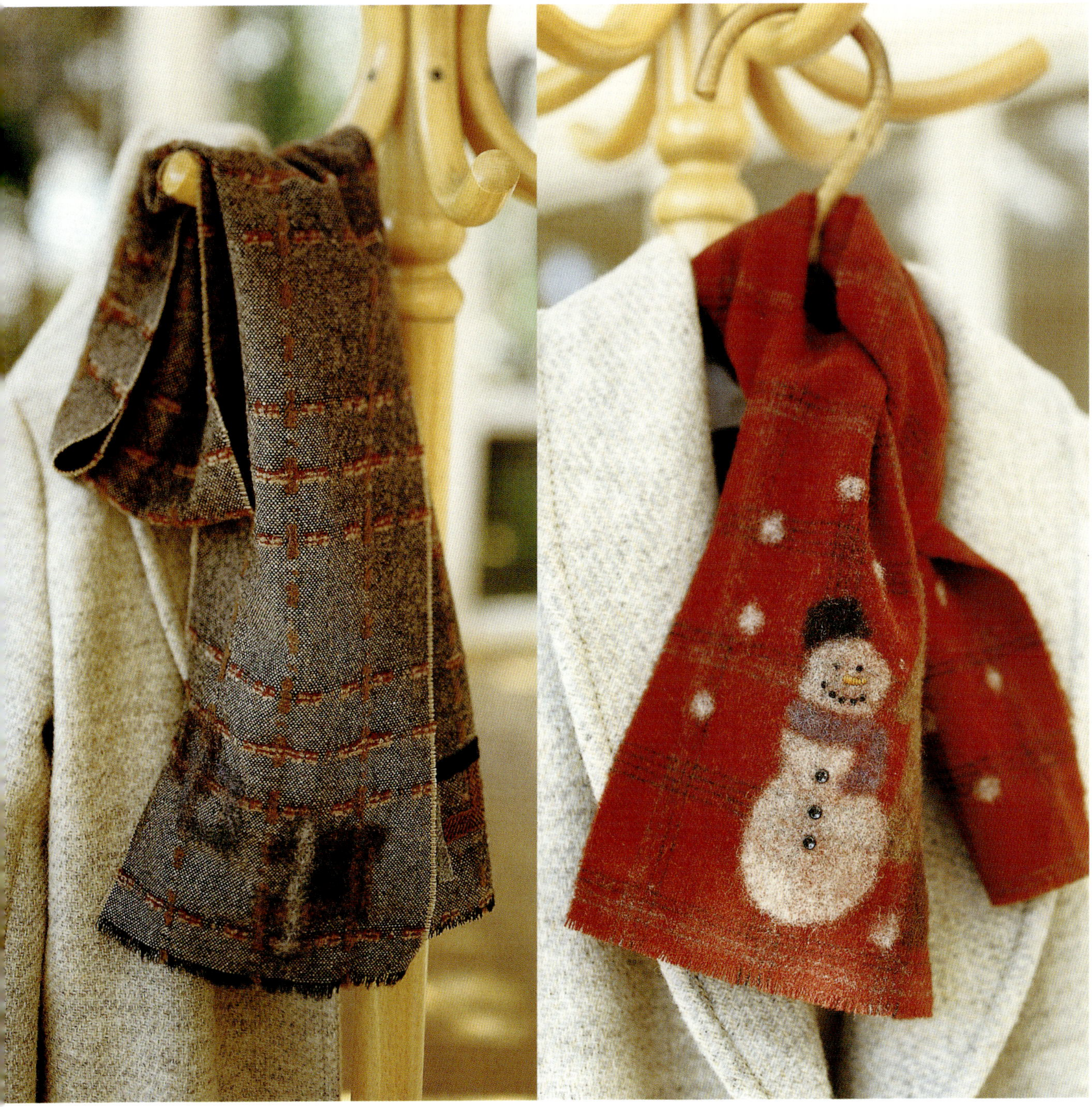

Designs bloom through to the right side of the scarves by needle-felting the appliqués from the wrong side.

⋯⋯> page 70

Coat rack/PROPS NOW

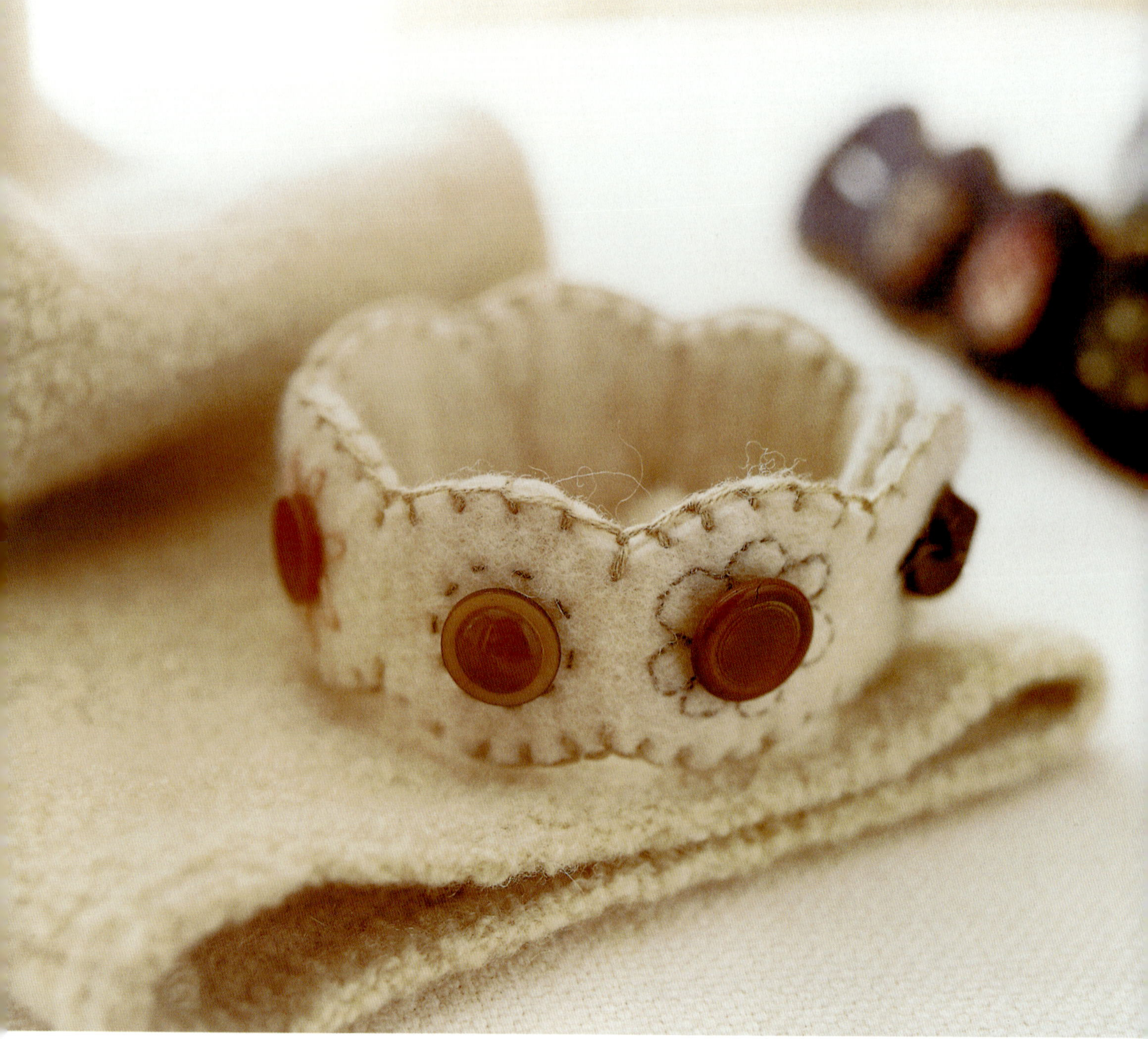

Adding appliqué, beads or embroidery, you can make cute bracelets out of wool. They can add a touch of interest to any outfit.

⋯⋯> page 71

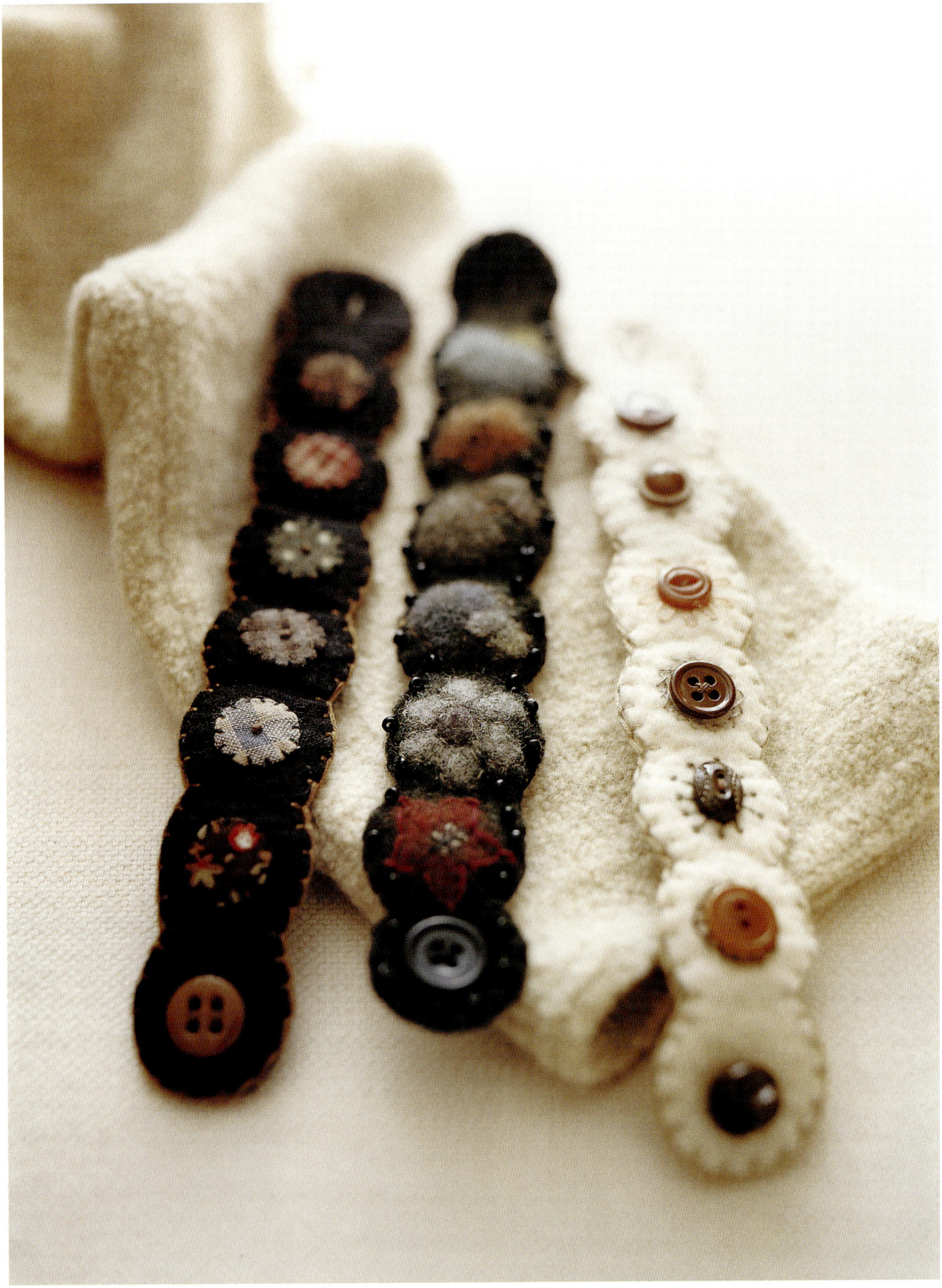

Wooleen Bracelets 13 14 15

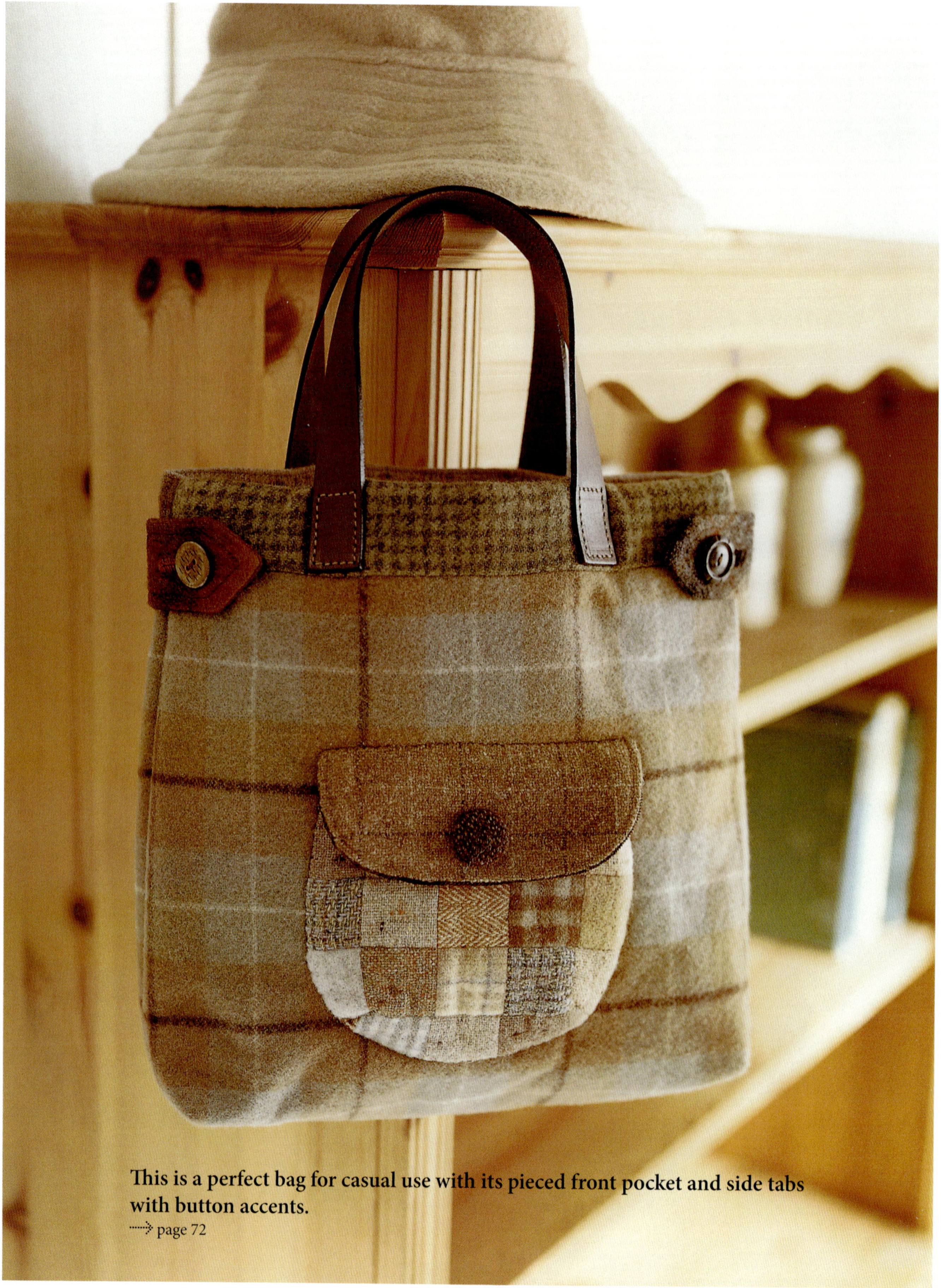

This is a perfect bag for casual use with its pieced front pocket and side tabs with button accents.

⋯⋯> page 72

These two mini-pouches shaped like a dog and cat have zippers in the back for easy access and are useful as a coin purse or for stashing small items.

→ page 74

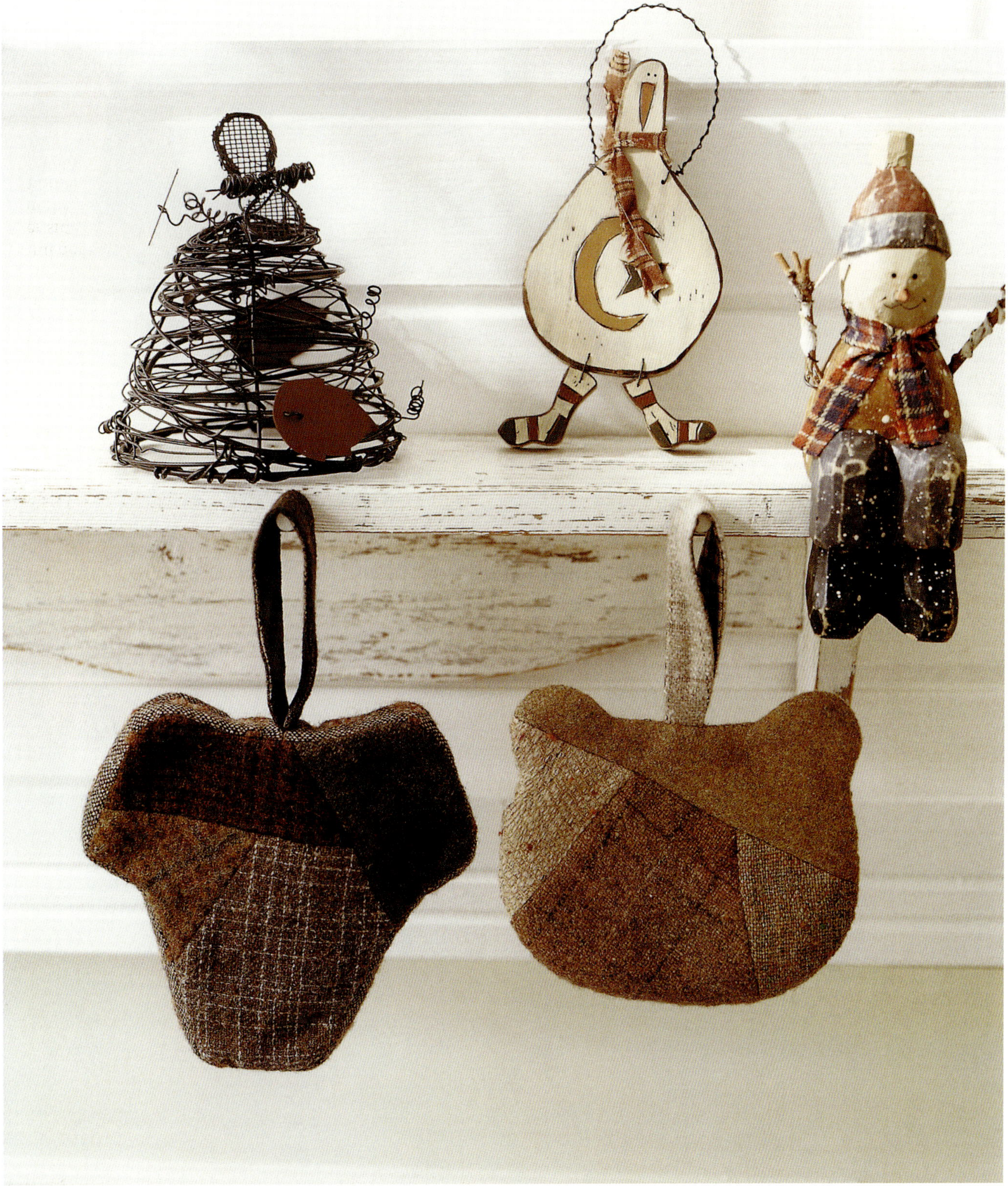

19 Gathered-Gusset Handbag

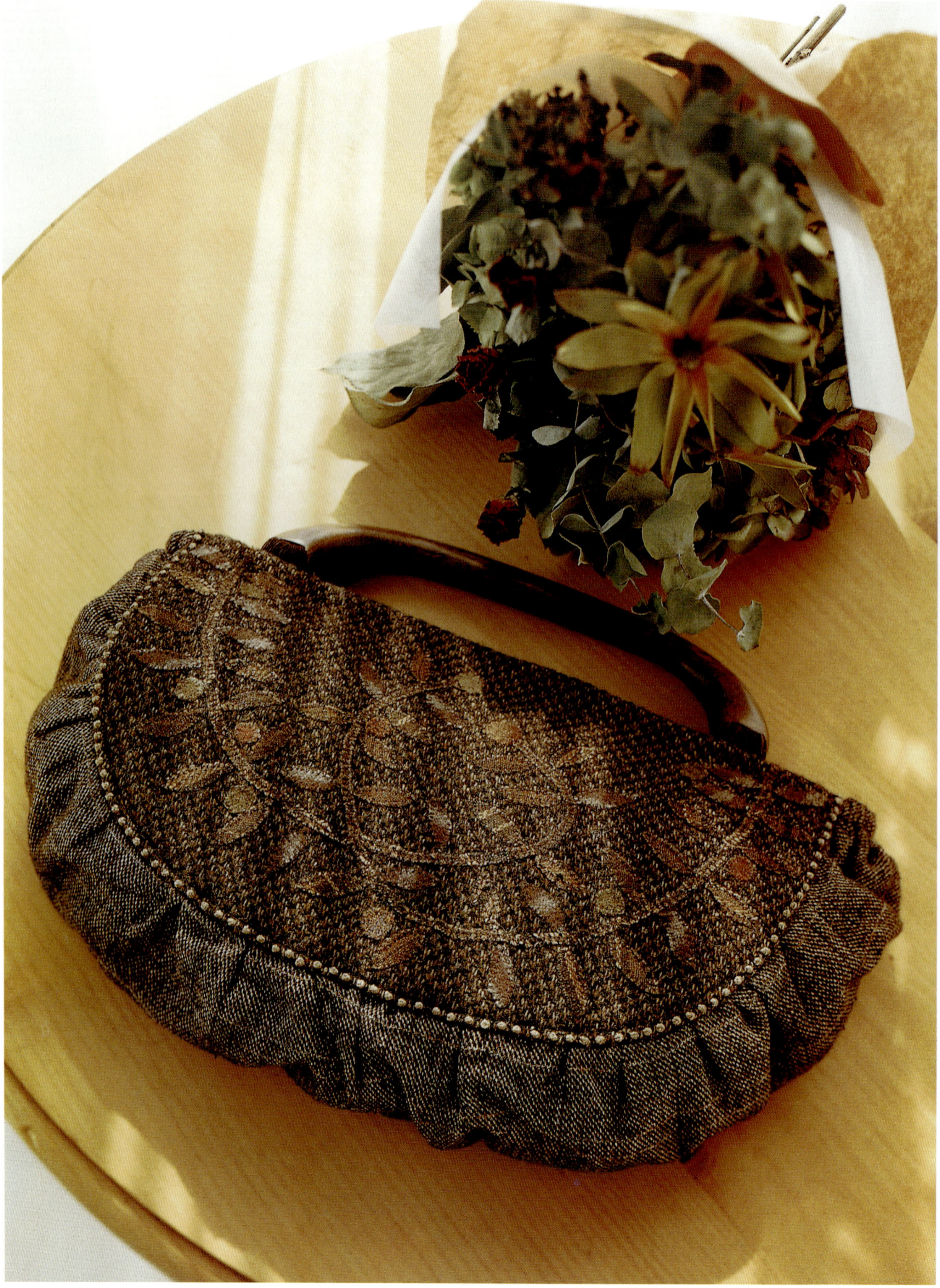

The stem and leaves appliqué is cut out of one piece of wool that gives the design a slightly irregular but light feel. The gathered gusset allows for more room inside.

⇢ page 76

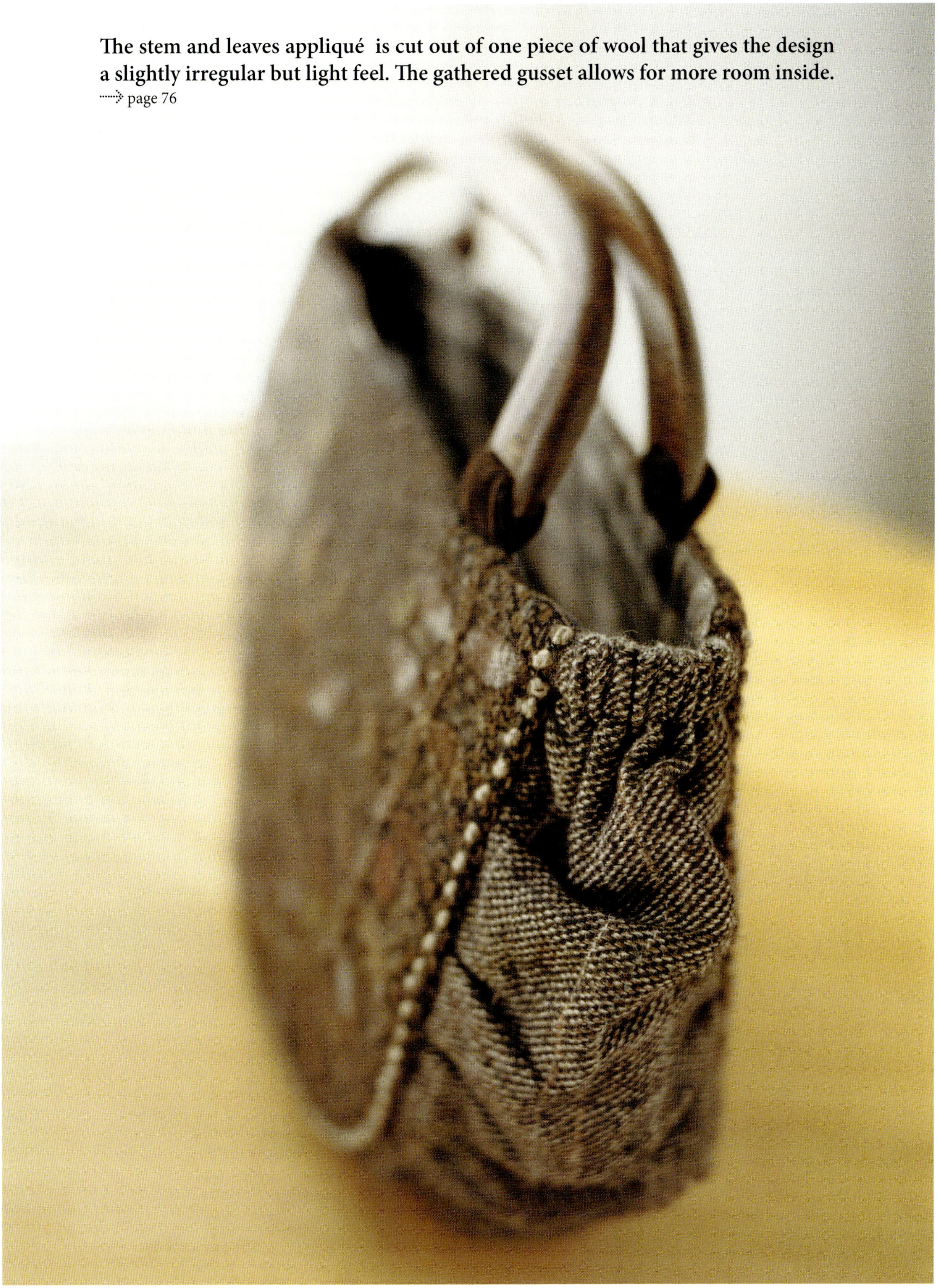

19

20 Floral Tea Cozy

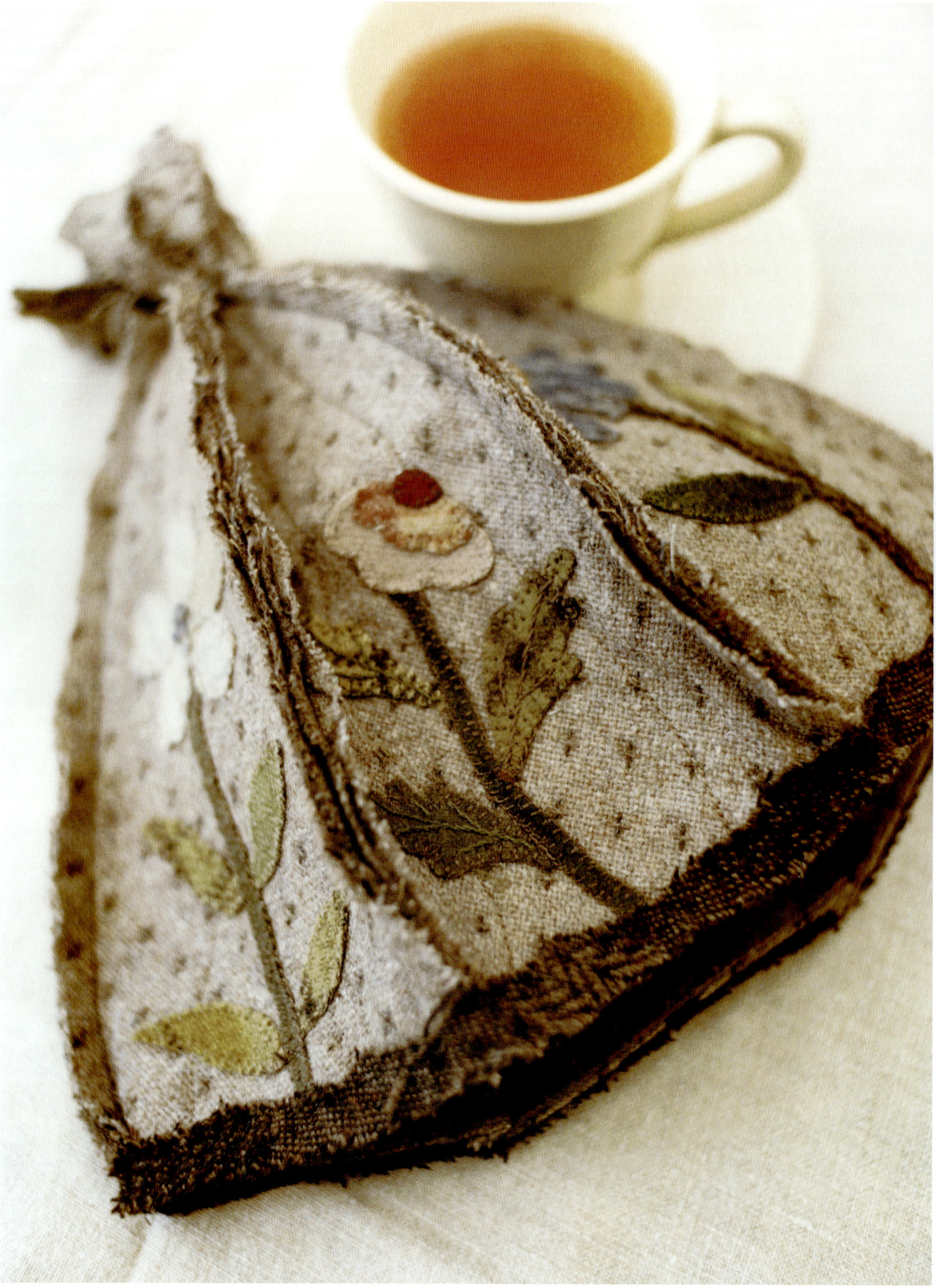

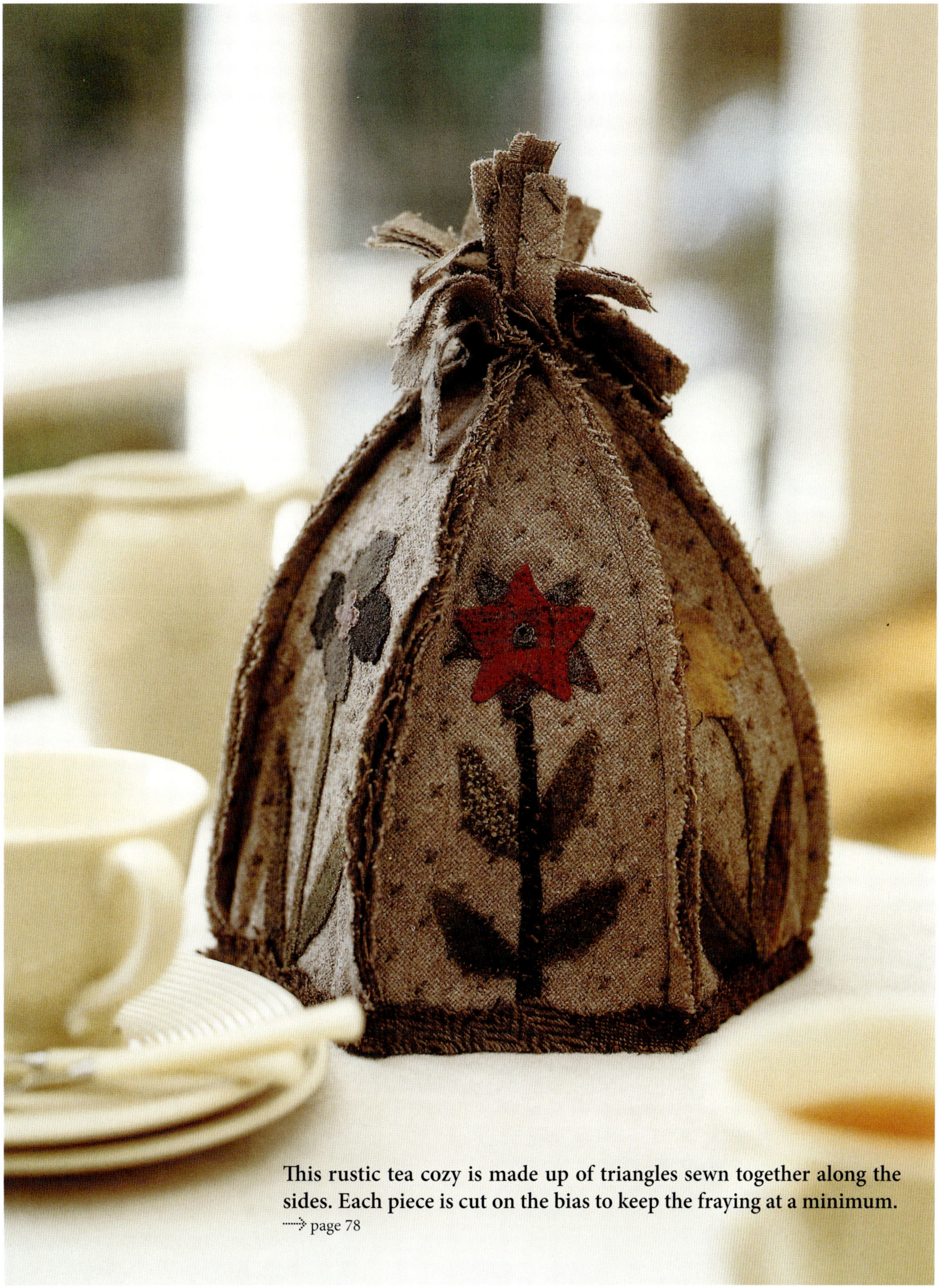

20

This rustic tea cozy is made up of triangles sewn together along the sides. Each piece is cut on the bias to keep the fraying at a minimum.

⇢ page 78

21 Hooked Rug Floor Mat

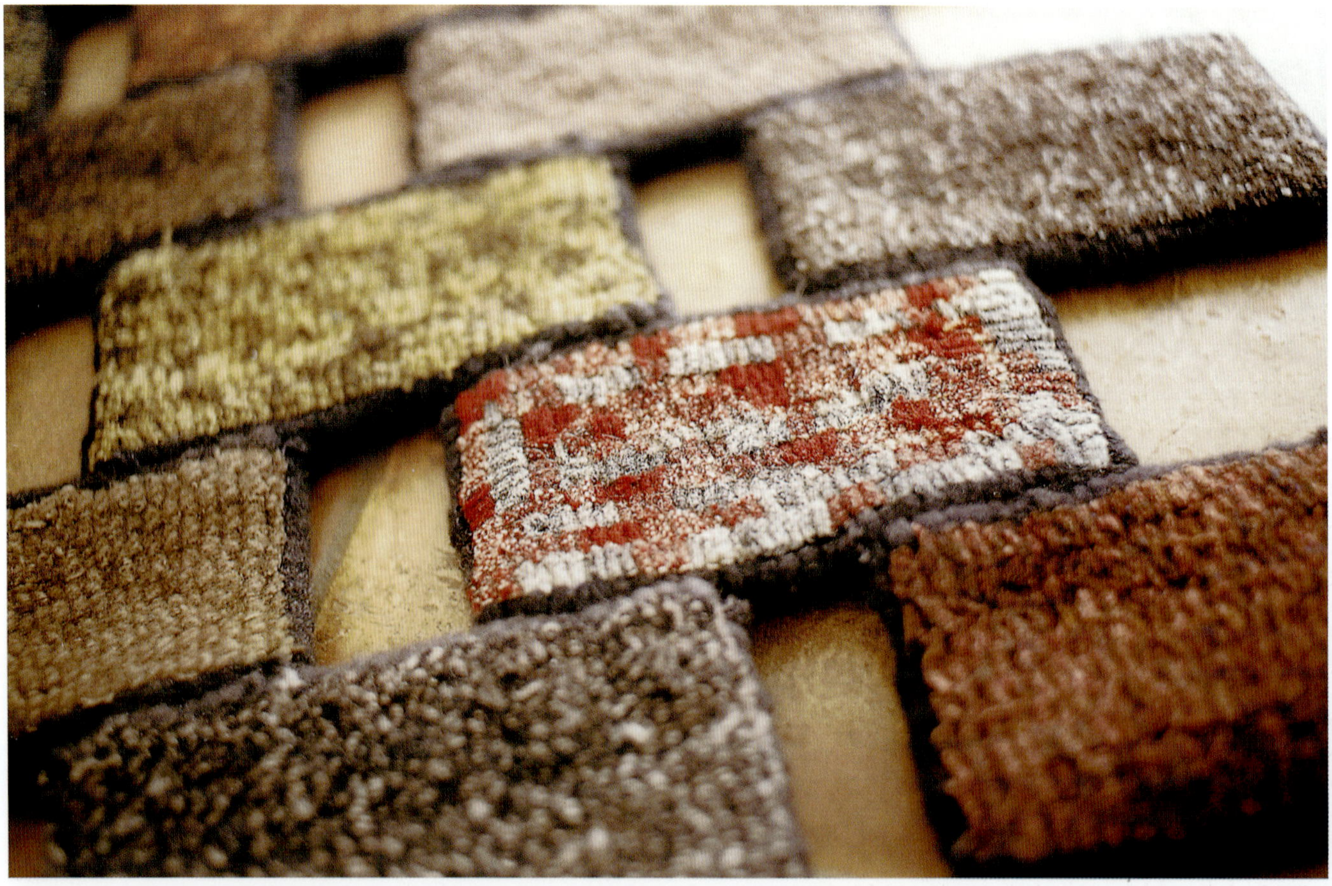

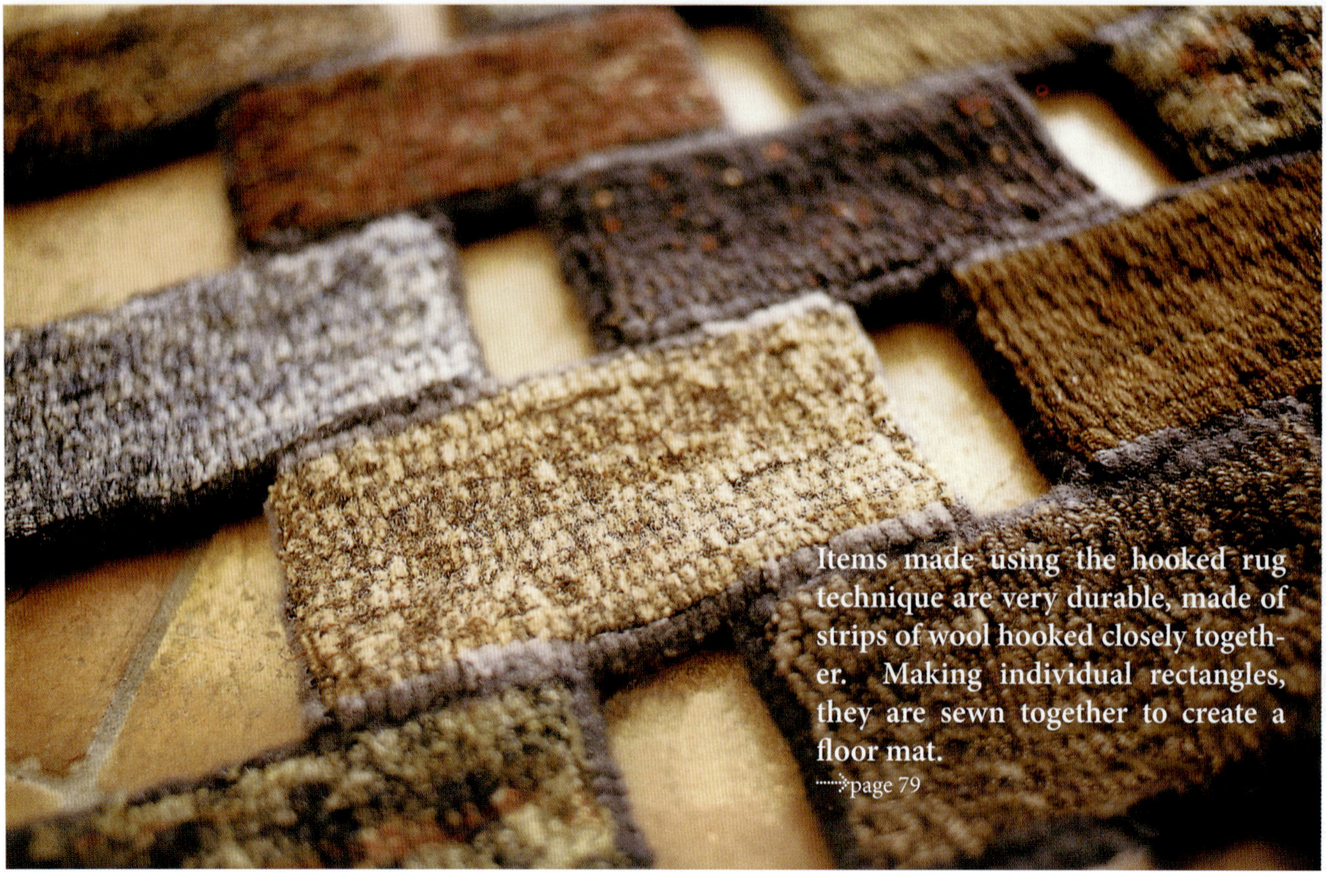

Items made using the hooked rug technique are very durable, made of strips of wool hooked closely together. Making individual rectangles, they are sewn together to create a floor mat.

⋯⋯➢page 79

◆ Rug Hooking

Rug hooking is a technique whereby wool, cut into strips, is pulled through a sturdy base fabric made up of canvas or burlap using a special hook, creating tightly packed loops of an equal height on the top.

1 You will need wool fabric that can be cut into a minimum width of 0.7 cm [¼"] by a length of 30 cm [11¾"], Canvas [6 count/cm] (14 count/inch), rug hook, a hoop.
2 Using a marker, draw the outline of the area where you will be filling in onto the the canvas. With your sewing machine, stitch approximately 2 cm [¾"] outside of the marked line.
3 If your design is square or rectangular, start from the edge; otherwise start from the center and move out. Holding the strip of wool between your left thumb and index finger under the canvas, push the hook down through the canvas and snag the strip in the hook.
4 Bring the hook up through the canvas, creating a loop approximately 0.5~0.7 cm [¼"] or your desired height.
5 Push down into the next hole and continue to bring the wool loops to the surface, the goal being a consistent height. When you come to the end of the strip, push the hook down into the same hole to begin working with the next strip.
6 Continue to work in a linear fashion for square or rectangular shapes, or radiating out from the center until the entire area is complete.
7 With sharp scissors, trim any ends to the same height as the loops.
8 Turn the project over and lay between a damp towel. Using an iron set to a wool setting, gently hold slightly above the wool to steam set in place, being careful not to flatten out the loops on the other side with pressure.
9 Cut the piece out, leaving approximately another 2 cm [¾"] outside of the sewn line. Fold in the canvas on top of the back of the project and carefully press. Cut a piece of backing fabric the same size as the finished piece, plus 2 cm [¾"] seam allowance and a piece of fusible interfacing to the same size as the project. Iron the interfacing to the wrong side of the backing; fold in the seam allowance and press.
10 With wrong sides together, match the edges of the back and hooked rug piece. Blindstitch the two together all the way around the edges to complete.

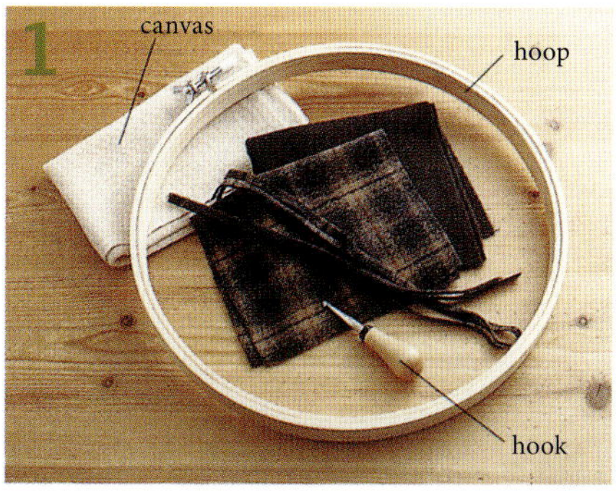

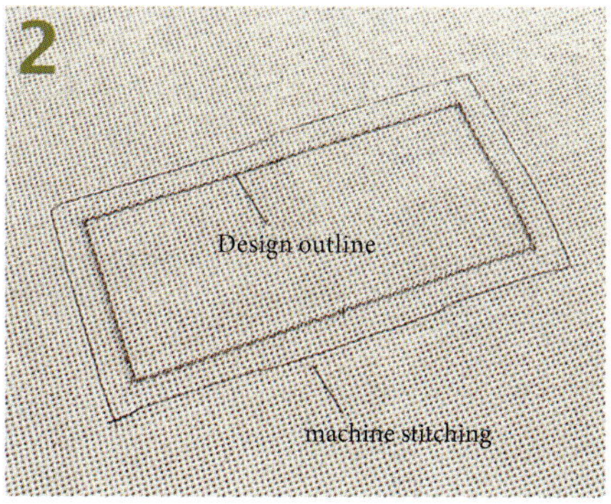

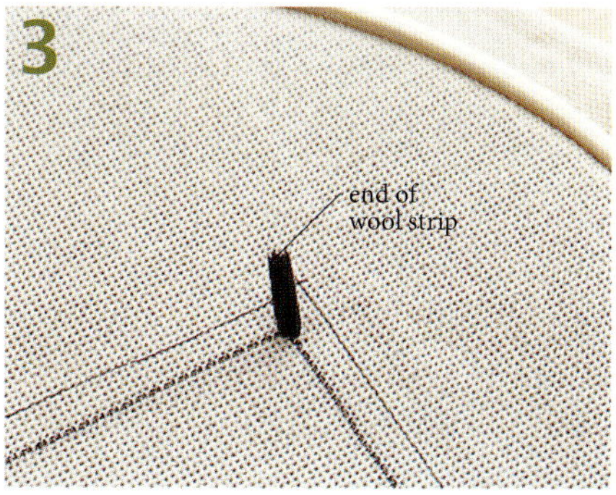

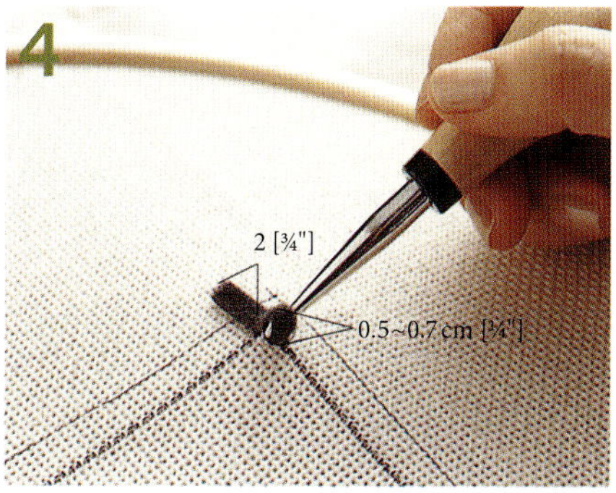

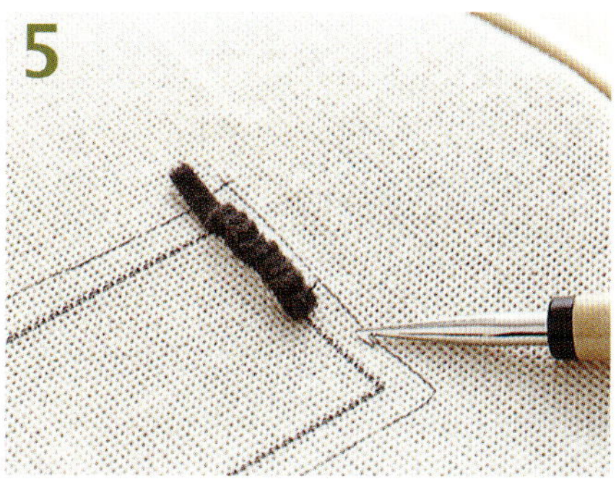

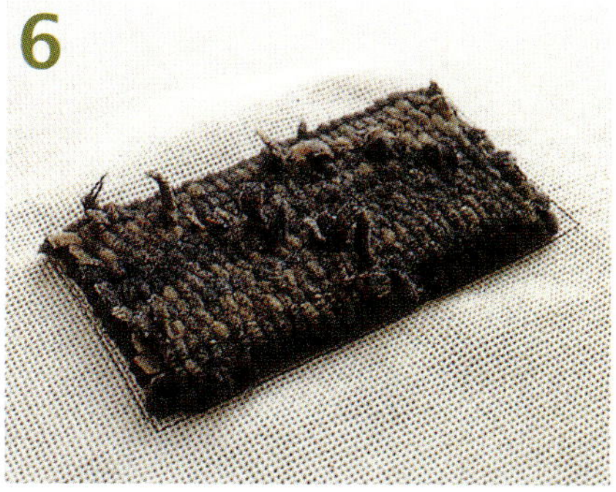

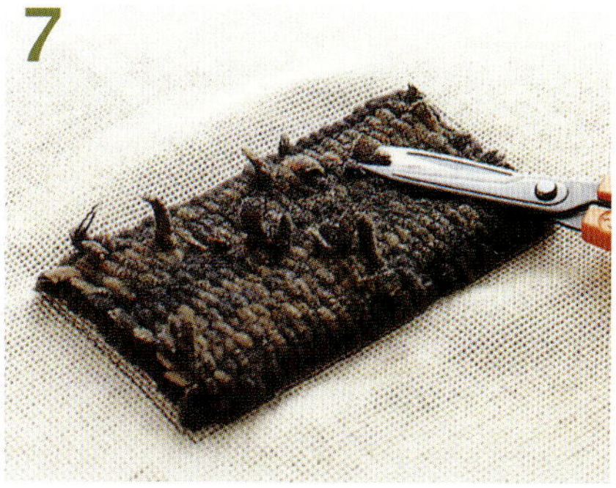

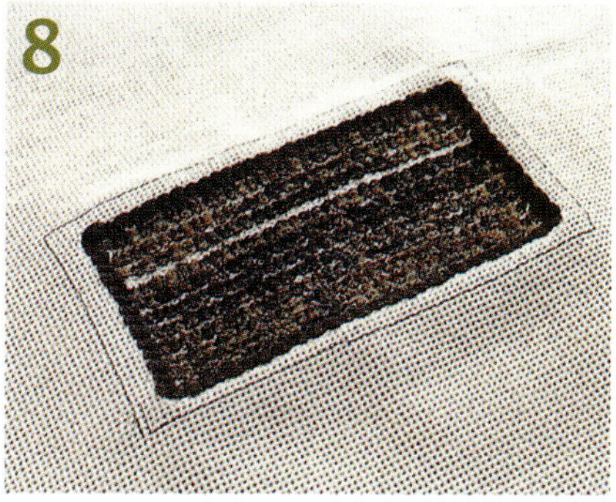

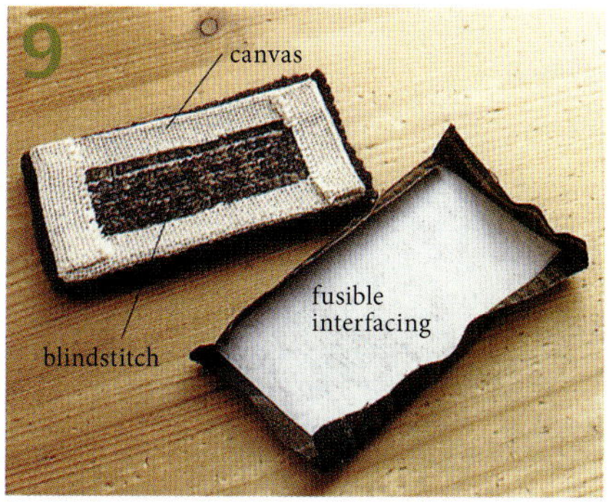

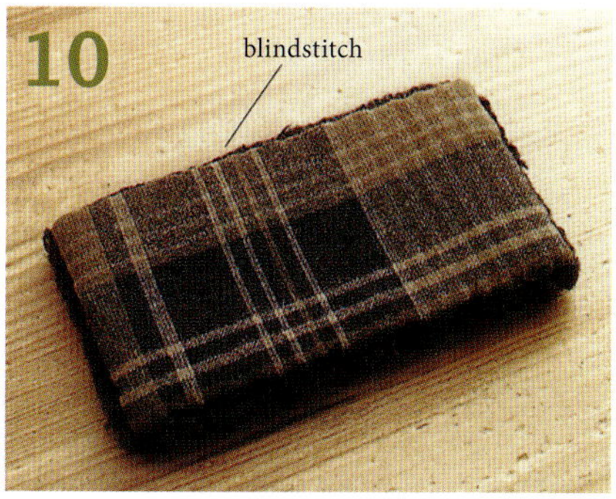

21

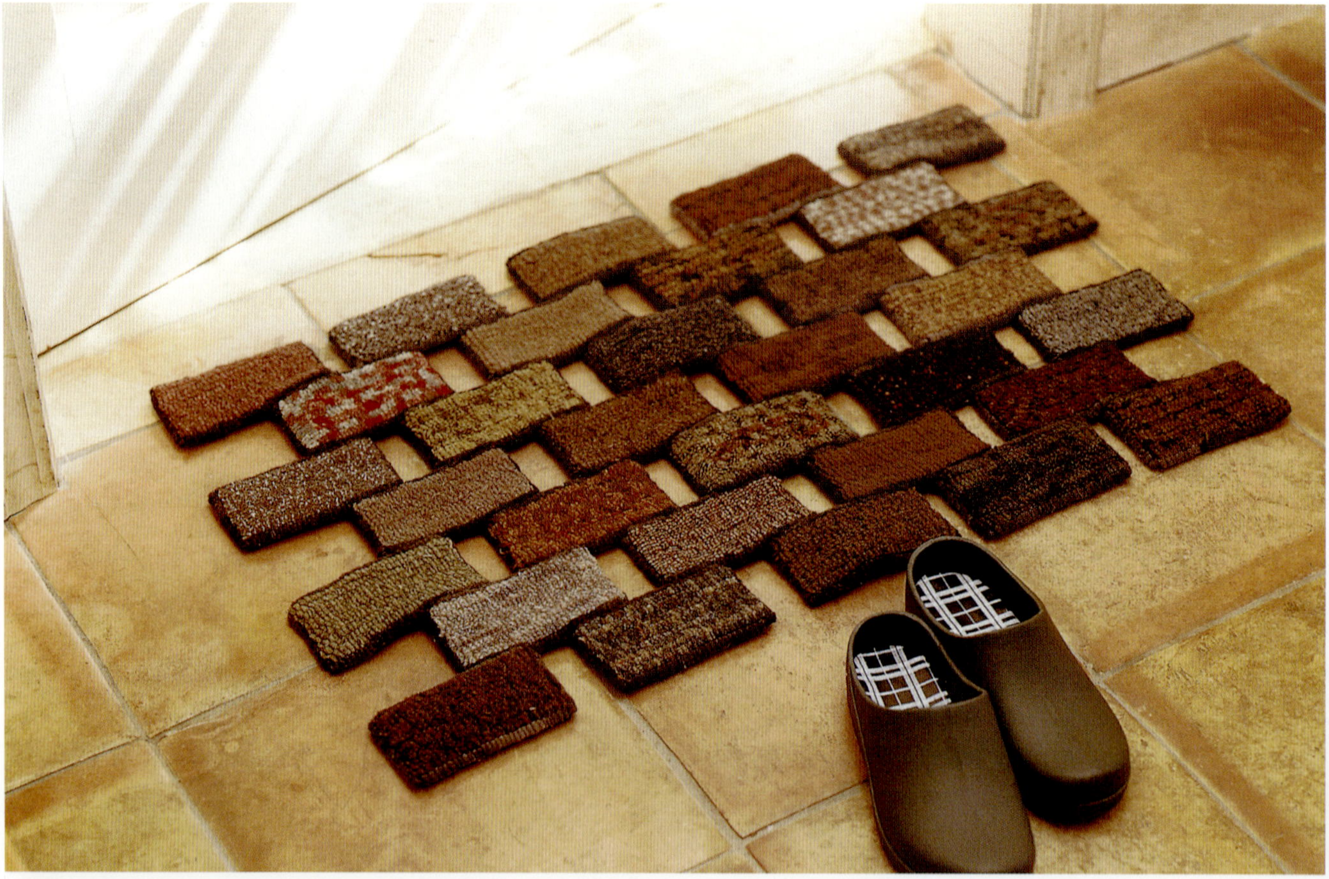

21

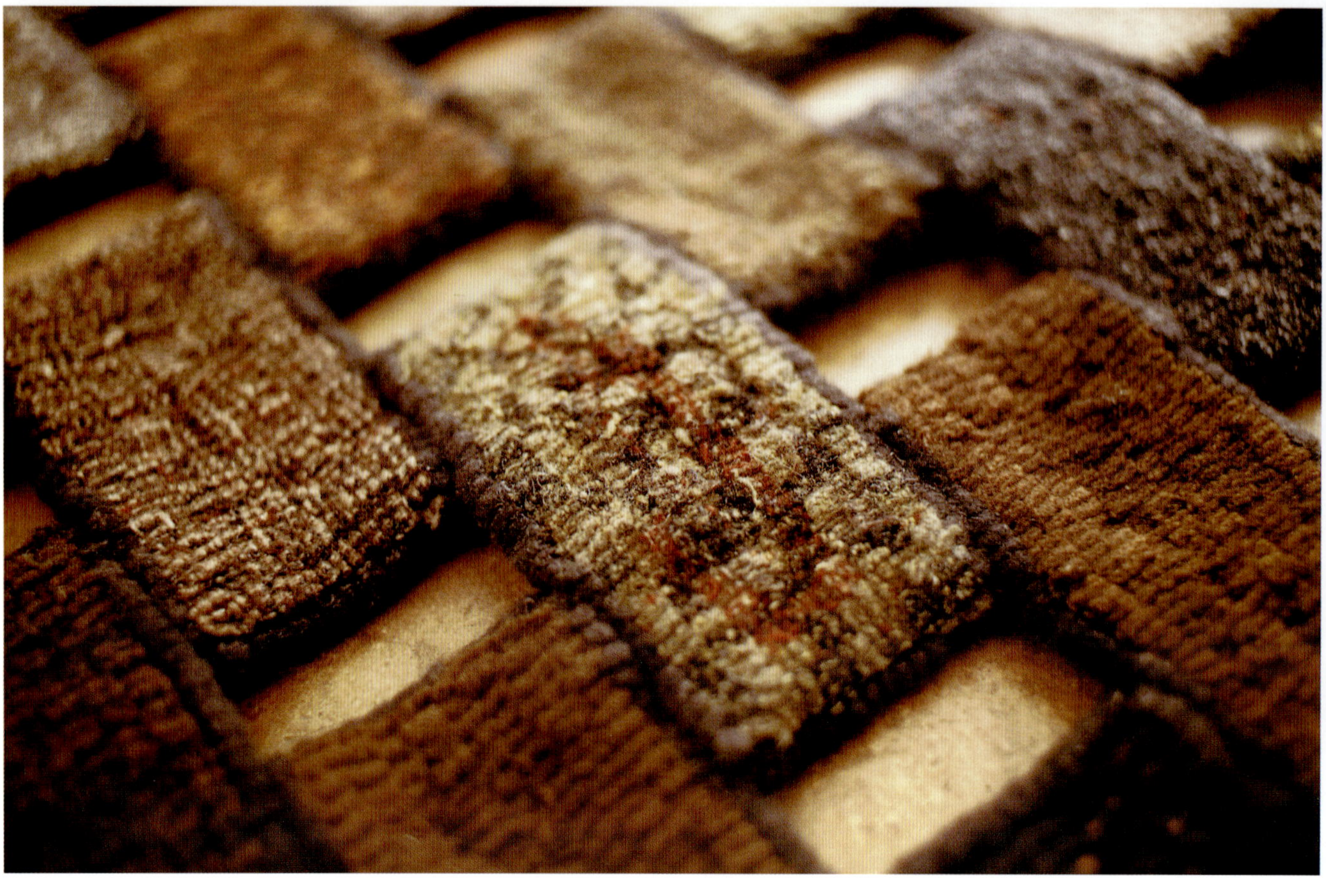

22 Turtle Pincushion

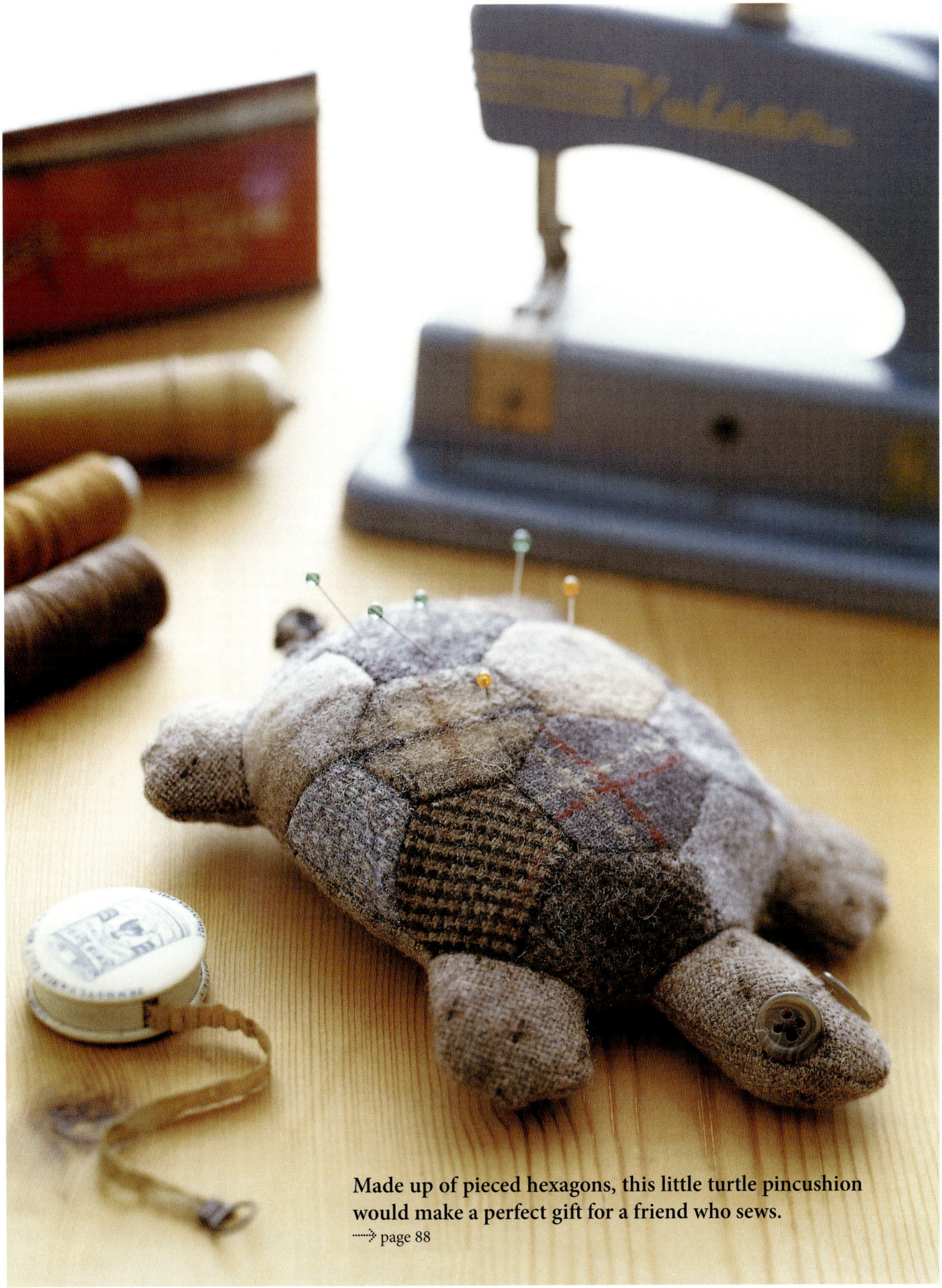

Made up of pieced hexagons, this little turtle pincushion would make a perfect gift for a friend who sews.

→ page 88

23 **Dog Rag Doll**

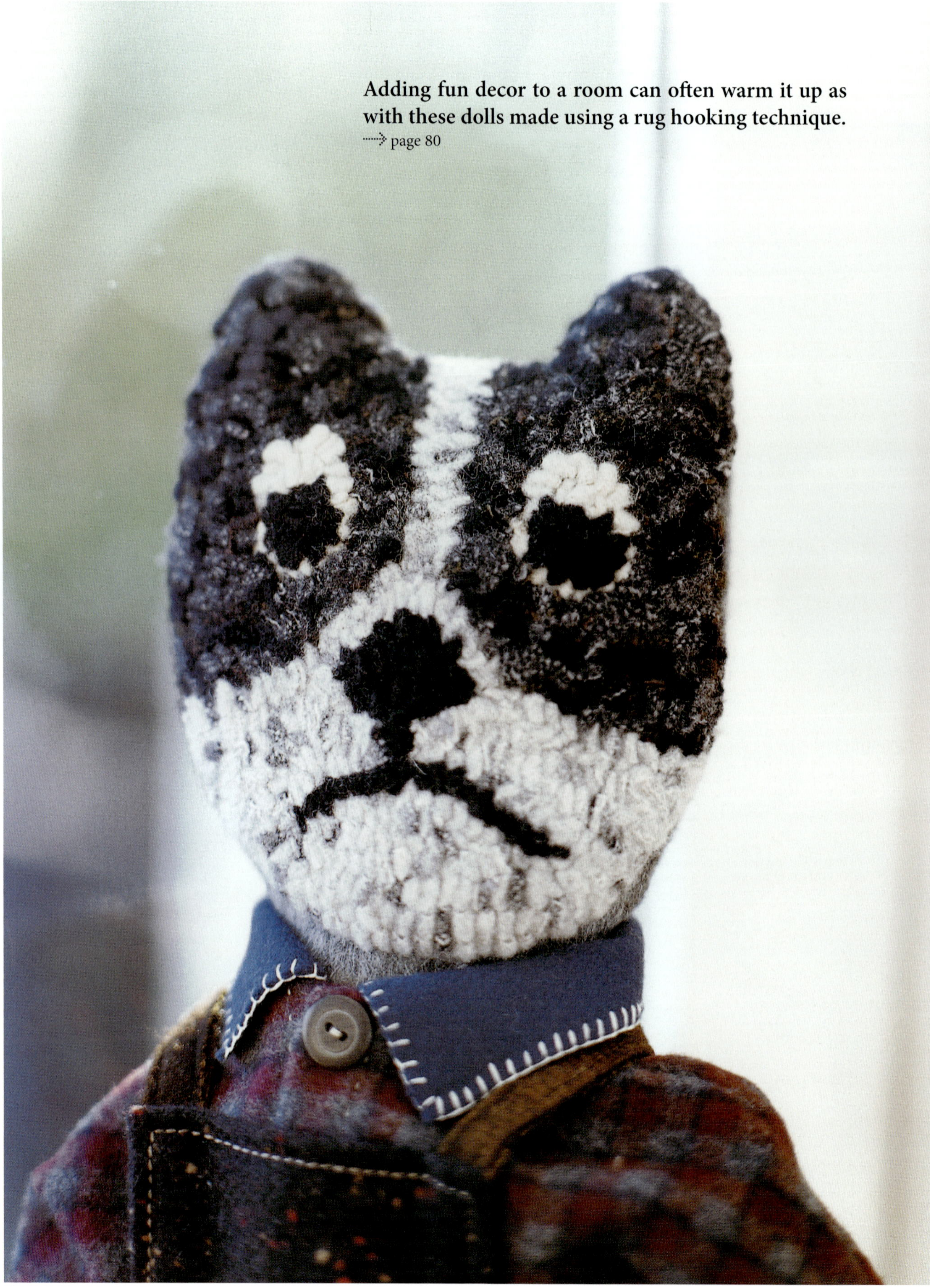

Adding fun decor to a room can often warm it up as with these dolls made using a rug hooking technique.

⋯⋯> page 80

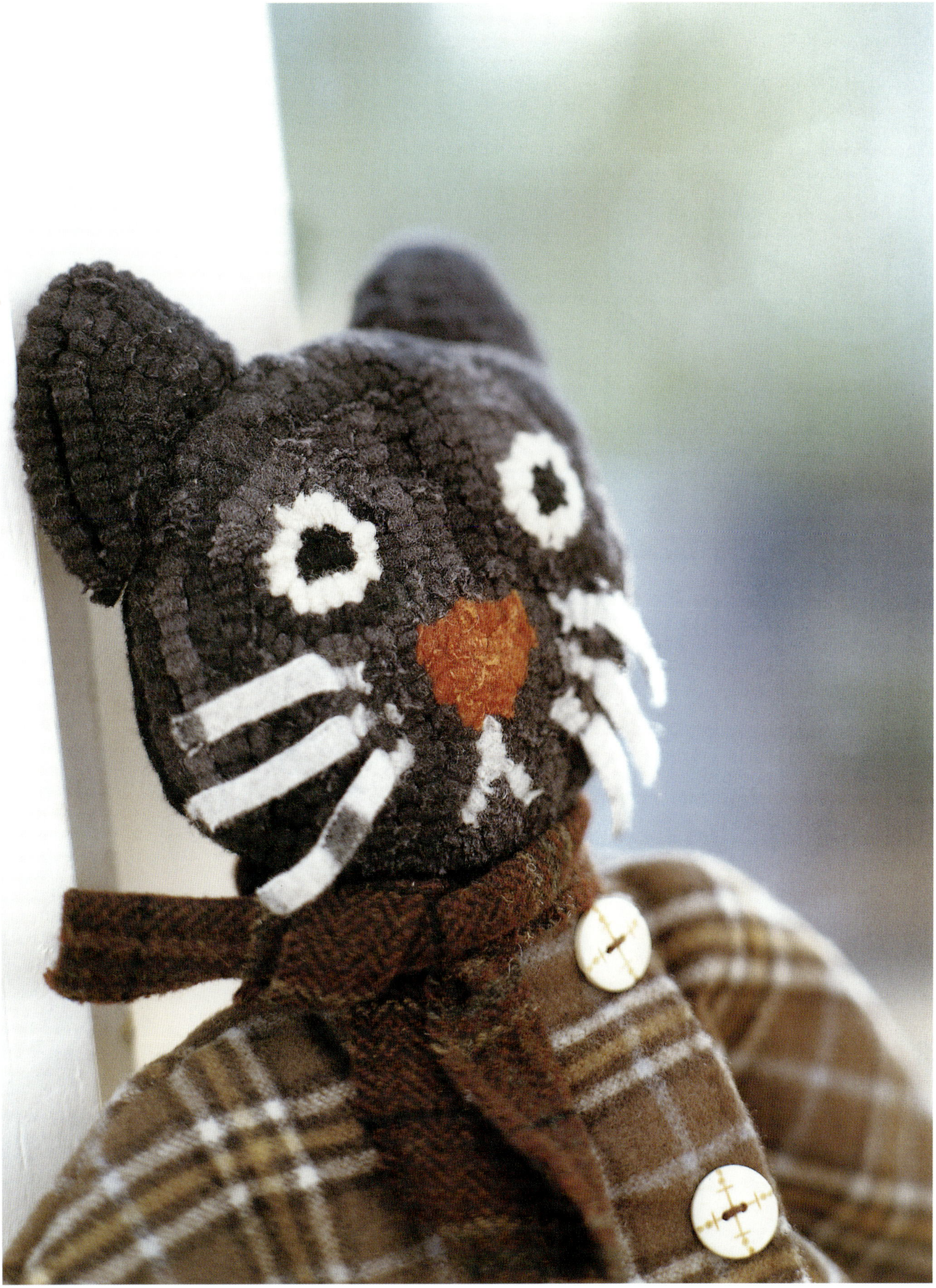

23
24

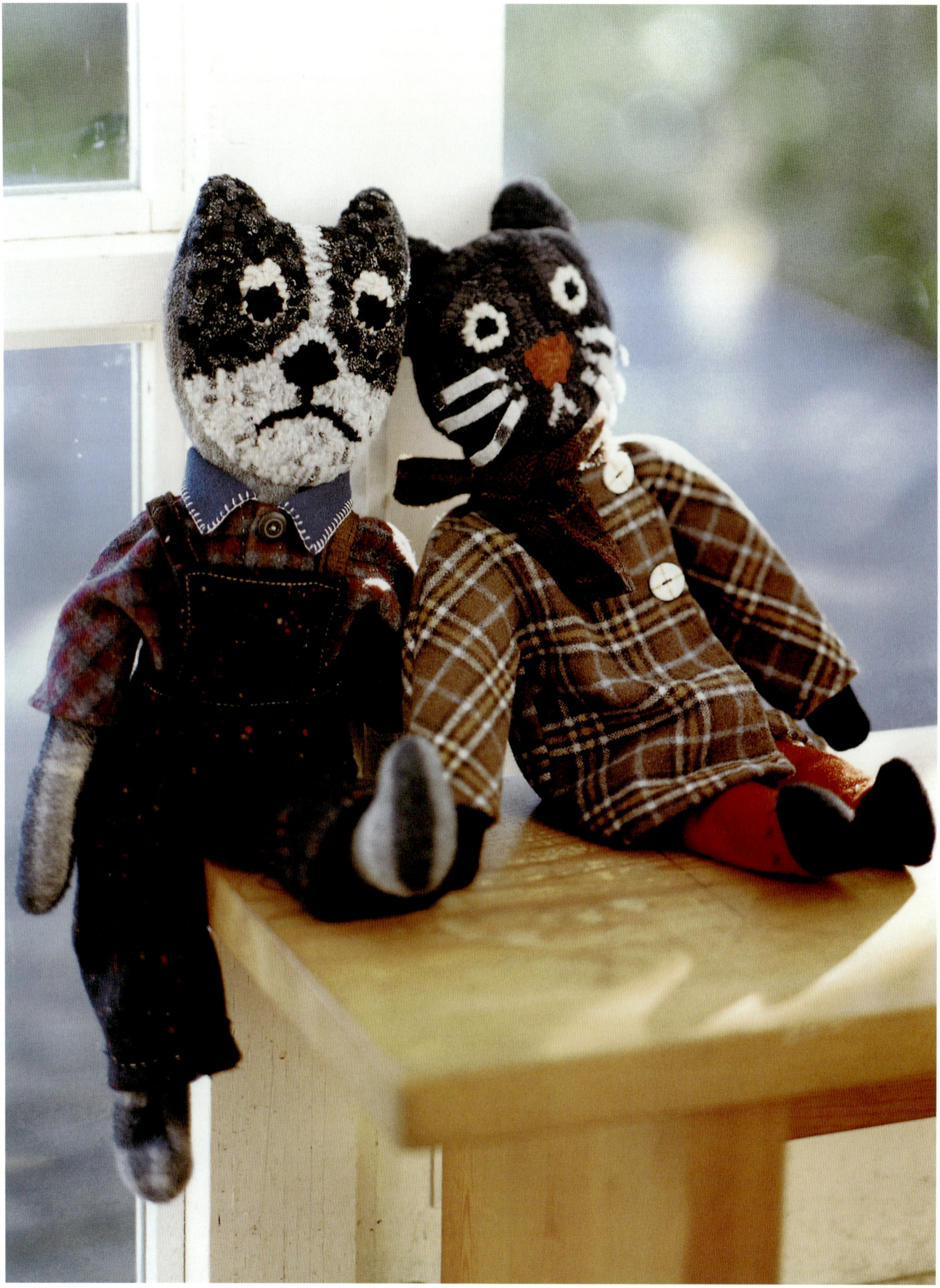

These flag cushions are fun and easy to make. Cut out each piece of the pattern by hand and stitch them together to give them a rustic appeal.

⟶ page 82

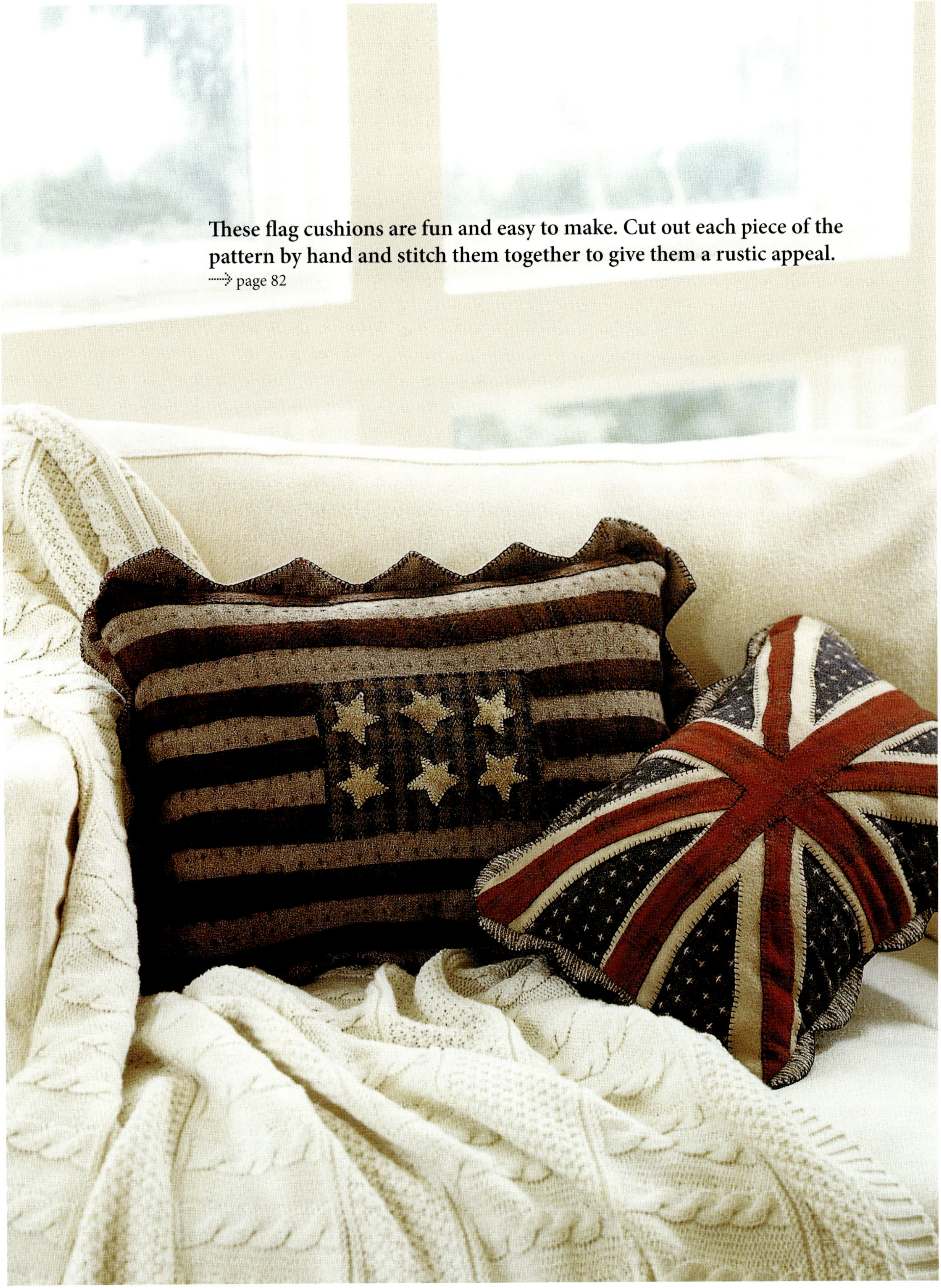

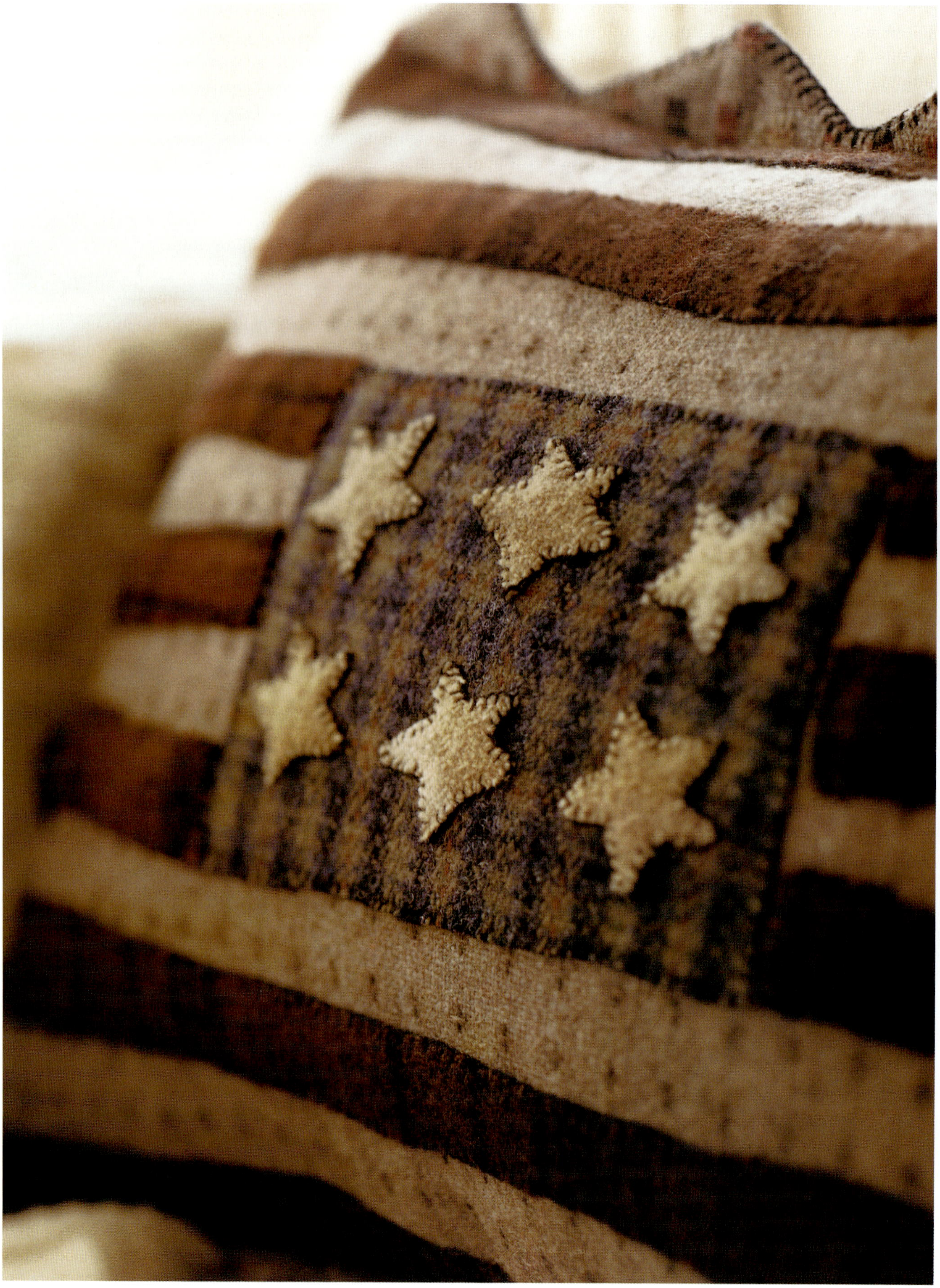

25

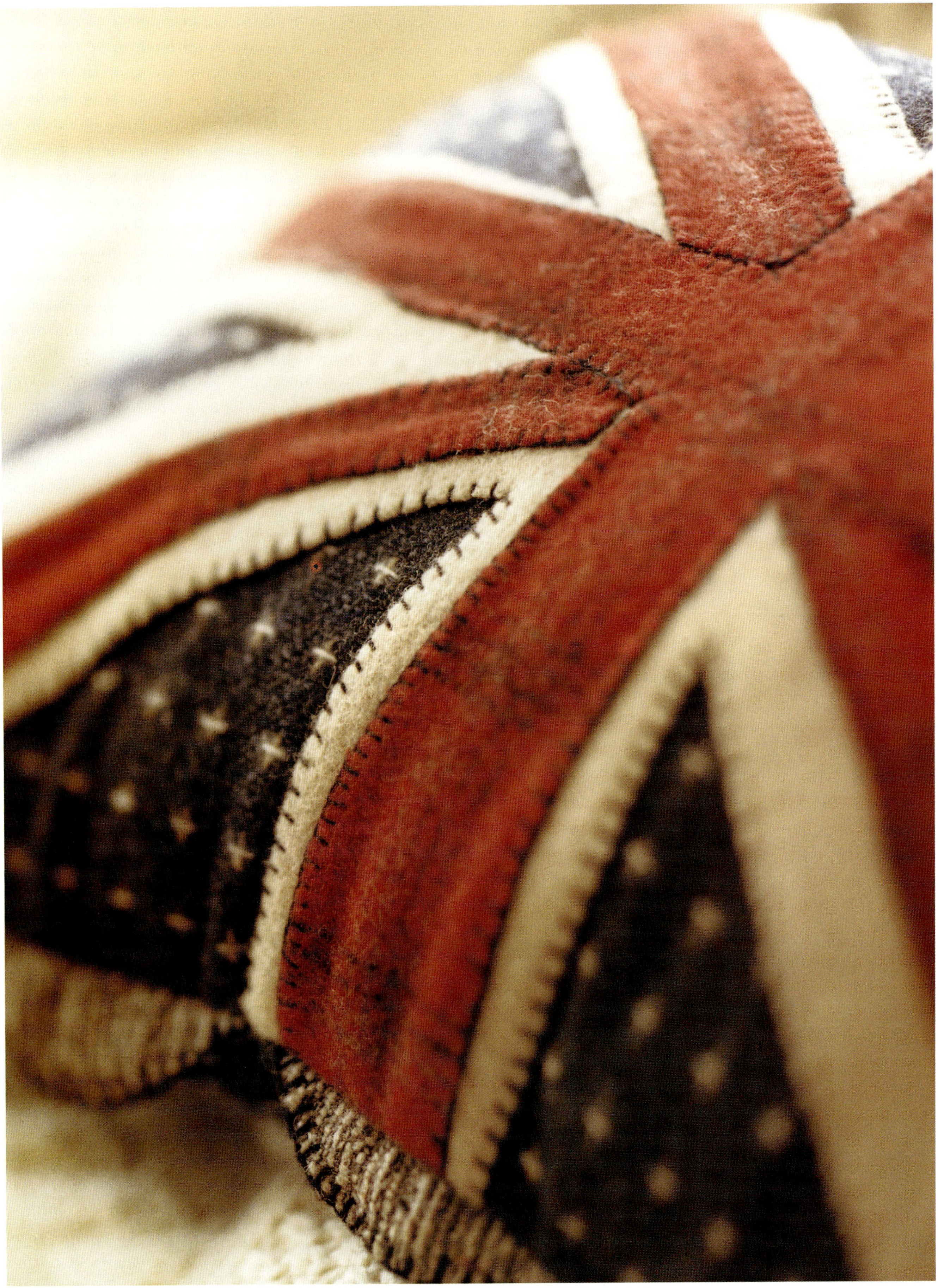

26

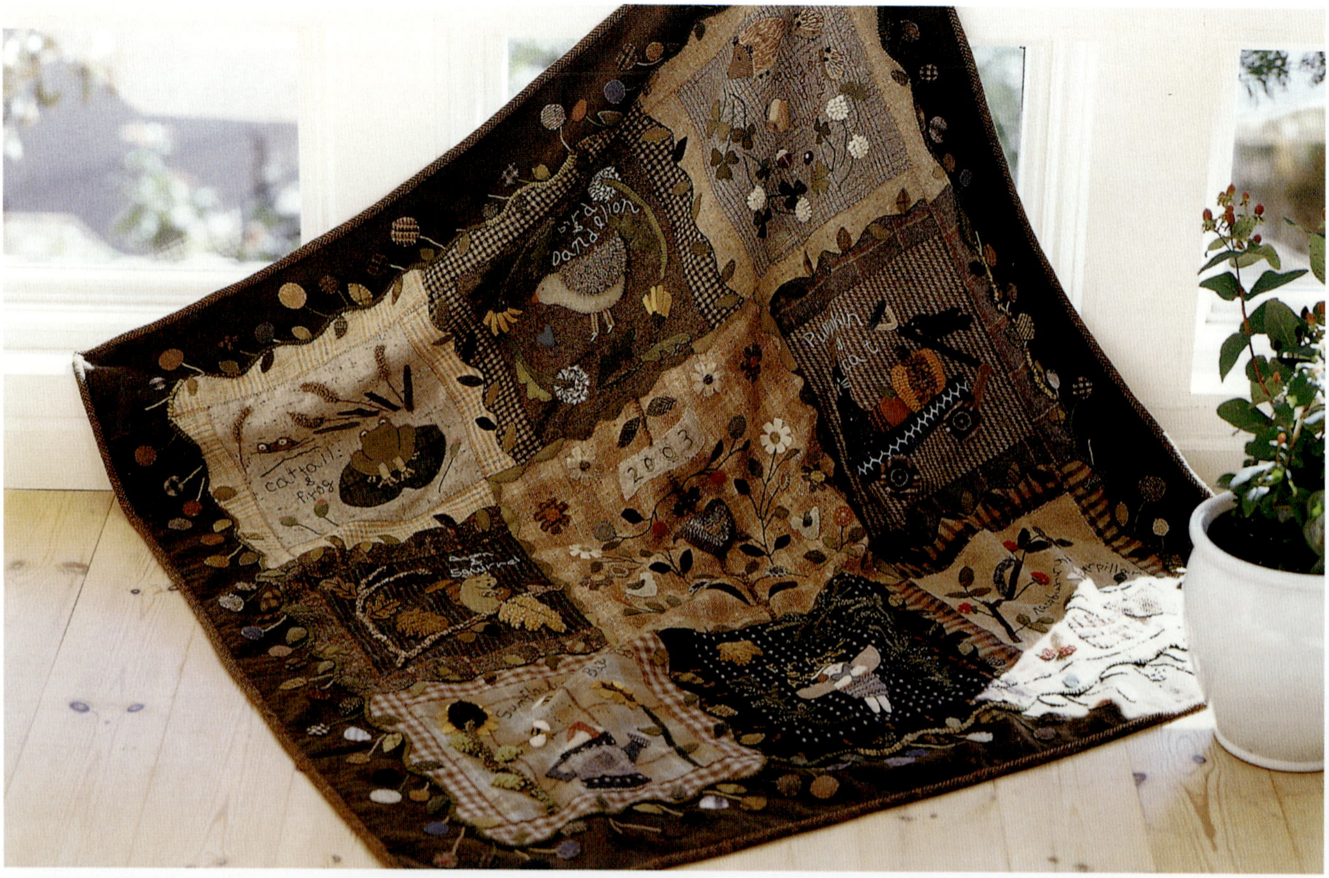

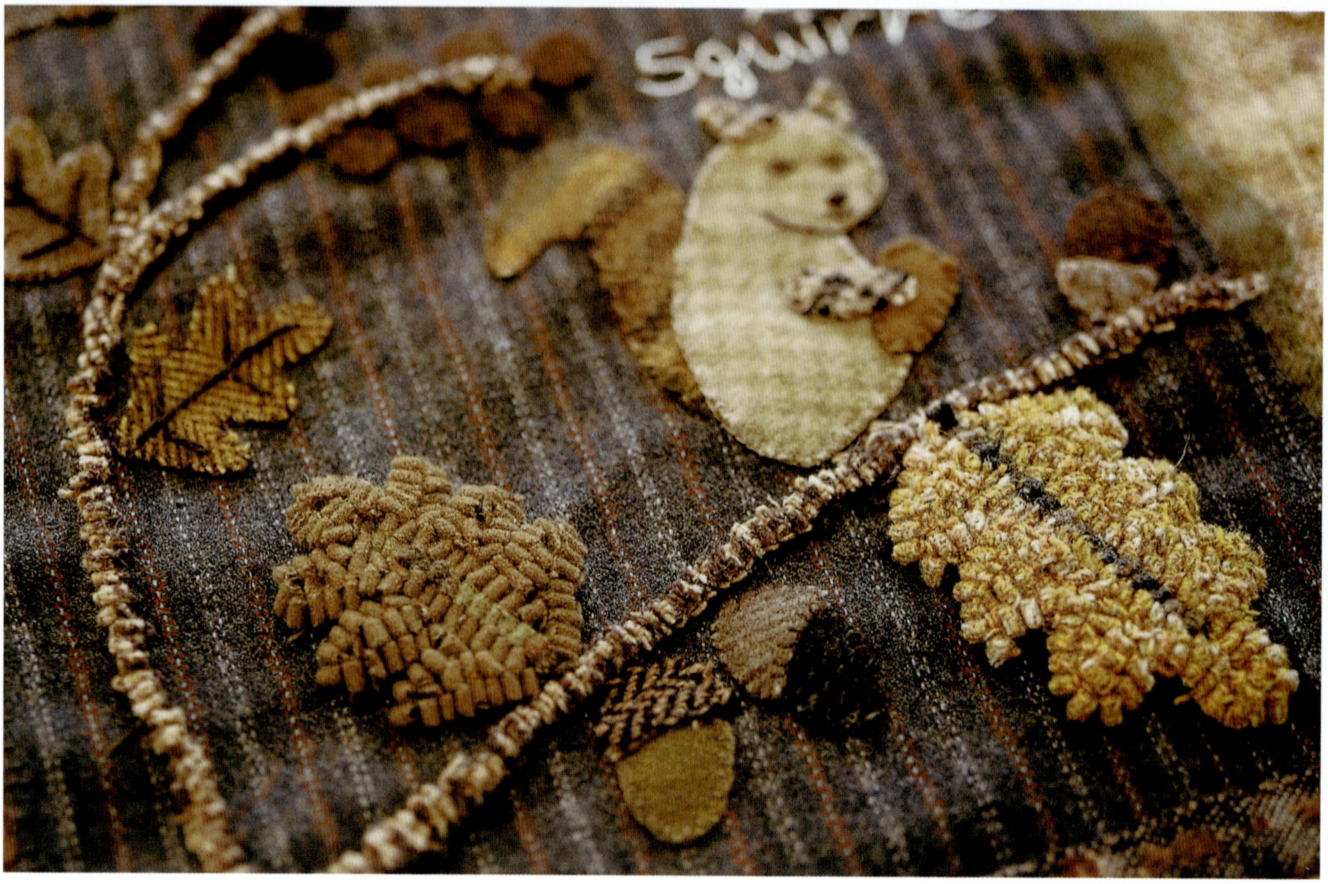

Almost appearing 3-dimensional, this lap quilt celebrates autumn with a combination of wool appliqué, rug hooking and embroidery elements.

⋯⋯› page 84

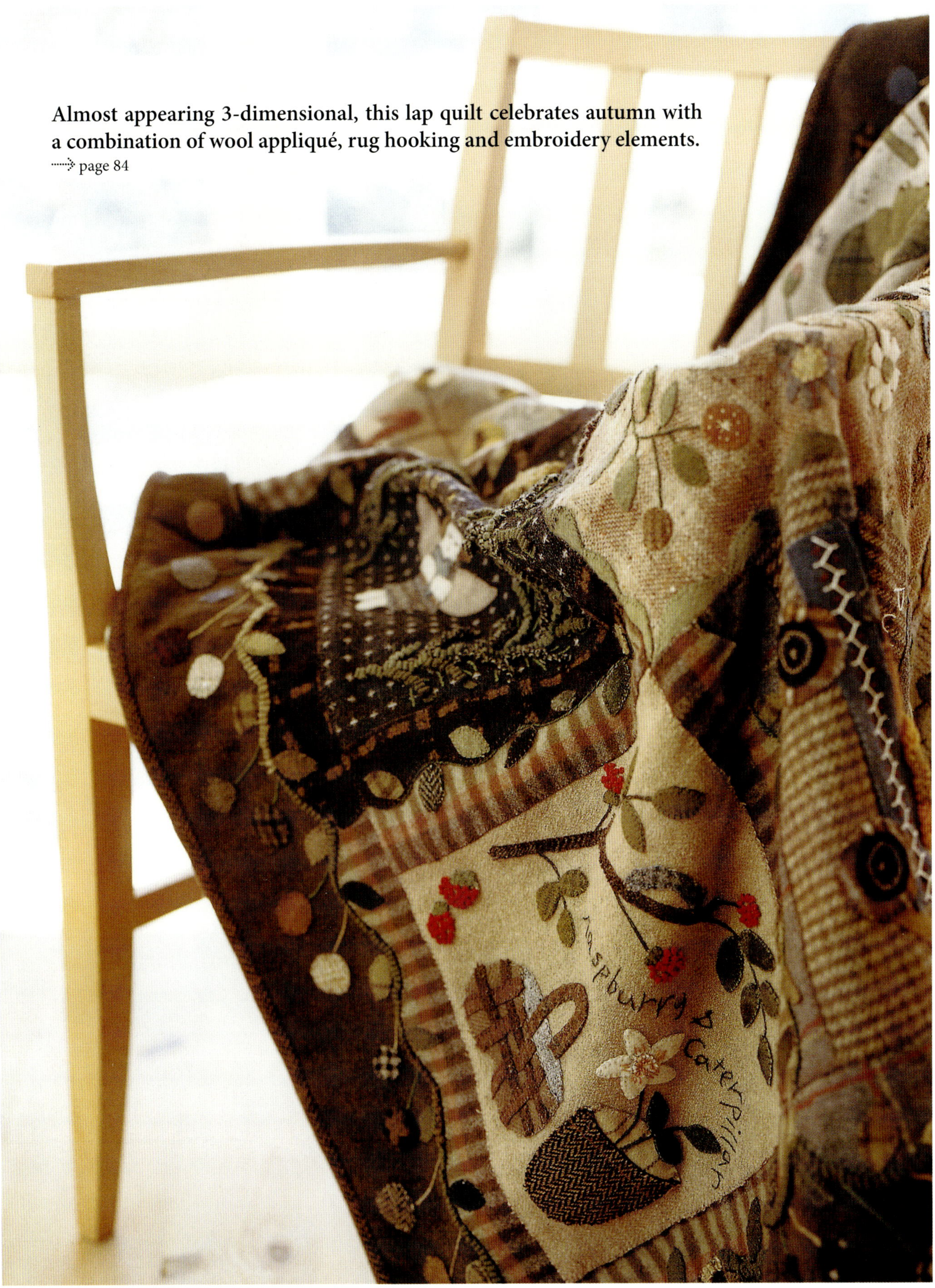

27

28 Shoulder Bag

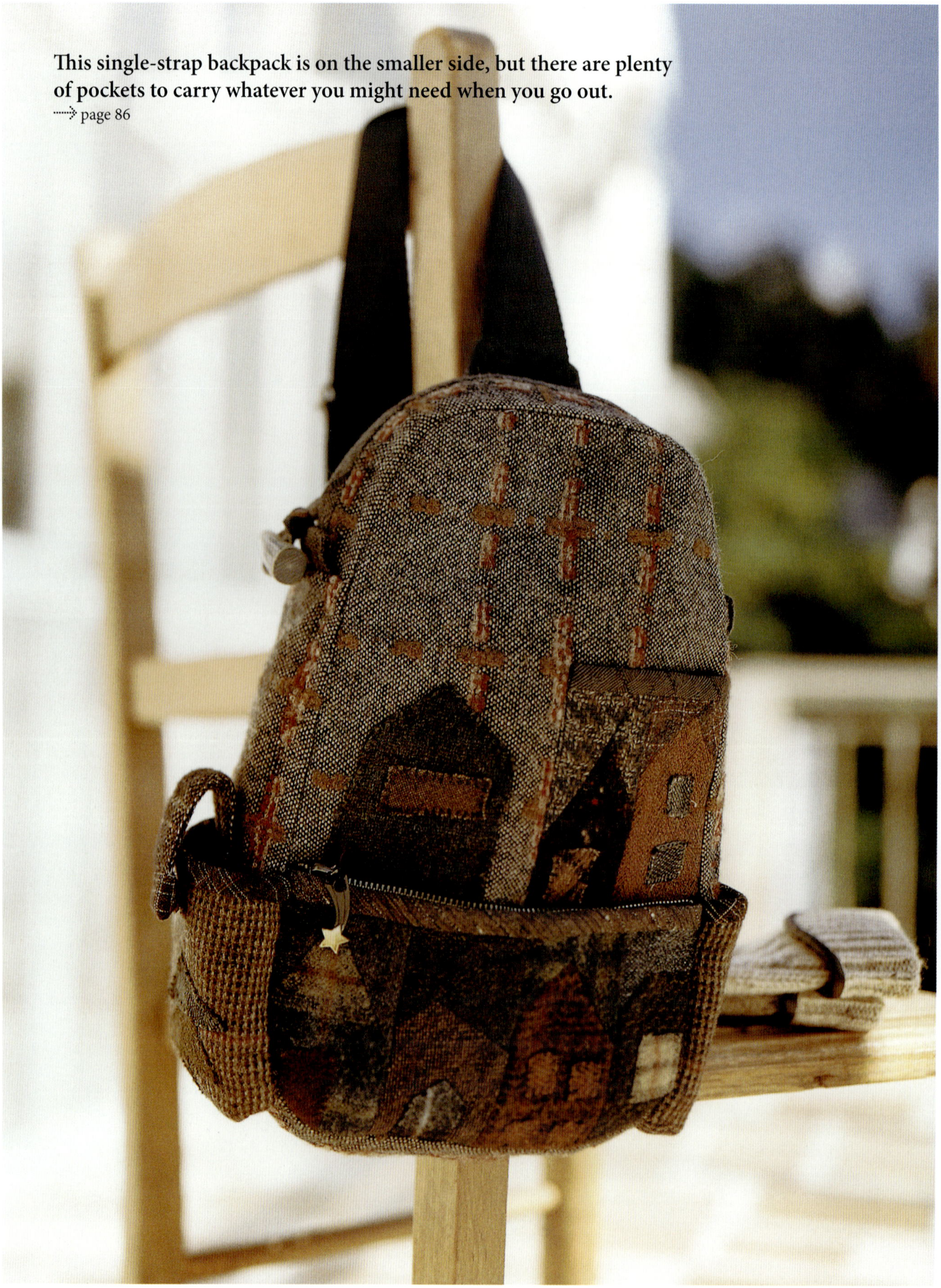

This single-strap backpack is on the smaller side, but there are plenty of pockets to carry whatever you might need when you go out.

⇢ page 86

Mini Peanut Pouch

29

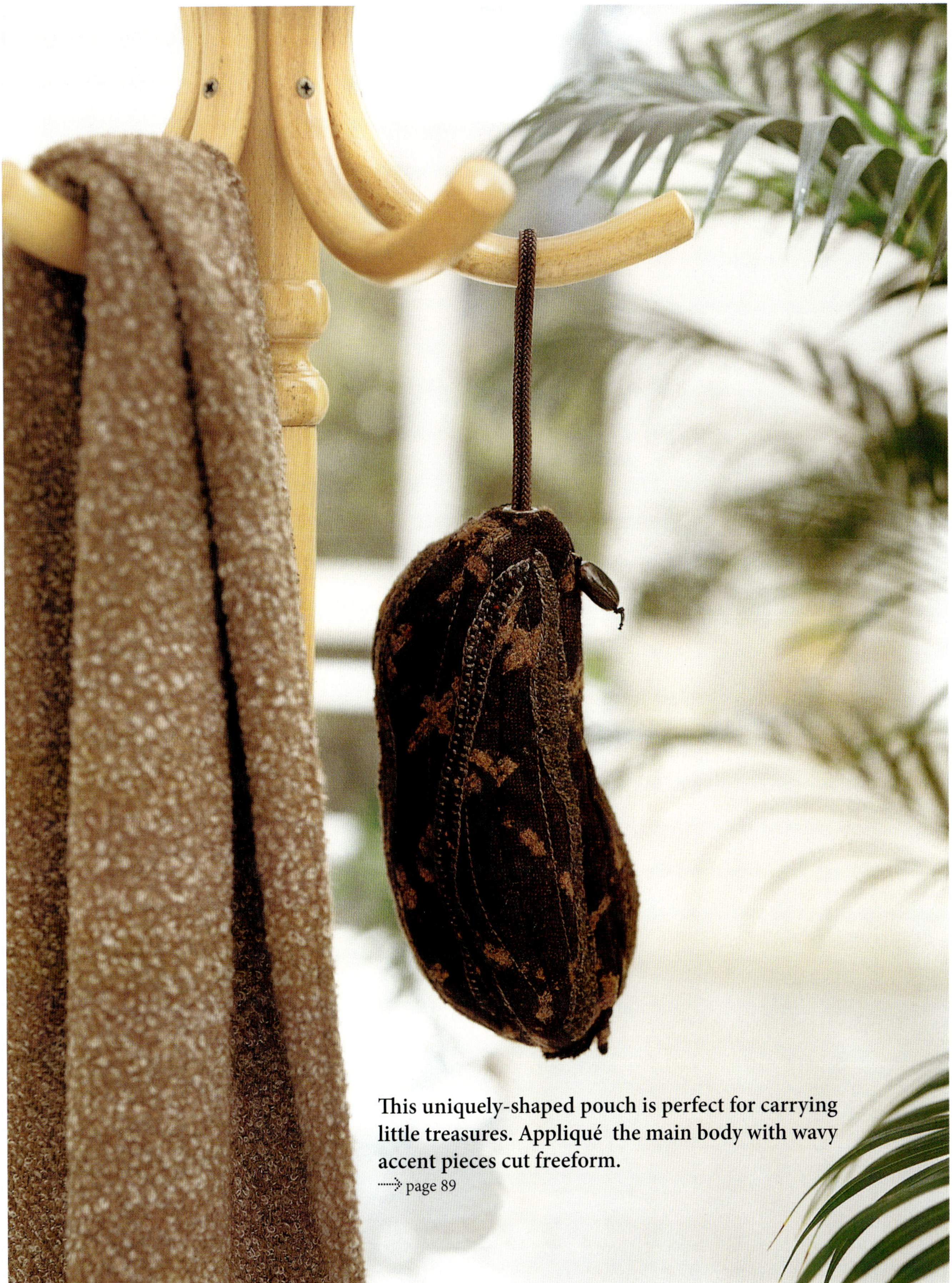

This uniquely-shaped pouch is perfect for carrying little treasures. Appliqué the main body with wavy accent pieces cut freeform.

⇢ page 89

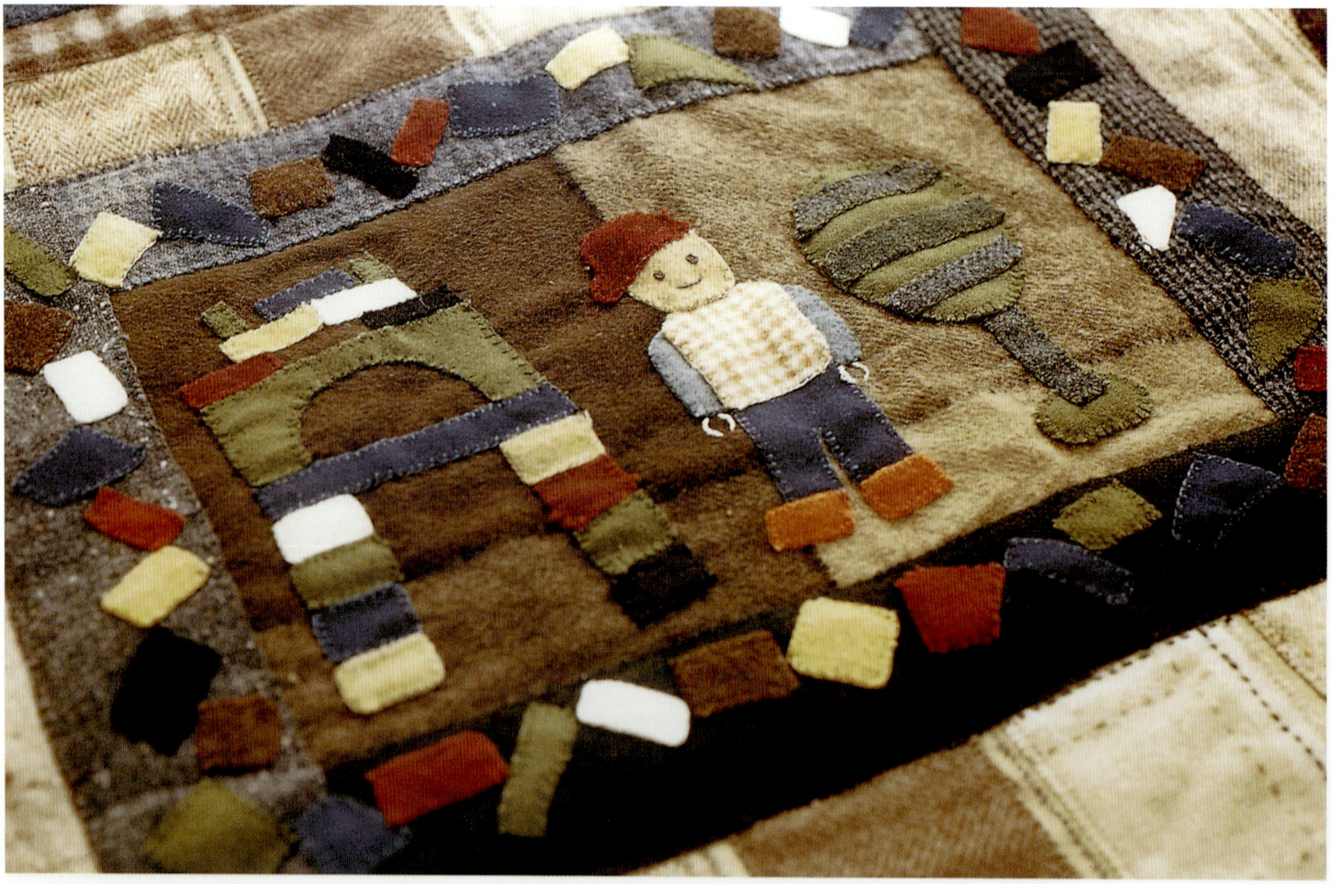

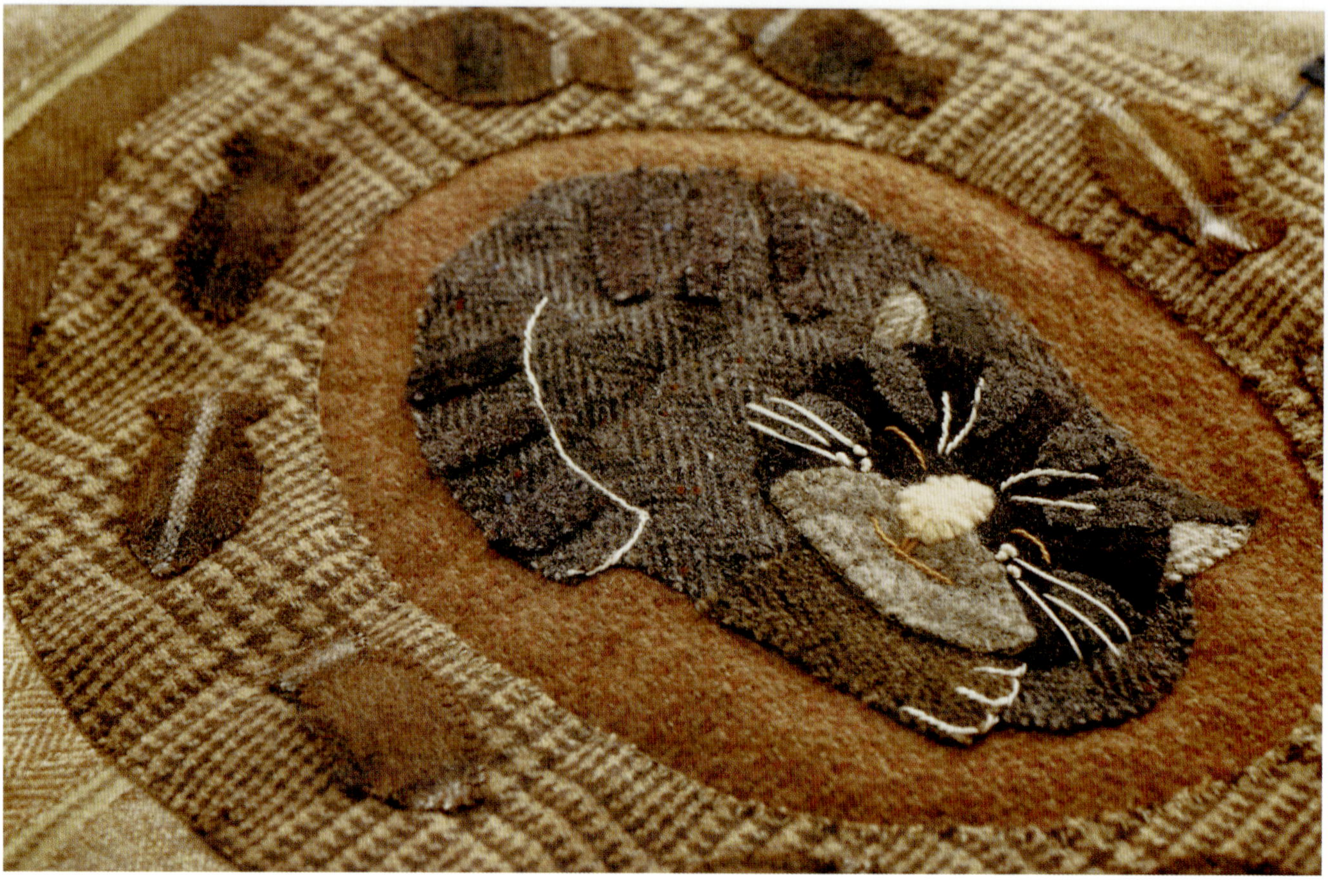

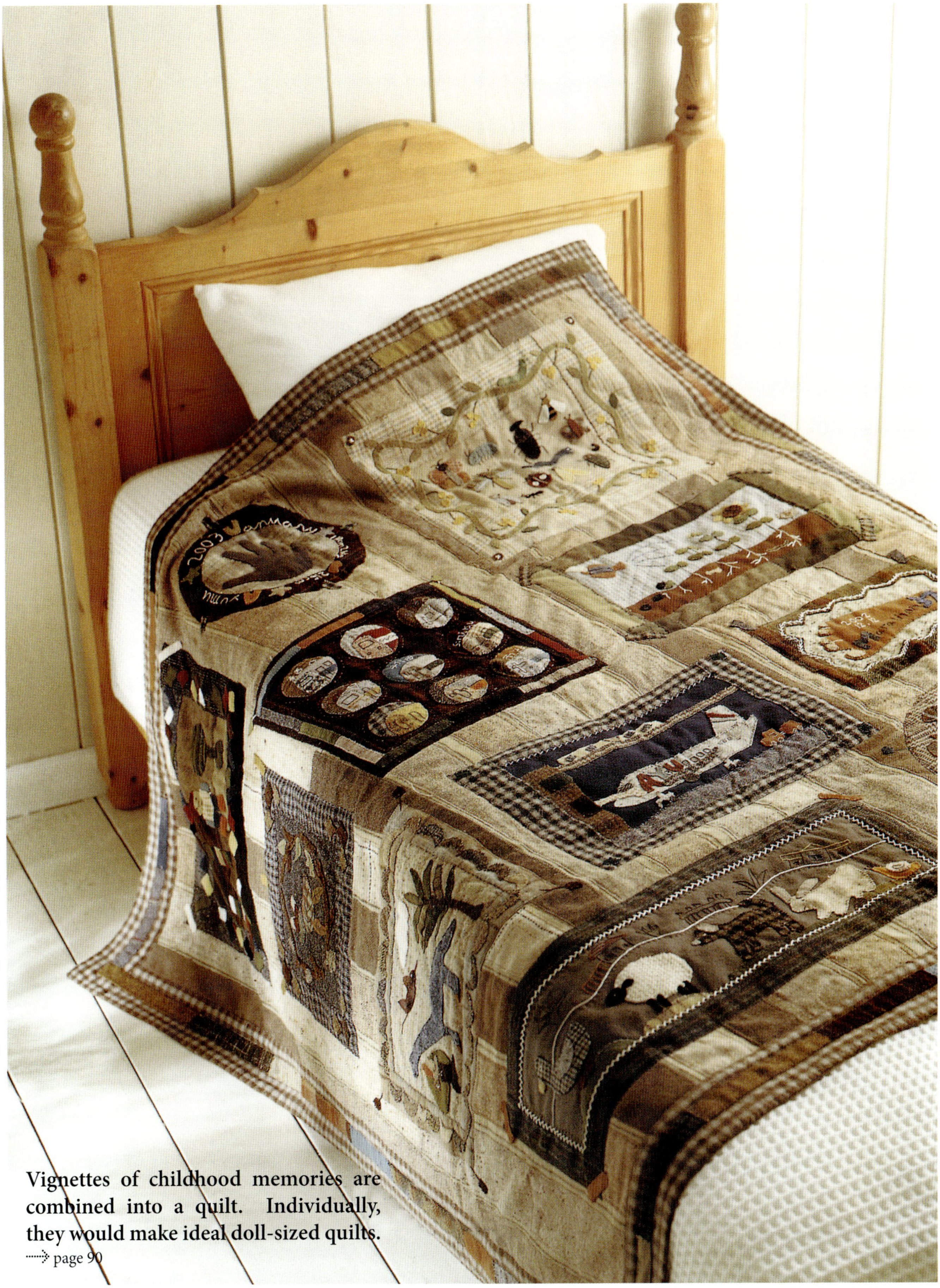

30

Vignettes of childhood memories are combined into a quilt. Individually, they would make ideal doll-sized quilts.

⇢ page 90

31 Autumn Foliage Placemat

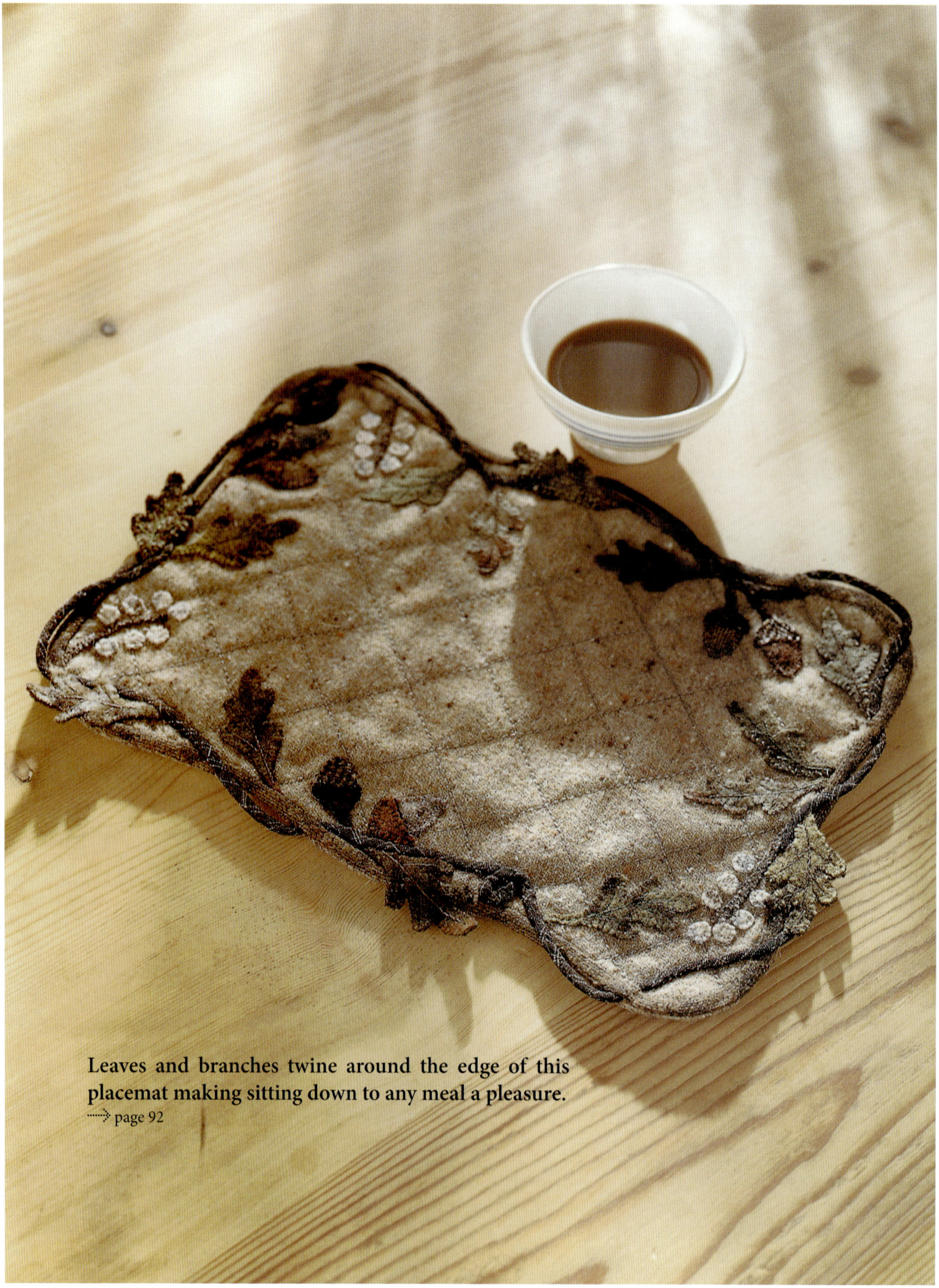

Leaves and branches twine around the edge of this placemat making sitting down to any meal a pleasure.
→ page 92

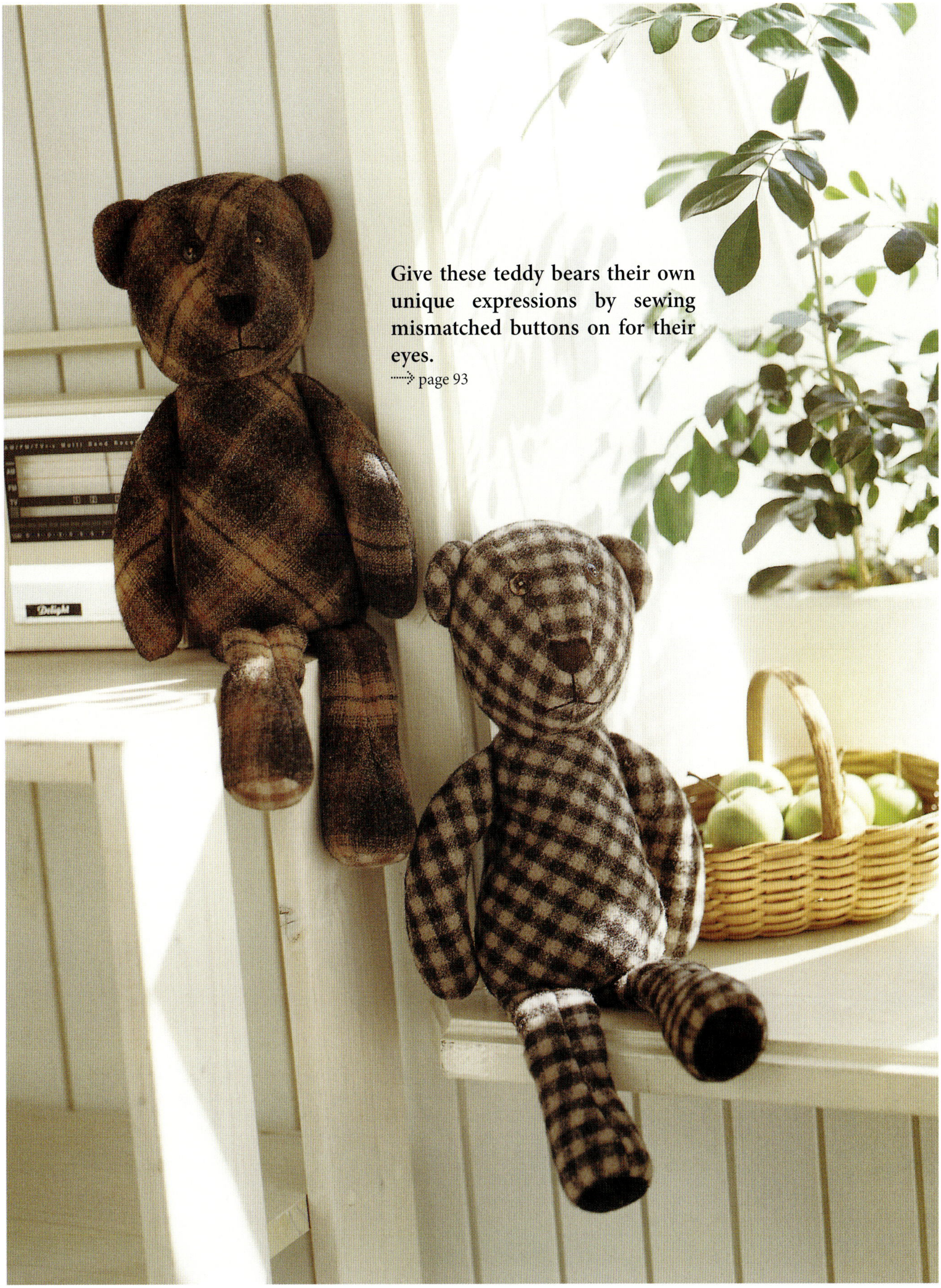

Give these teddy bears their own unique expressions by sewing mismatched buttons on for their eyes.

⇢ page 93

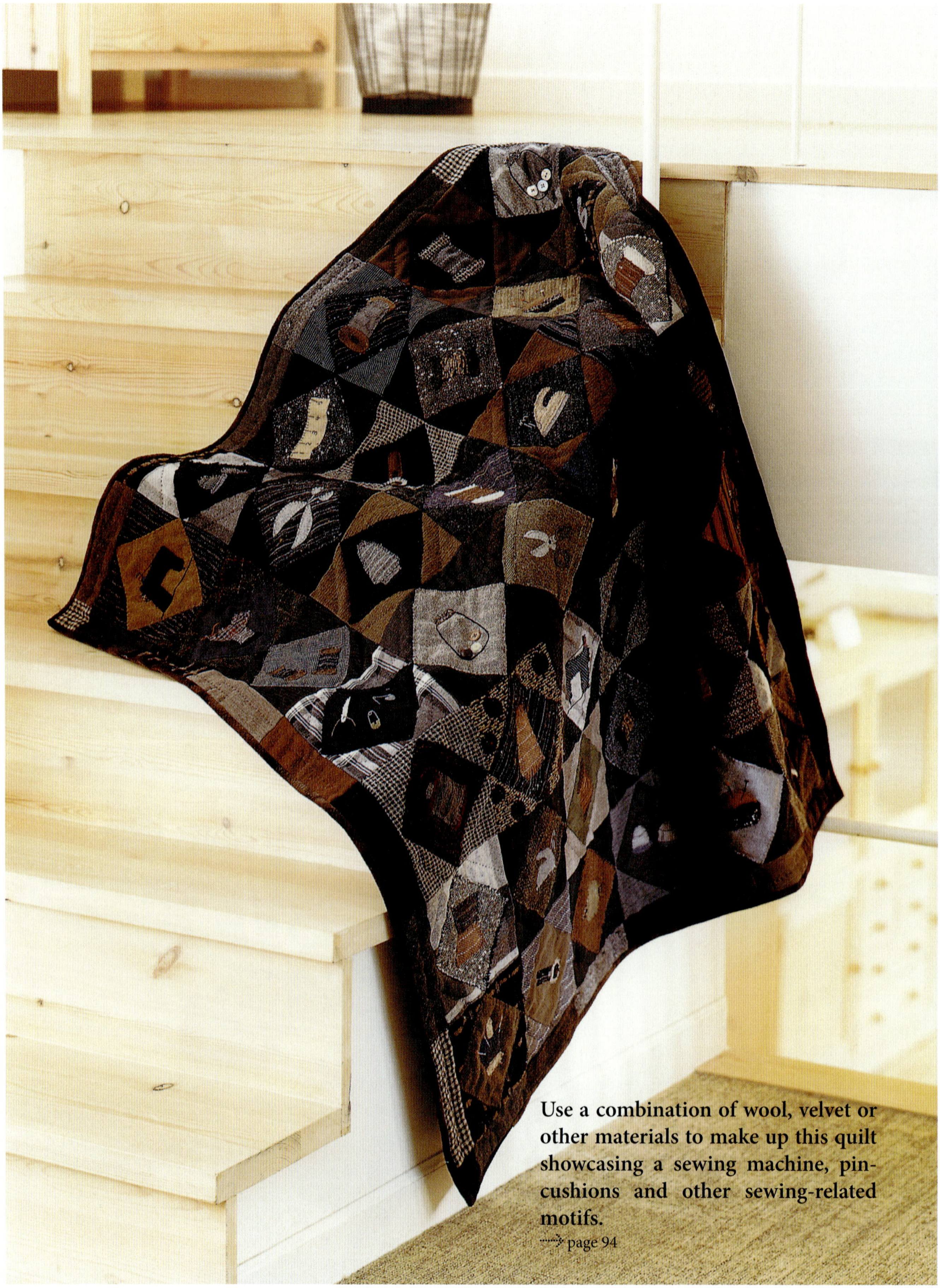

Use a combination of wool, velvet or other materials to make up this quilt showcasing a sewing machine, pin-cushions and other sewing-related motifs.

⇢ page 94

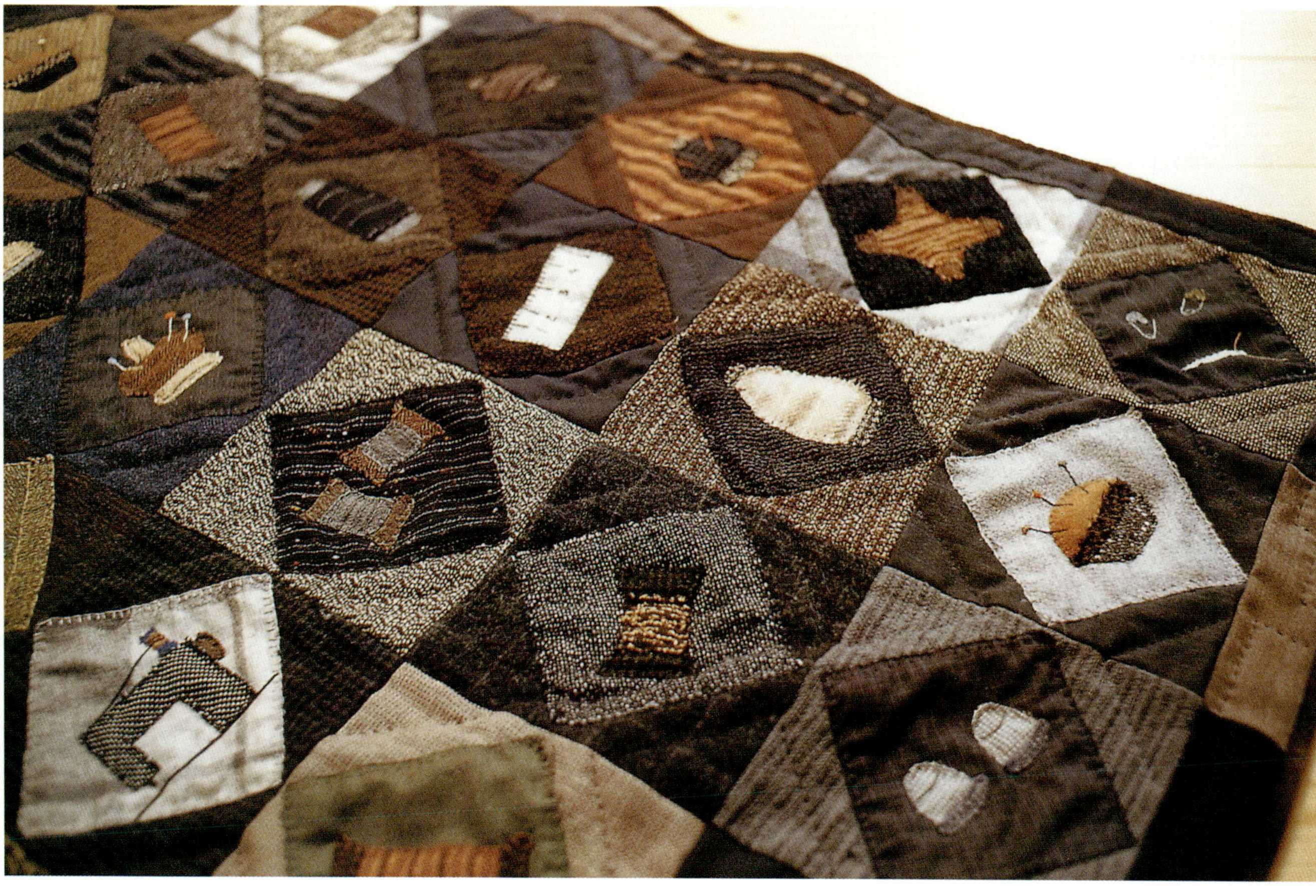

34

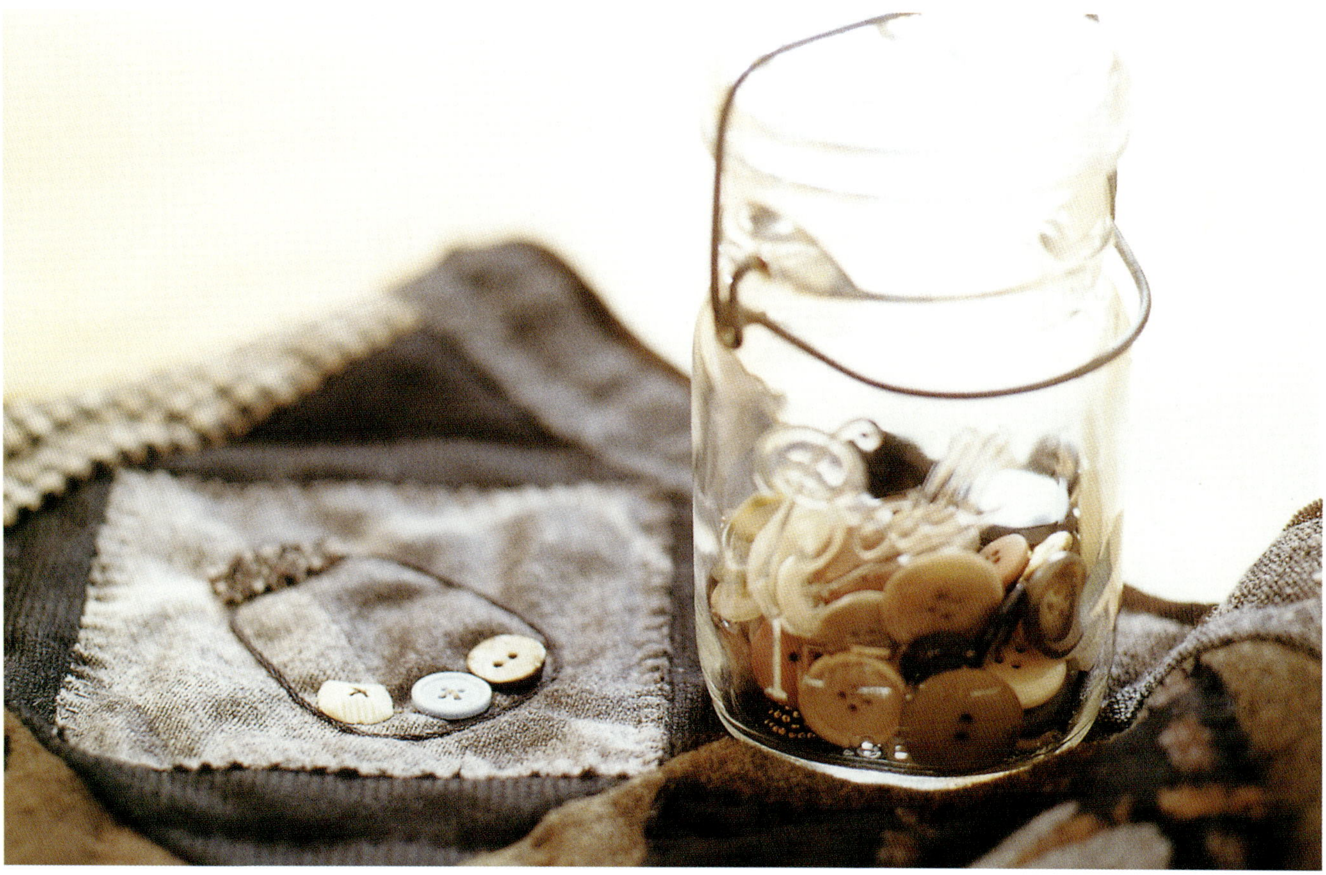

Essential Notions

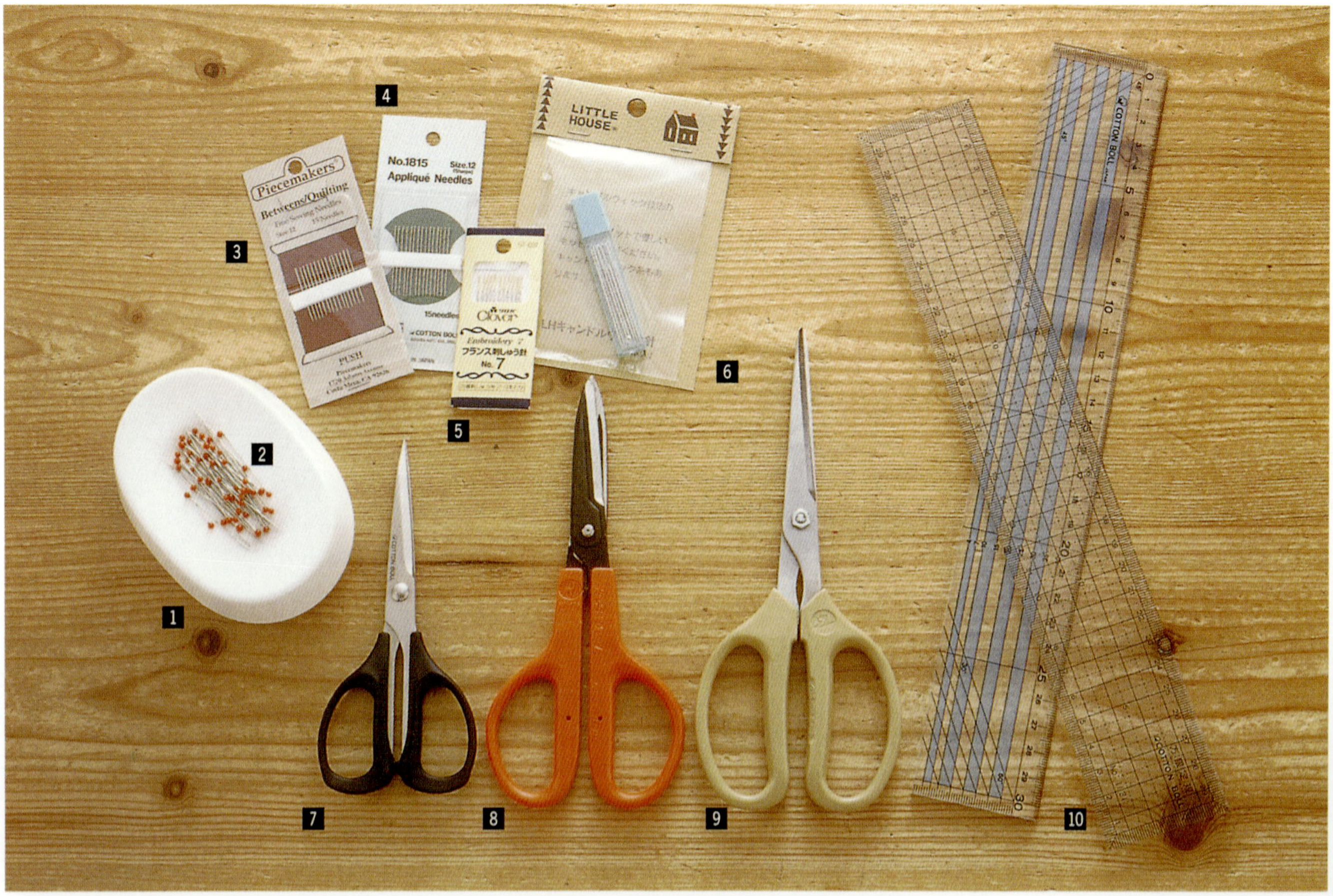

Materials

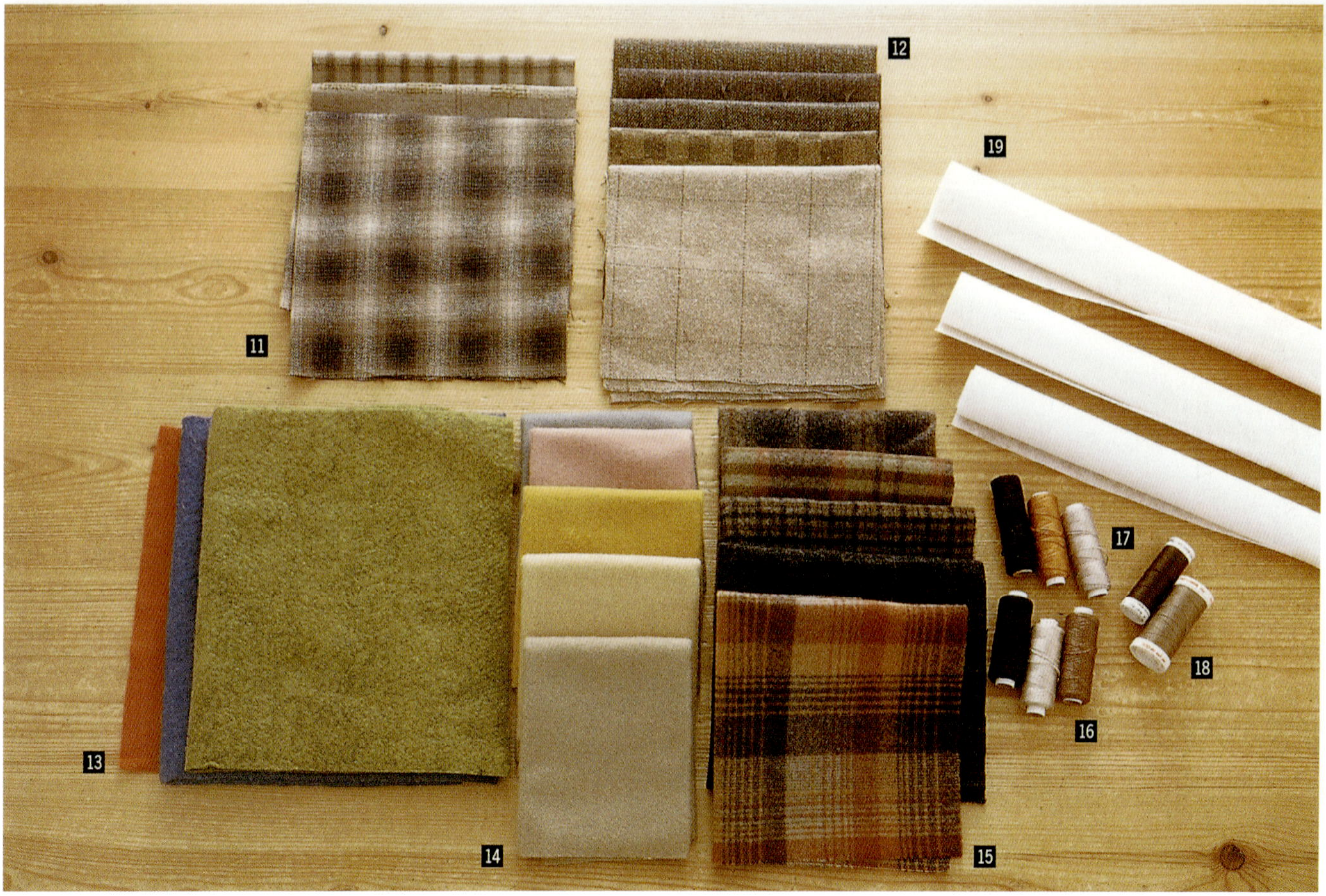

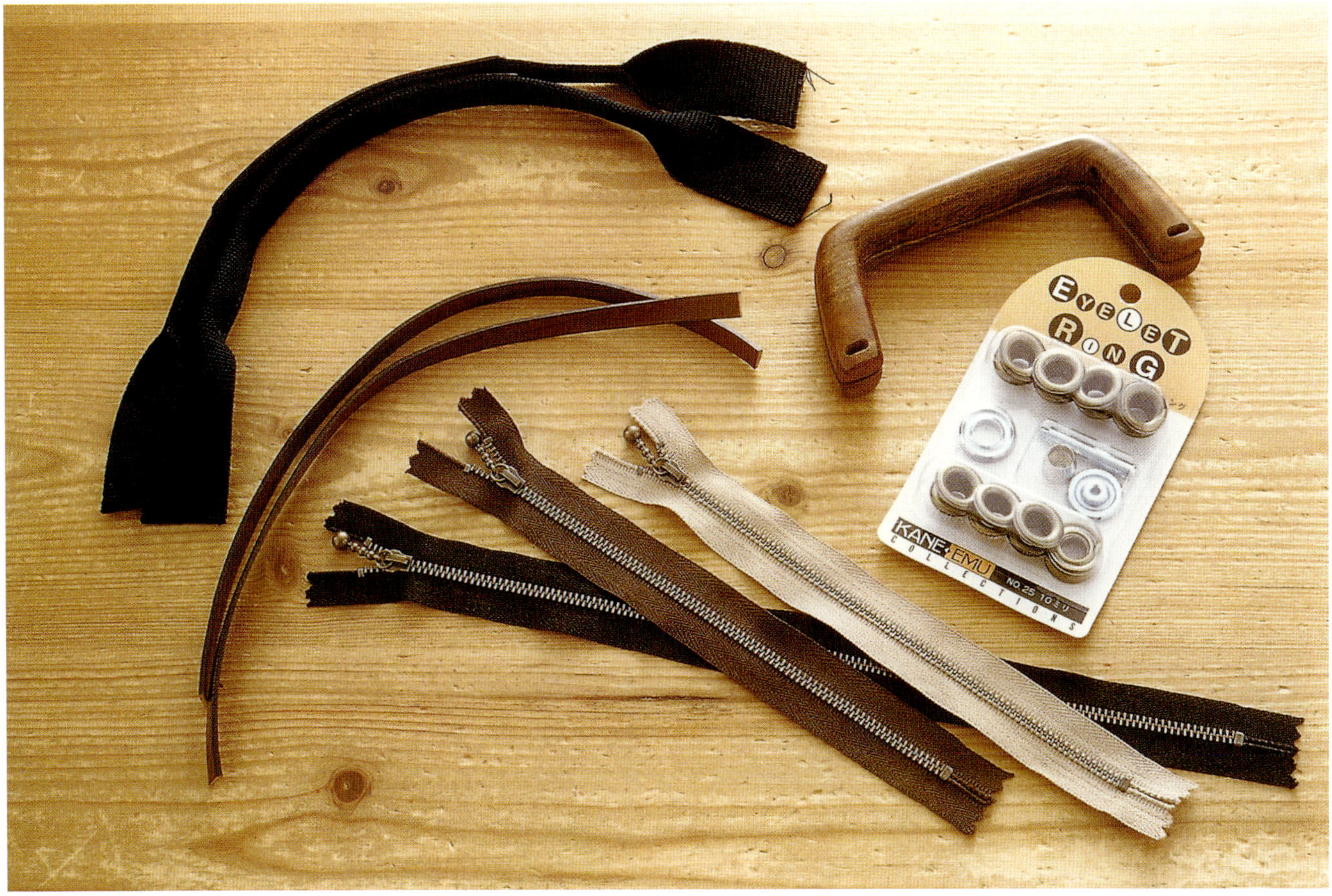

Essential Notions

Necessary tools for wool projects.

1 **Magnetic Pincushion**
Conveniently keeps your pins and needles handy.

2 **Straight Pins**
An easy-to-use longer straight pin with a small head.

3 **Quilting Betweens Needles**
Shorter than sharps, used for quilting.

4 **Sharps Needles**
For general hand-sewing or stitching.

5 **Embroidery Needle**
Perfect for embroidery stitches.

6 **Embroidery Needle** (large eye)
Needles used for candlewicking have larger eyes and are easier to thread when using perle cotton.

7 **Scissors** (a pair specifically for thread)

8 **Scissors** (a pair specifically for paper)

9 **Scissors** (a pair specifically for fabric)
They will last longer if each pair is used for specific things, such as for paper, fabric or thread.

10 **Rulers**
Used to trace straight lines when transferring patterns. Rulers with markings made for quilters are useful.

Materials

11 **Cotton (homespun)**
Use for lining bags and other projects.

12 **Lightweight Wool**
Mainly used when stitching appliqués.

13 **Felted Wool**
Richly colored, they add depth and texture to your designs.

14 **Felt**
Another option with a variety of colors to choose from.

15 **Light to Mid-weight Wool**
Most used for patchwork and/or larger appliqués. Use recycled or new material.

16 **Perle Cotton**
Used to emphasize hand-stitching or embroidery on wool appliqué.

17 **Embroidery Thread**
Used for embroidery stitches. If you can buy 2-strand on a spool, it can also be used in your sewing machine.

18 **Sewing Thread**
Used for piecing or stitching; appropriate for either hand-sewing or machine sewing.

19 **Fusible Interfacing**
Used to add body or stiffness to a fabric. (lightweight, medium weight, heavyweight)

Bag-Making Accessories

The appearance of bags are impacted by what kind of handles, closures and other accessories you add. Look at the overall balance of the bag (size, shape, etc.) when you choose your handles. There are a variety of options to choose from (from the top left): cloth/woven, leather, and wood.

Zippers always come with metal pulls, but it is fun to experiment with adding your own zipper pulls made out of waxed cords or beads. You can also buy buckles, eyelet rings or grommets that have directions on how to use them. Experiment and have fun!

Fly Stitch

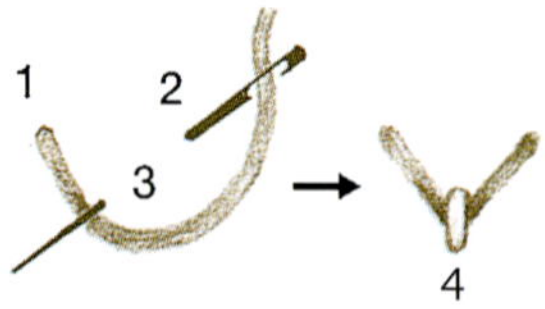

Colonial Knot Stitch

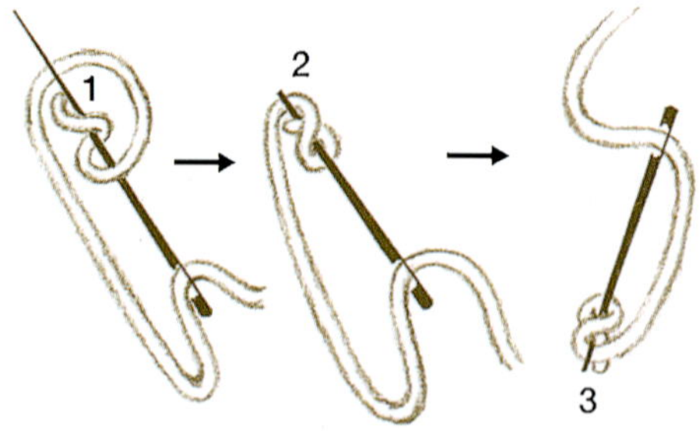

Outline Stitch

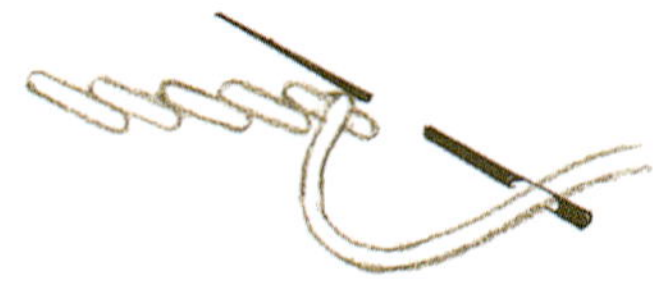

Cross Stitch

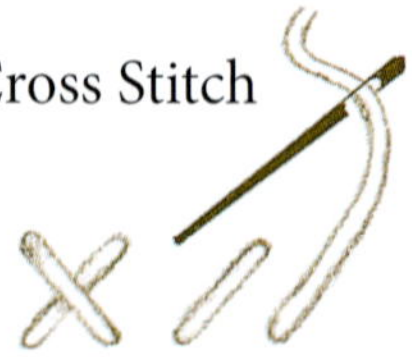

Honeycomb Stitch

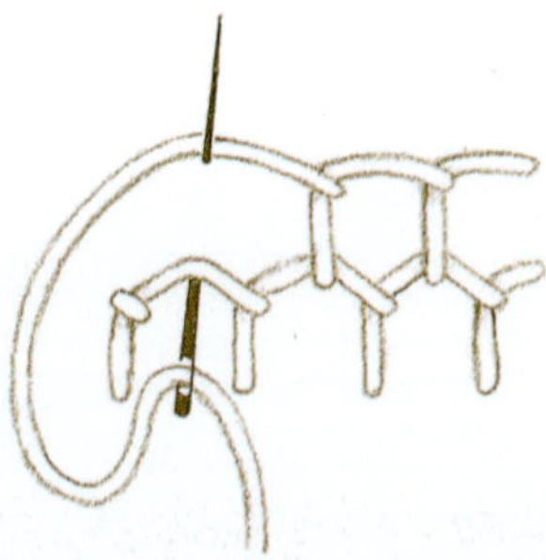

Lazy Daisy Stitch

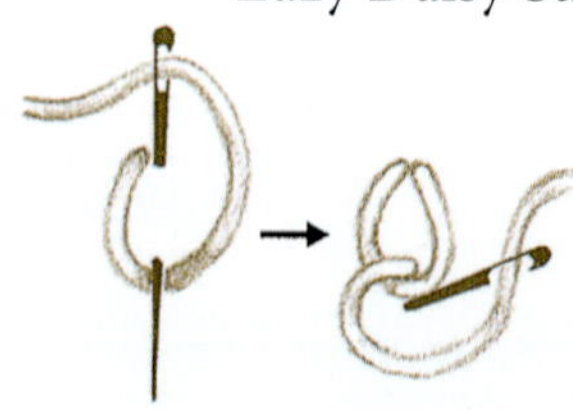

Herringbone Stitch

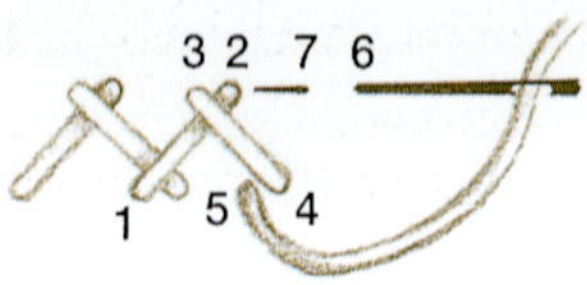

Blanket Stitch

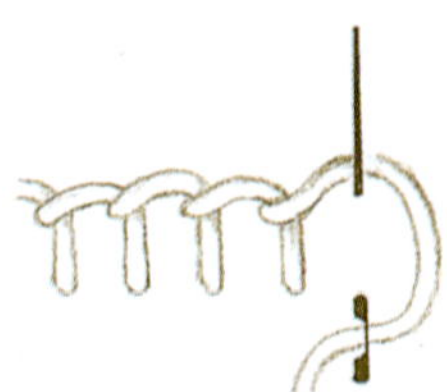

Daisy Knot Stitch

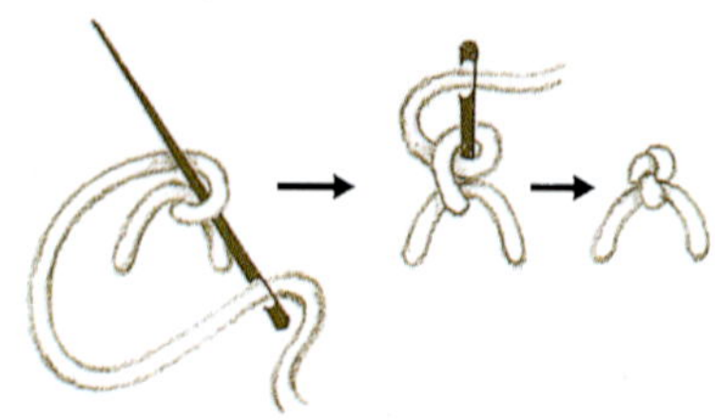

Straight Stitch

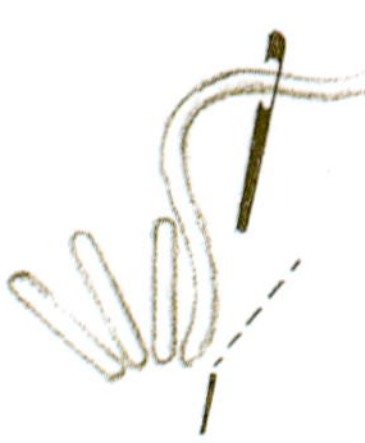

Double Cross Stitch

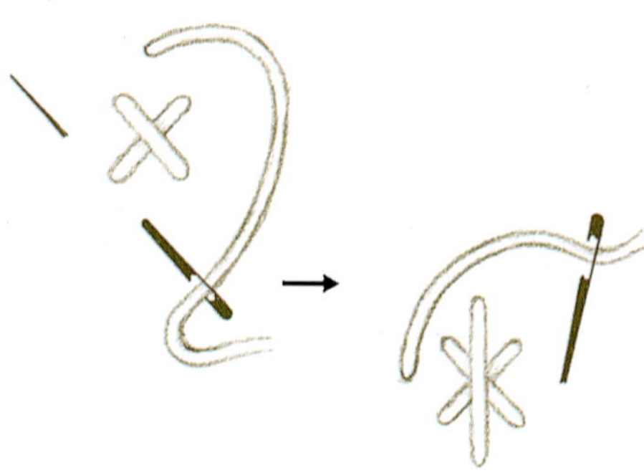

Feather Stitch

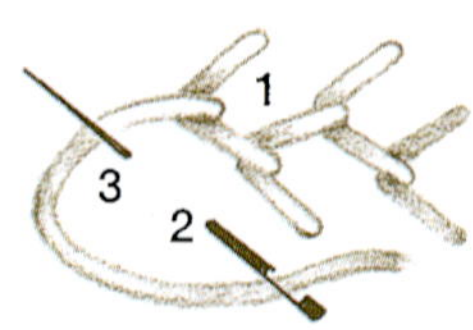

Running Stitch

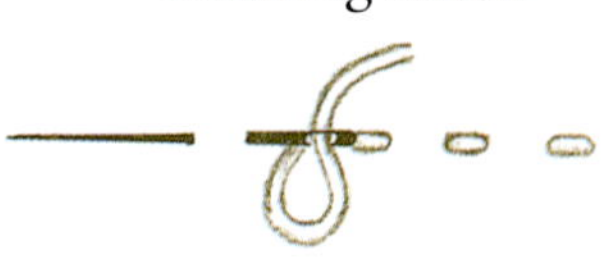

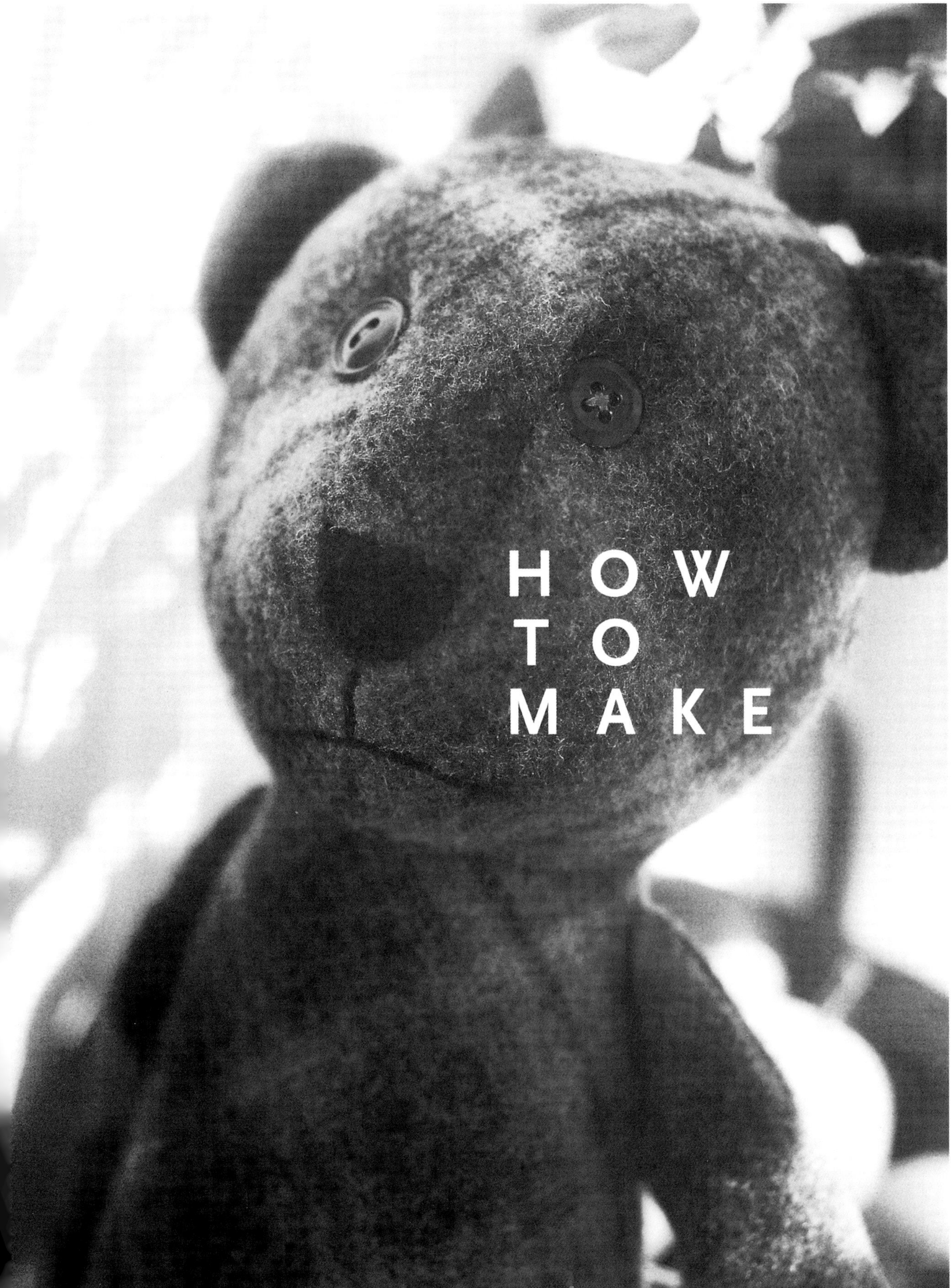

HOW TO MAKE

1 ↓ 34

1

Basketweave Handbag

page 5 - Pattern Sheet A (brown)

Materials

Wool (horizontal tubes)
  Fabric A - 40 × 40 cm [15¾" × 15¾"]
  Fabric B - 25 × 40 cm [9¾" × 15¾"]
  Fabric C - 20 × 40 cm [7⅞" × 15¾"]
Wool (vertical tubes) - 60 × 50 cm [23⅝" × 19¾"]
Lightweight wool (backing for tubes) - 100 × 80 cm [39⅜" × 31½"]
Wool (side gusset - bias) - 30 × 20 cm [11¾" × 7⅞"]
Wool (bag bottom, cut 2) - 35 × 30 cm [13¾" × 11¾"]
Lightweight wool
  (outer bag opening, facing) - each 4.5 × 80 cm [1¾" × 31½"]
  (bag opening bias binding) - 3 × 80 cm [1¼" × 31½"]
Lightweight wool (handle loops) - 40 × 35 cm [15¾" × 13¾"]
Homespun (lining) - 90 × 90 cm [35⅜" × 35⅜"]
Fusible interfacing (heavyweight) - 80 × 30 cm [31½" × 11¾"]
Fusible interfacing (medium weight) - 30 × 30 cm [11¾" × 11¾"]
Fusible interfacing (lightweight) - 25 × 10 cm [9¾" × 4"]
Flannel (for bag opening) - 2.5 × 80 cm [1" × 31½"]
Handles - 1 pair

1a Make the fabric tubes

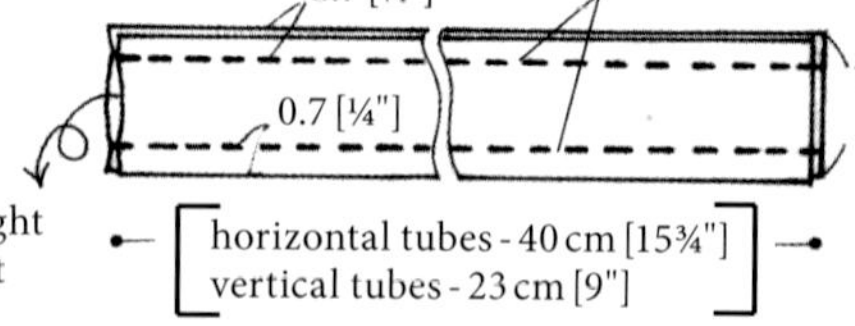

make 20 horizontal tubes; 34 vertical tubes

↓

machine embroider down the center of each tube with desired stitch

2a Weaving the tubes together

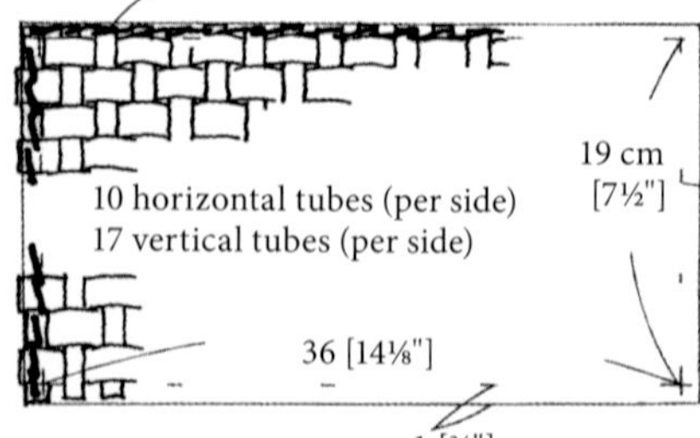

make 2 (front and back pieces)

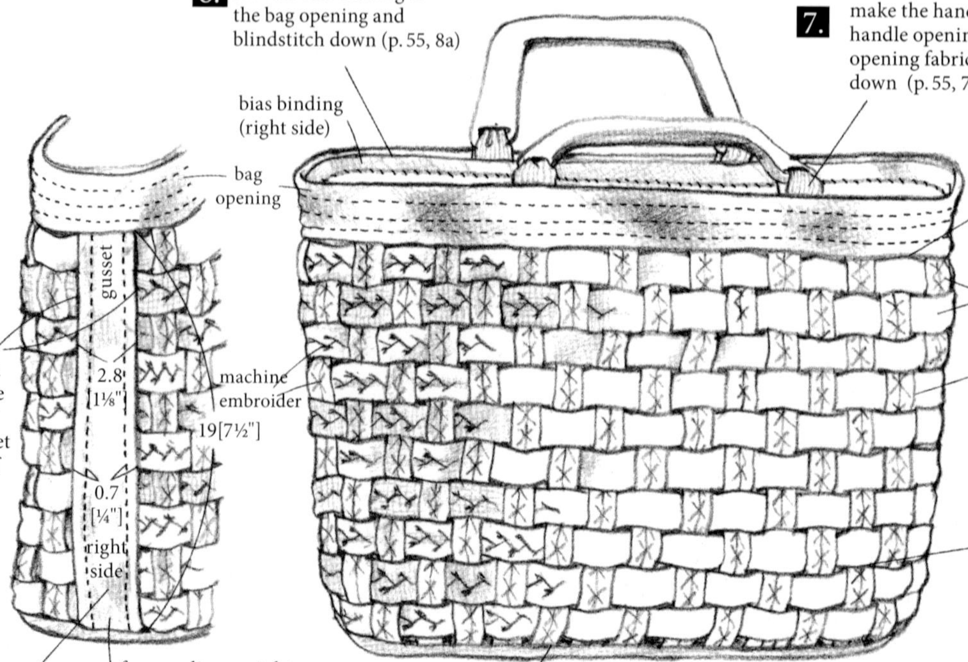

3a sewing the gussets to the front and back pieces

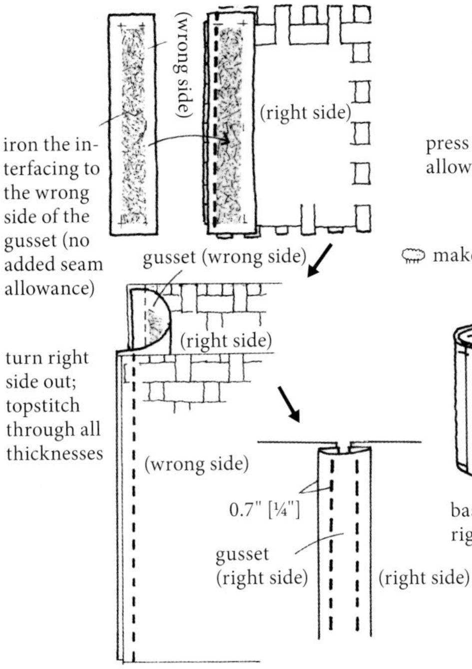

4a making the bag lining (cut 2 pieces)

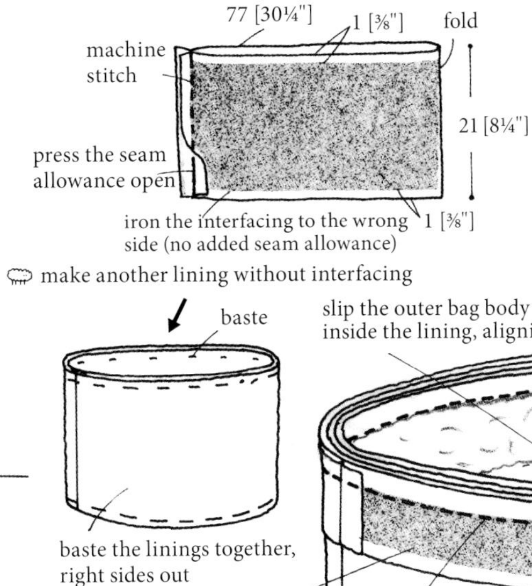

6a making and attaching the bag opening to the main bag body (cut 2 pieces)

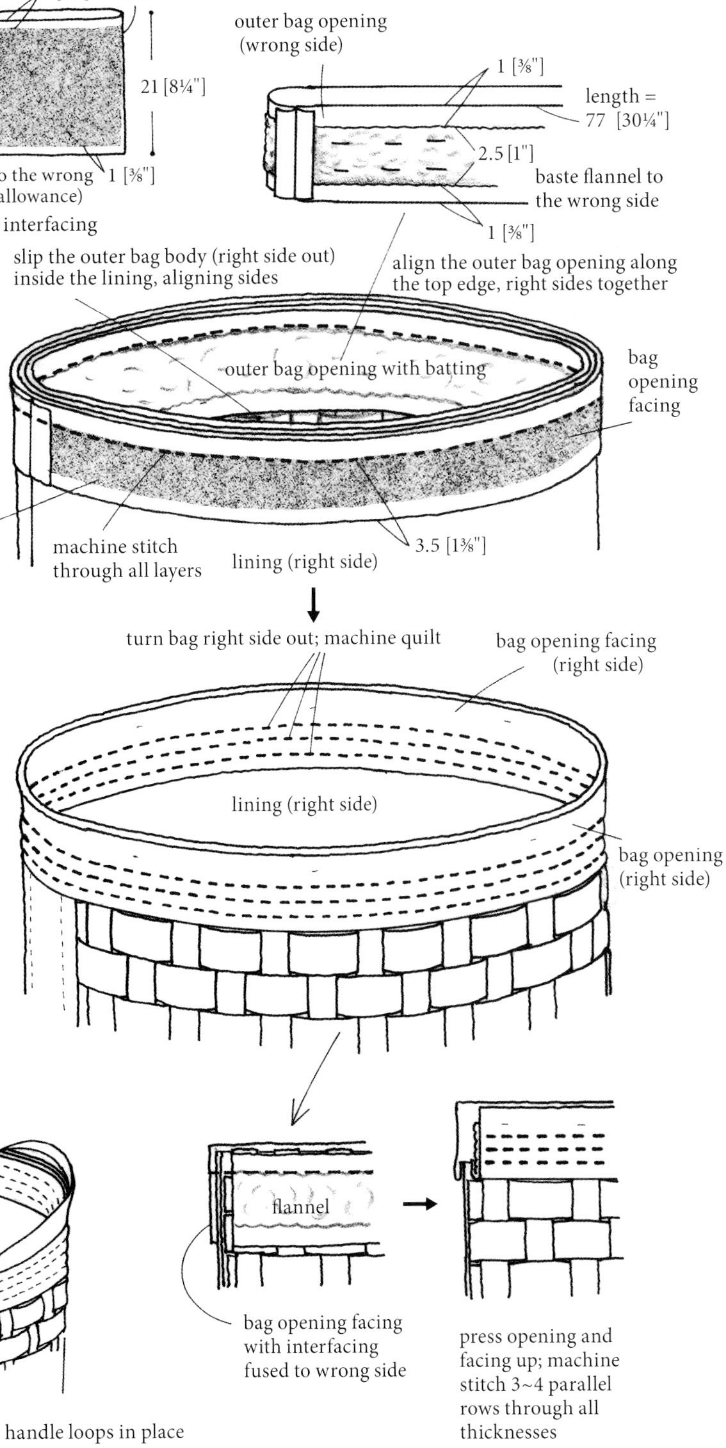

7a & 8a make the handle loops; sandwich between bag opening seams and stitch

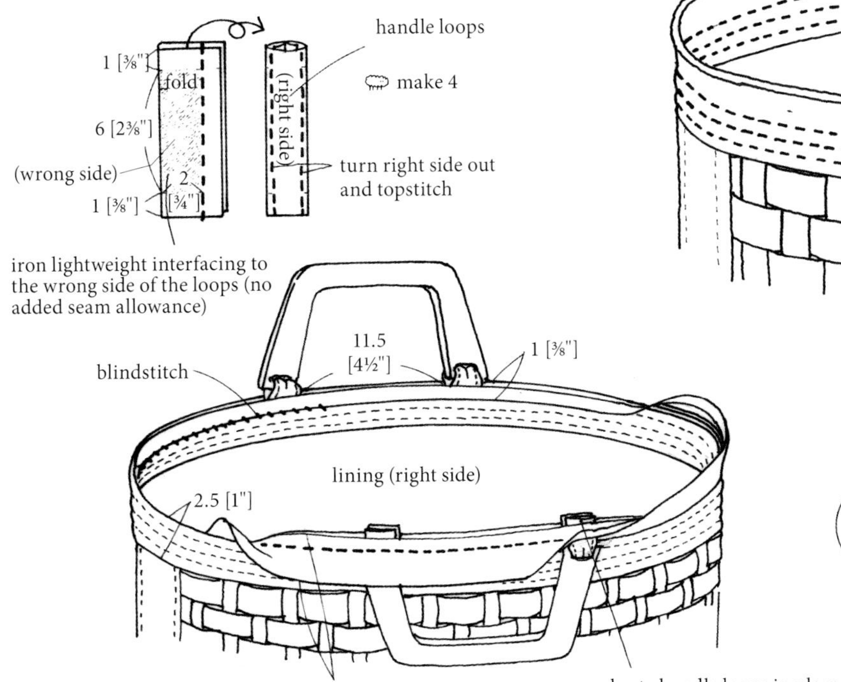

cut the bias binding out of the same fabric as the bag opening/facing; center handles and position and baste handle loops in place; with right sides together and aligning raw edges, stitch the bias binding to the bag opening, catching the handle loops in between; fold bias binding to the inside, covering the raw edges; blindstitch to the inside bag opening facing to complete the bag

❷

Semi-Circle Handbag

page 6 - Pattern Sheet A (brown)

Materials

Wool
(bag front, cut on bias) 40 × 40 cm [15¾" × 15¾"]
(bag back) 40 × 35 cm [15¾" × 13¾"]
(pocket) 45 × 25 cm [17¾" × 9¾"]
Wool (lining for bag front, bag back, pocket) 40 × 90 cm [15¾" × 35⅜"]
Wool (bias binding) 60 × 60 cm [23⅝" × 23⅝"]
Fusible interfacing (heavyweight) - 60 × 40 cm [23⅝" × 15¾"]
Heavy woven webbing (handle) - 3 × 80 cm [1¼" × 31½"]
2 Leather strips (handle center) - 1.5 × 13.5 cm [⅝" × 5¼"]
Assorted scraps of wool (appliqué)
Embroidery thread - moss green, beige
Perle cotton - dk brown, moss green, black

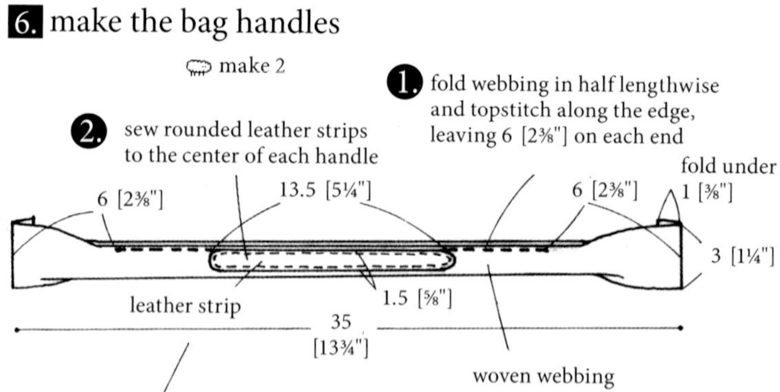

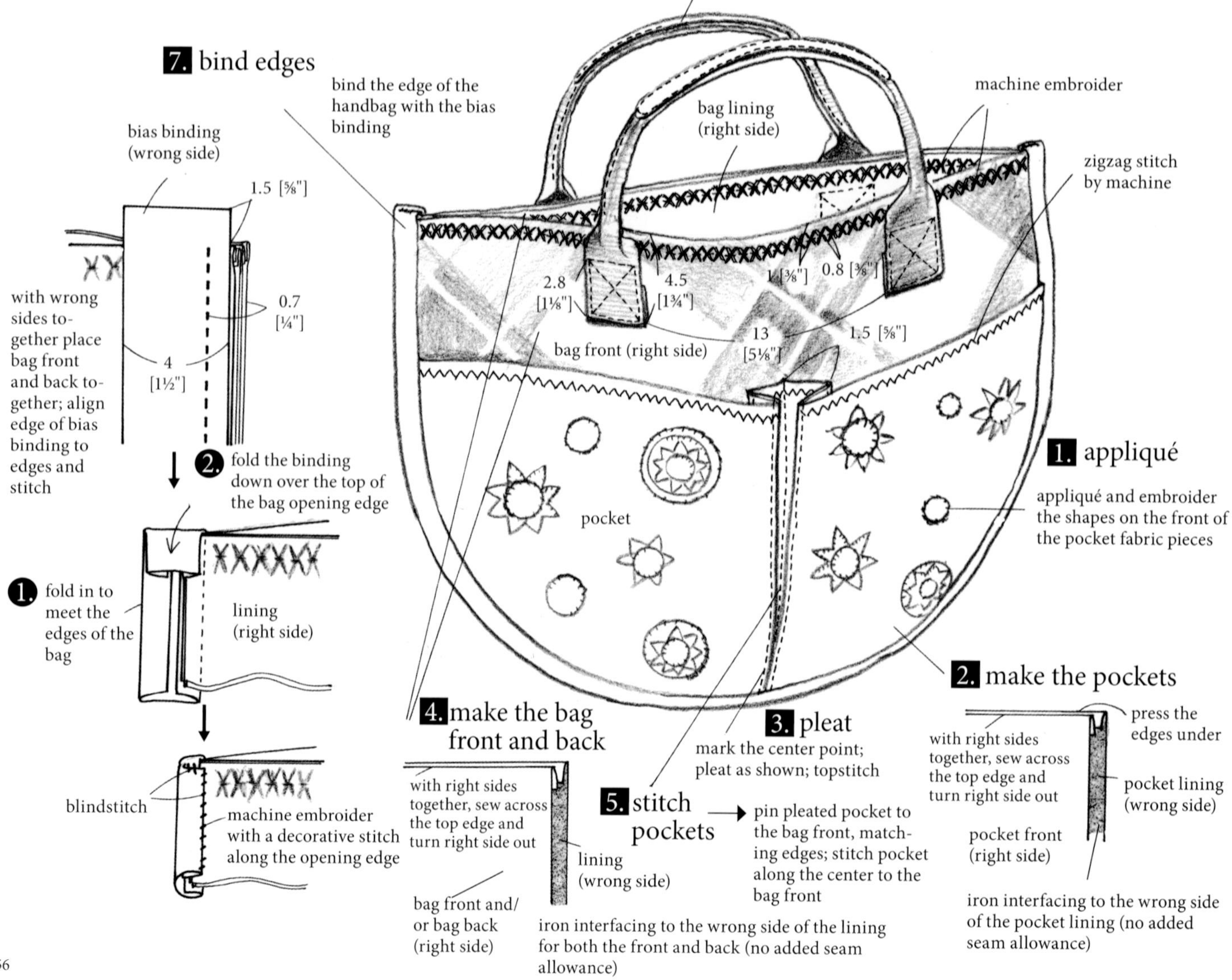

3

City Skyline Pouch

⇢ page 10 - Pattern Sheet A (brown)

Materials

Wool
(front upper section, pouch back) - 25 × 25 cm [9¾" x 9¾"]
(front lower section, zipper tab) - 25 × 15 cm [9¾" x 5⅞"]
Wool (bias binding) - 4 × 47 cm [1½" x 18½"] cut from a piece of 40 × 40 cm [15¾" x 15¾"]
Wool (lining for pouch front, pouch back, pocket) - 25 × 45 cm [9¾" x 17¾"]
Assorted scraps of wool (appliqué)
Fusible interfacing - 25 × 15 cm [9¾" x 5⅞"]
1 Zipper - 17 cm [6"]
Embroidery thread - black, grey

4. sew the pouch front to the pocket lining

❷ carefully cut a slit in the lining for the zipper opening

❸ fold the edges of the lining under to the wrong side and blindstitch around the zipper opening

❶ align the pocket lining to the back of the pouch front; baste around the edges

3a machine stitch the zipper to the upper and lower sections

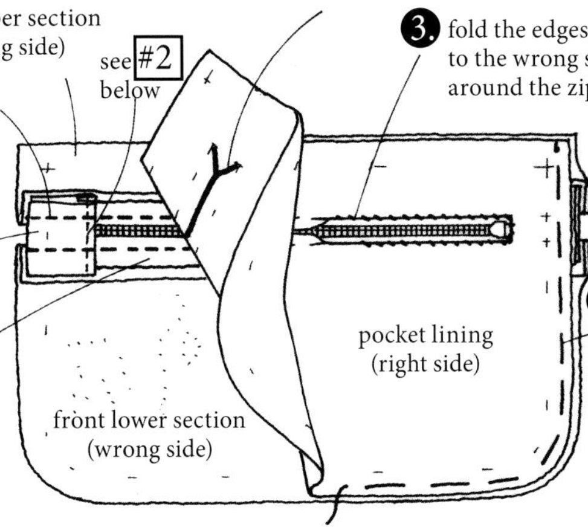

5. sew pouch together

align top edges and machine stitch through all layers

fold pouch back over right side out; press and align edges

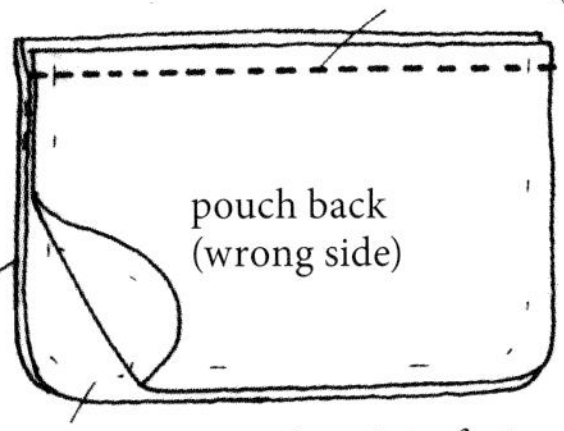

iron interfacing to the wrong side of the pouch back (no added seam allowance)

2. zipper

measure the length of the zipper; sew the zipper tab fabric to each end of the zipper

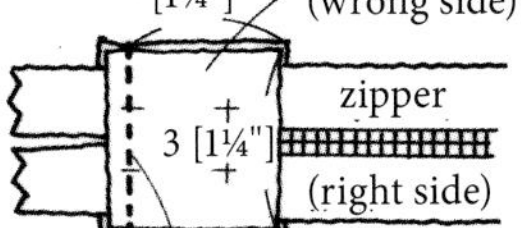

with right sides together sandwich the end of the zipper between the tabs

↓

sew and fold back over to cover the ends of the zipper tape

6. embroider by machine

embroider through the pouch front and also the pouch back with a stitch of your choice

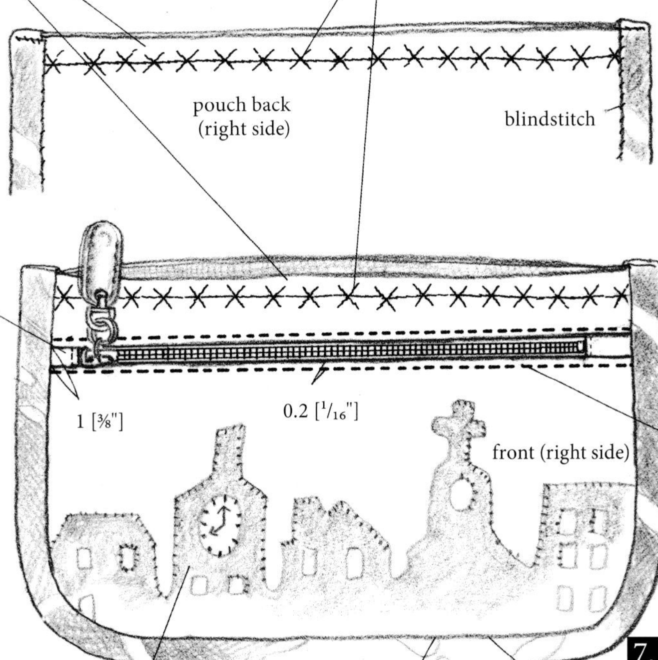

3. insert zipper

insert the zipper by sewing it, right sides together, to the front upper and lower sections; topstitch close to teeth (3a, above)

7. bind the edges

with wrong sides together baste the front and back together around the outer edge; bind the edges with the bias strip; blindstitch the binding down to finish the pouch

1. appliqué

appliqué the city skyline to the front lower section (p. 52)

4

Embroidered Drawstring Bag

⋯> page 11 - Pattern Sheet A (brown)

Materials

Wool (outer bag)
(bag opening for drawstring out of bias, cut 2) - 25 × 5 cm [9¾" × 2"]
Assorted scraps (14 vertical pieces for bag body, bag bottom, cut 2) - each 20 × 20 cm [7⅞" × 7⅞"]
Wool (lining for bag body, bottom) - 60 × 20 cm [23⅝" × 7⅞"]
Homespun (lining for bag opening, cut 2 from a contrasting color) - 25 × 5 cm [9¾" × 2"]
Fusible interfacing (lightweight) - 15 × 10 cm [5⅞" × 4"]
Cord (drawstring, cut 2) - 0.4 cm × 35 cm [¼" × 13¾"]
2 Wooden beads - (for ends of drawstring)
Embroidery thread - various shades of brown

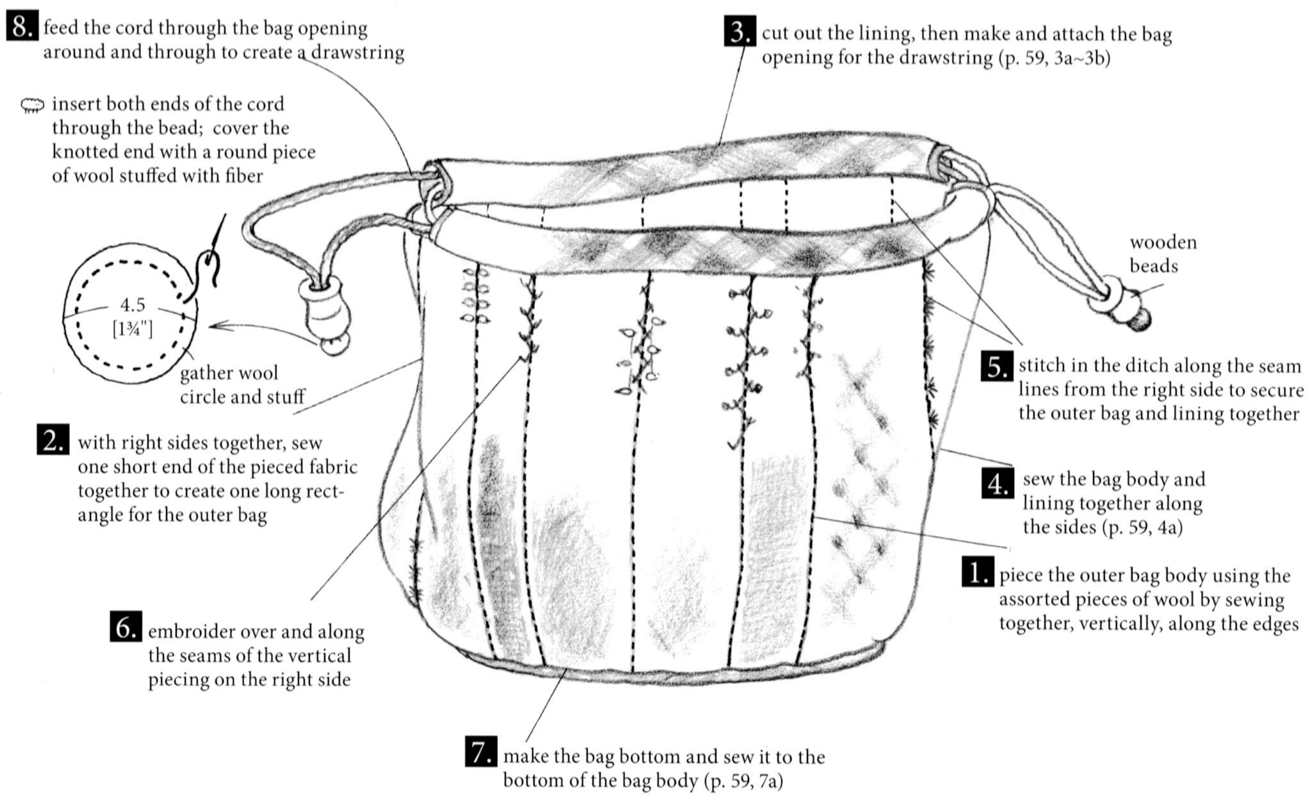

3a the lining

cut out the lining the same size as the large pieced rectangle made in steps 1~2

3b make the bag opening for the drawstring

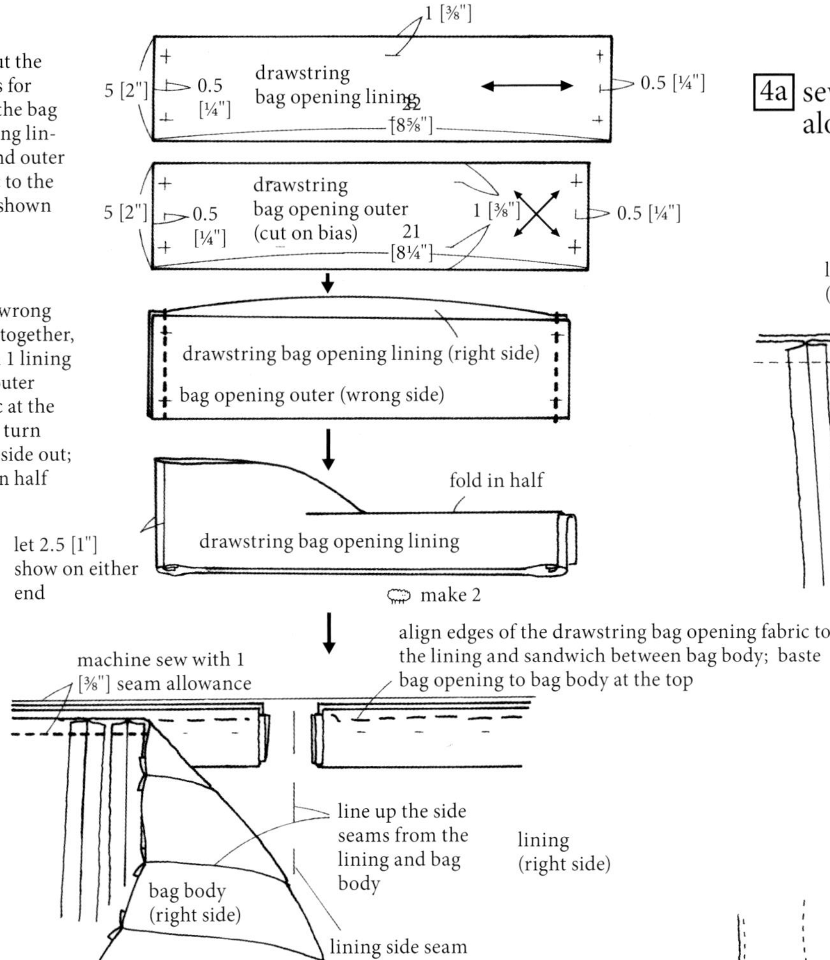

4a sew the bag body and lining together along the sides

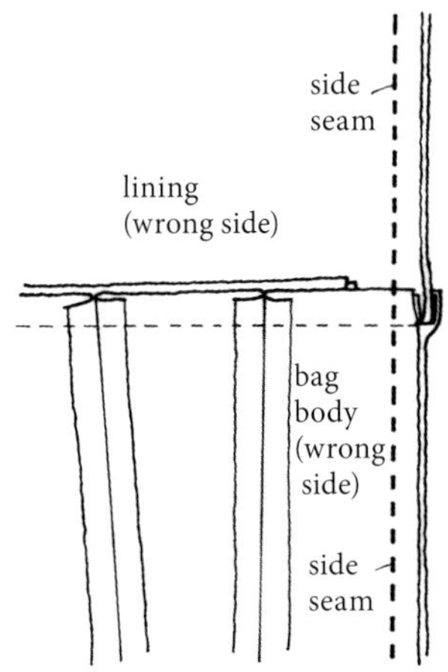

with right sides together, open out the bag and lining and align the side seams; sew the side seam in one continuous line; turn right side out, then fold the lining back inside the bag along the top seam to create a cylinder shape

7a make the bag bottom and sew it to the bottom of the bag body

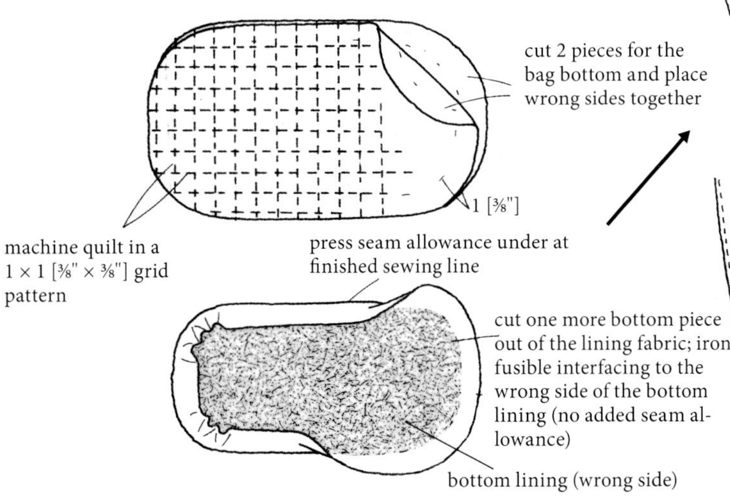

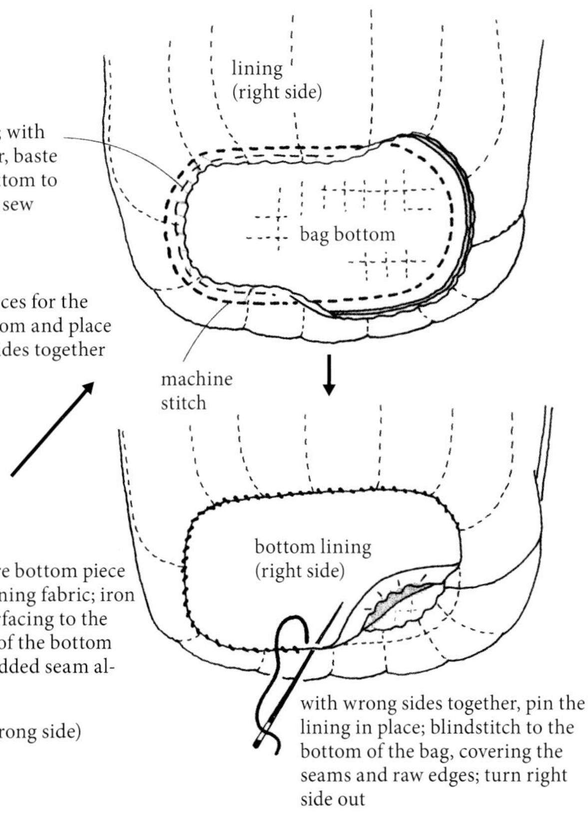

5

Crazy Quilt Boston Bag

→ page 12 - Pattern Sheet A (brown)

Materials

Assorted fat quarters and scraps of wool (piecing for outer bag)
Homespun (lining) - 50 × 60 cm [19¾" × 23⅝"]
Homespun (bias binding) - 4 × 140 cm [1½" × 55⅛"] cut from a piece of 40 × 40 cm [15¾" × 15¾"]
Fusible interfacing (heavyweight; for body, gusset, zipper opening) - 40 × 70 cm [15¾" × 27½"]
Woven webbing (handle) - 4 × 44 cm [1½" × 17¼"]
1 Zipper - 30 cm [11¾"]
Narrow cord (zipper pull) - 10 cm [4"]
Wooden beads - (zipper pull, 2 each) - length 2.5 cm [1"]; diameter 0.5 cm [¼"]
Embroidery thread - assorted colors for crazy quilting stitches

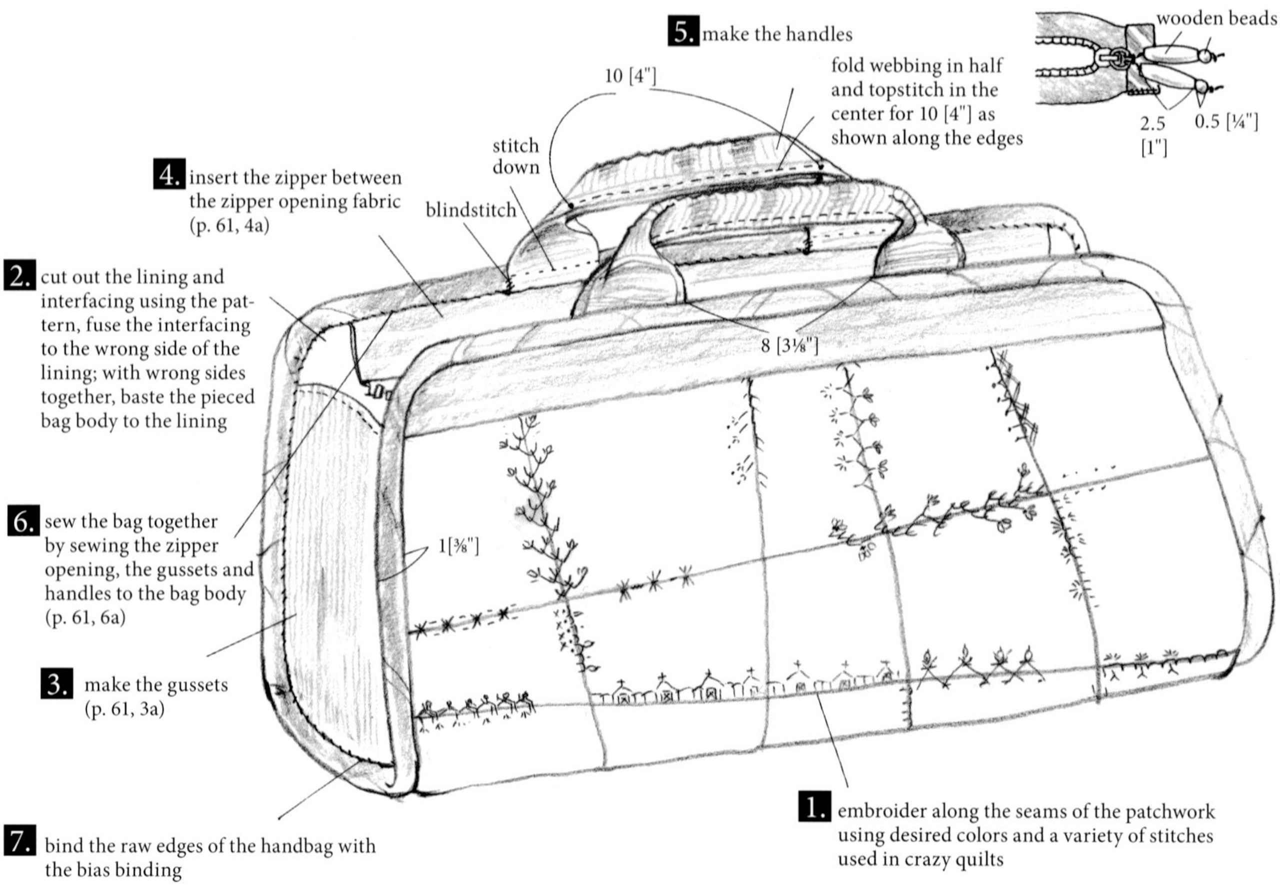

3a make the gussets

cut out the pieces for the gussets
(2 outer and 2 linings)

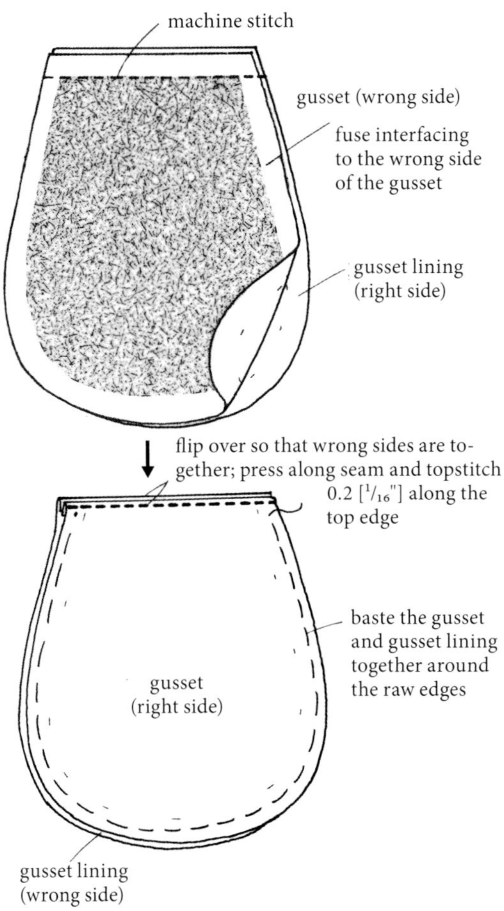

4a sew the zipper to the zipper opening fabric

cut out the pieces for the zipper openings (2 outer and 2 linings)

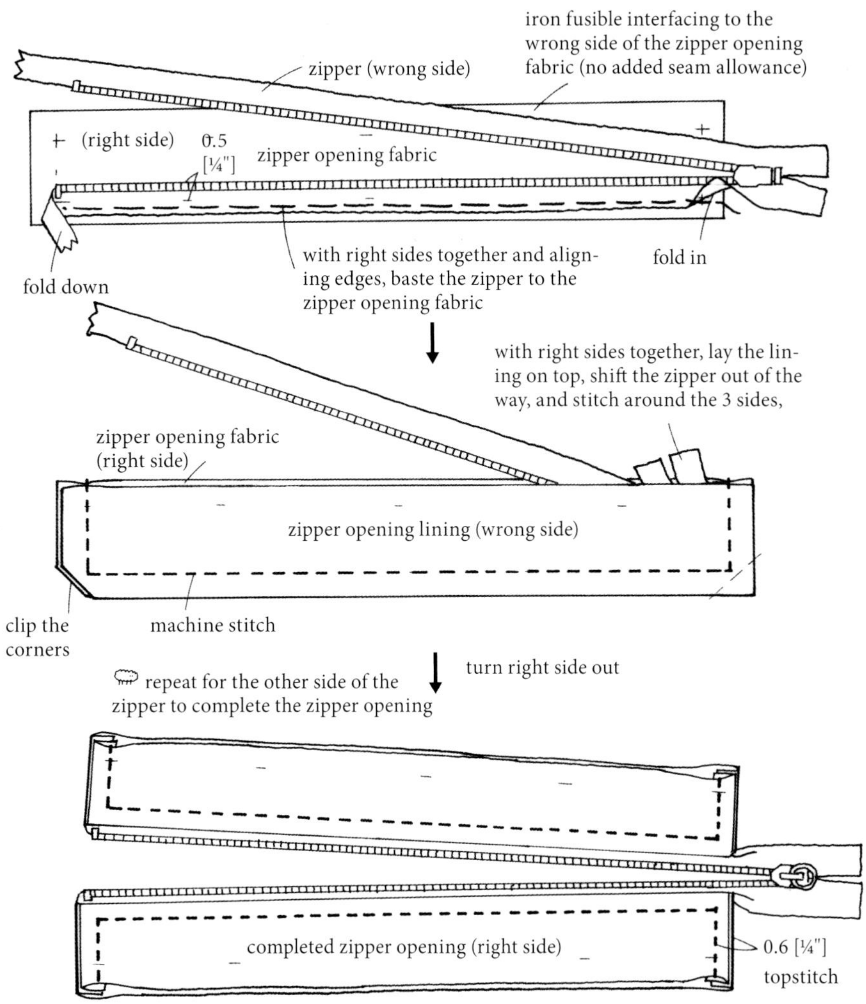

6a sew the handbag together

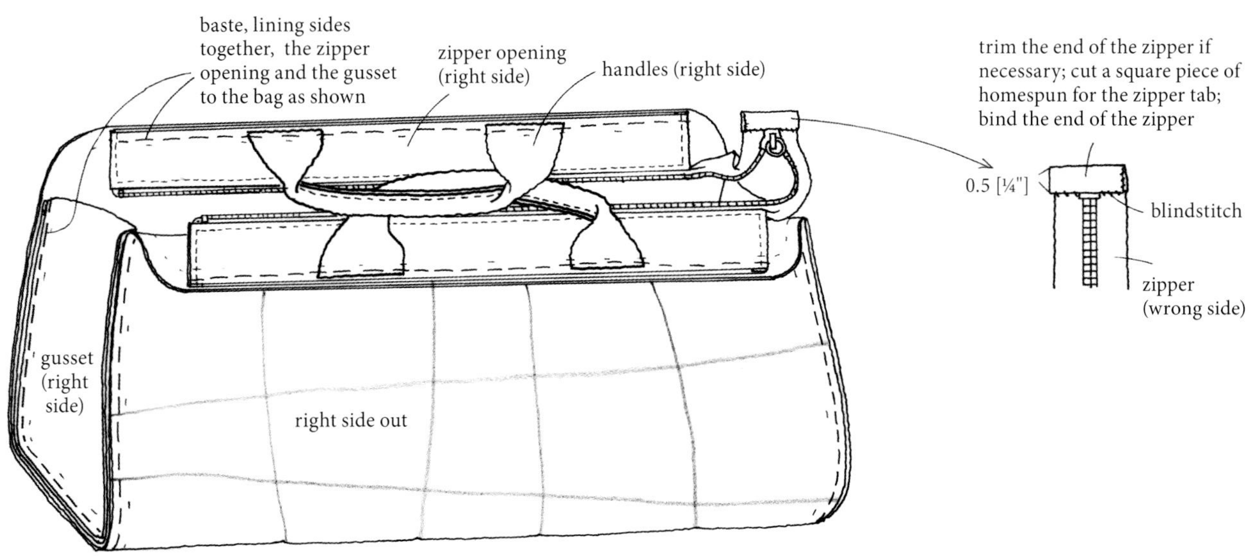

6

Woolen Tiles Handbag

⋯⋯> page 14 - Pattern Sheet A (brown)

Materials

Wool - checkerboard pattern
(bag body) - 80 × 30 cm [31½" × 11¾"]
(handle loops, flap binding) - 20 × 20 cm [7⅞" × 7⅞"]
(zipper opening, on bias) - 3.5 × 23 cm [1⅜" × 9"]
cut from a piece of 25 × 25 cm [9¾" × 9¾"]
Assorted fat quarters and scraps of wool (piecing for flap)
Lightweight wool (lining for bag body, flap, handle facing, and gusset binding) - 40 × 110 cm [15¾" × 43¼"]
Fusible interfacing (lightweight) - 65 × 60 cm [25⅝" × 23⅝"]
Batting (low loft, dense) - 70 × 60 cm [27½" × 23⅝"]
1 Zipper - 17 cm [6"]
Handles - 1 pair
Magnetic Closure (1 set) - 1.8 cm [⅝"] diameter
Clear template plastic - 2.5 × 15 cm [1" × 5⅞"]

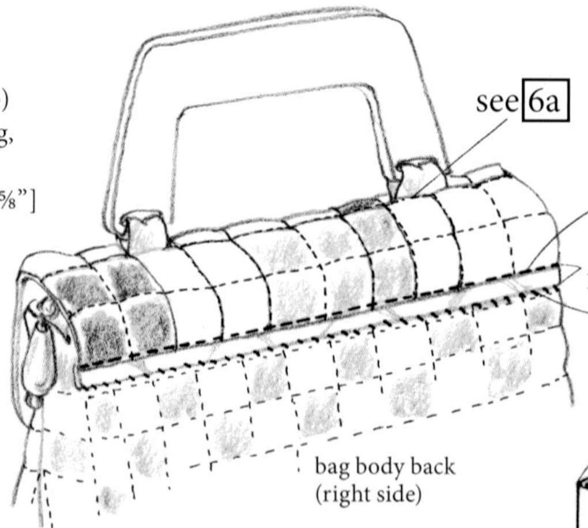

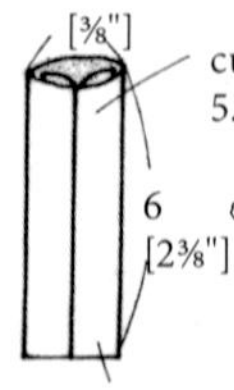

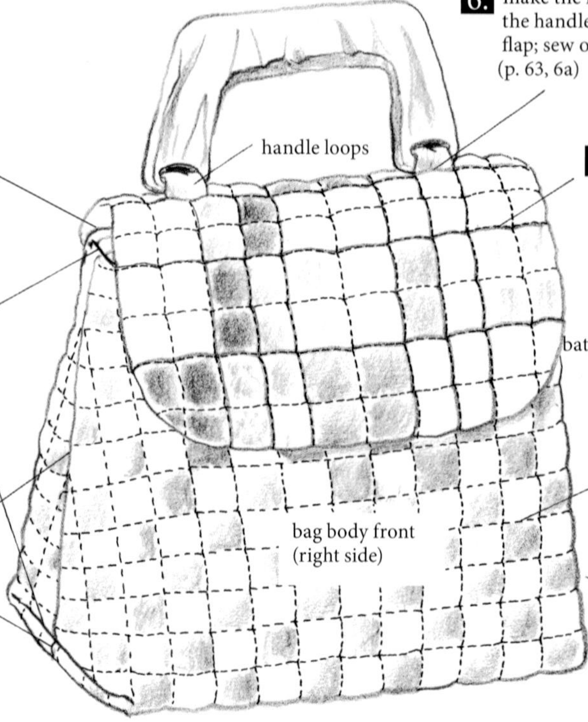

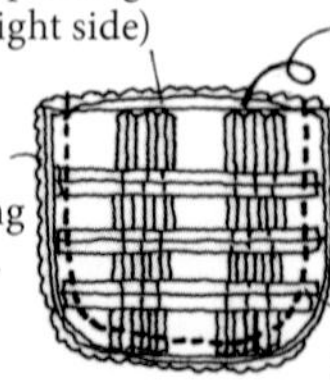

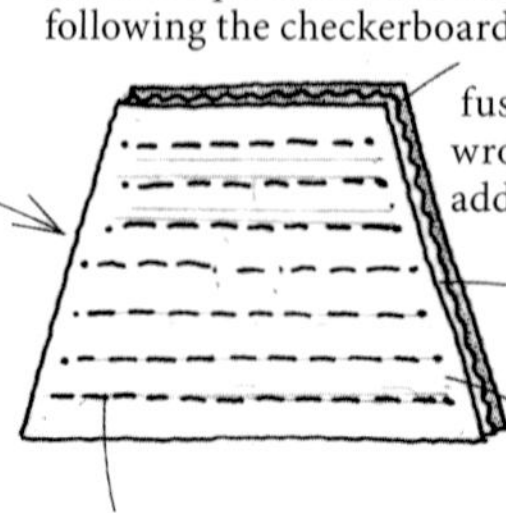

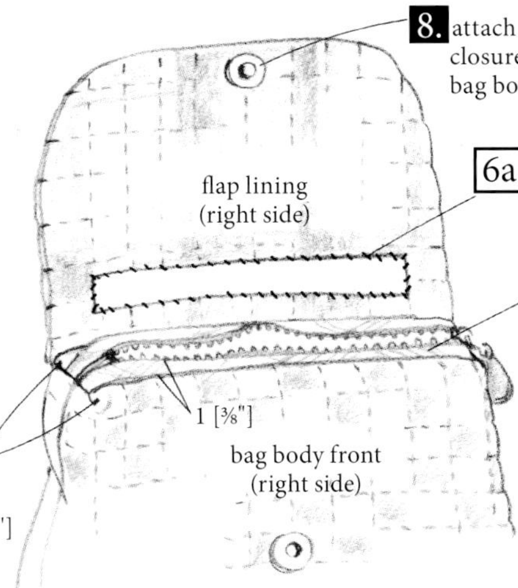

9. use heat on the wool to help set the shape when the bag is completed

2a sew in the zipper at the top of the bag body front and back

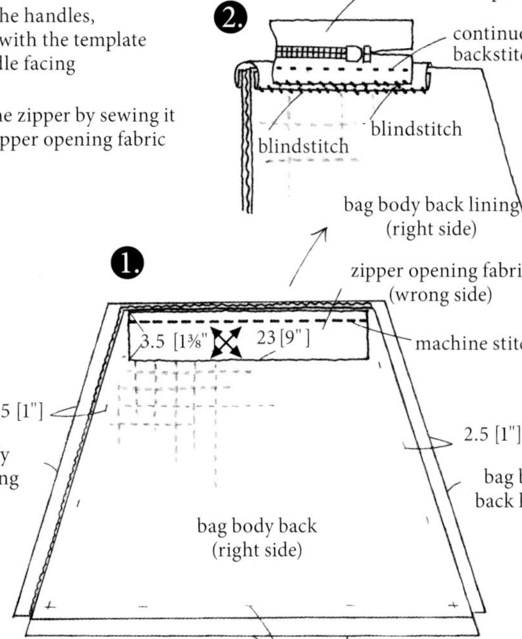

3a sew the side and bottom seams

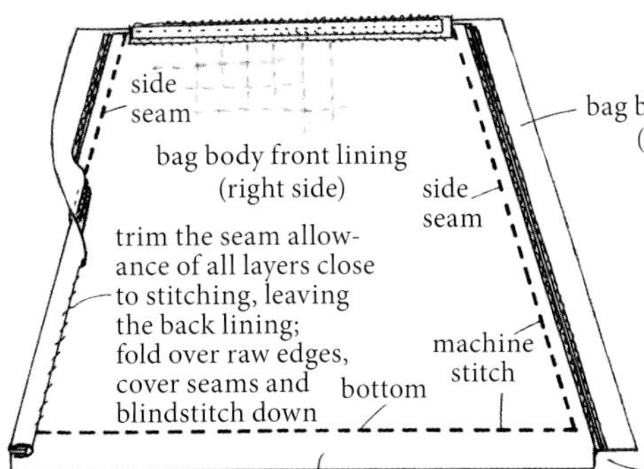

6a bind the flap edge and attach the handles

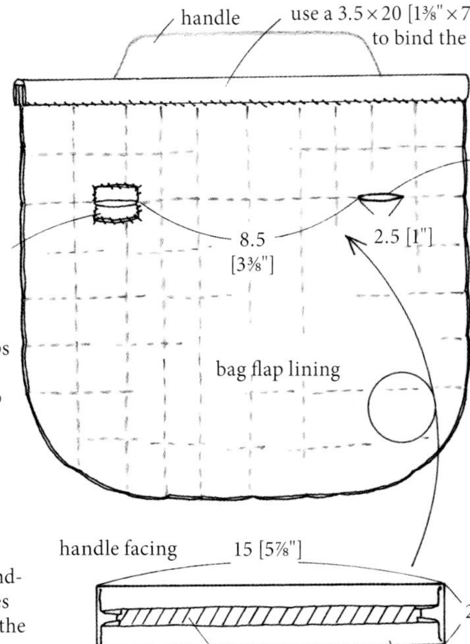

4a create the gussets

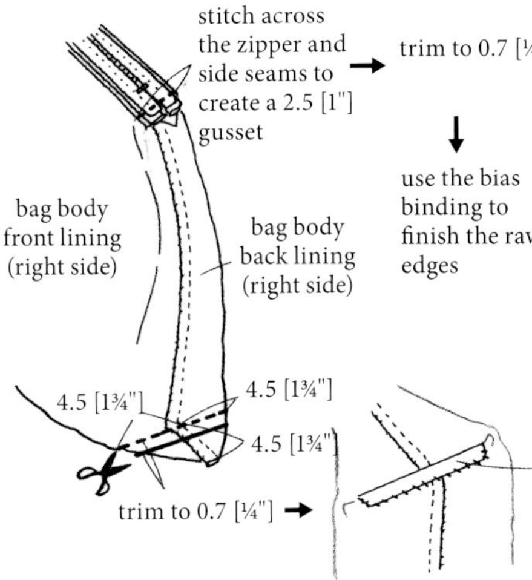

❼

Patchwork Mini-Handbag

⋯> page 15 - Pattern Sheet A (brown)

Materials

Wool - sm check pattern (upper front section) - 20 × 10 cm [7⅞" × 4"]
Assorted fat quarters and scraps of wool
(pieced lower front section) - 25 × 30 cm [9¾" × 11¾"]
(binding for zipper covering) - 3.5 × 20 cm [1⅜" × 7⅞"]
(bag back) - 25 × 30 cm [9¾" × 11¾"]
(gusset, cut 2 on bias) - 10 × 35 cm [4" × 13¾"]
cut from a piece of 40 × 30 cm [15¾" × 11¾"]
Wool (lining, pocket facing) - 35 × 80 cm [13¾" × 31½"]
Fusible interfacing (medium weight for bag front) - 25 × 30 cm [9¾" × 11¾"]
Fusible interfacing (lightweight for bag back, gusset) - 65 × 35 cm [25⅝" × 13¾"]
1 Zipper (metal teeth) - 14 cm [5½"]
4 Leather strips (handles) - 0.8 × 30 cm [⅜" × 11¾"]
Woven cotton tape (zipper pull) - 0.5 cm [¼"]
1 Button (zipper pull) - 2.5 cm [1"]
Embroidery thread - dk brown

make the front, the back and the gusset separately and then assemble the pieces into the bag

Steps 1~6	make the front of the bag
Steps 7~8	make the back of the bag (facing page)
Steps 9~10	make the gusset

2 strips of leather (0.8 × 30 [⅜" × 11¾"]) are attached on each side of the bag to make the handles

pinch together each corner and stitch 0.7 cm [¼"] along the opening edge

2. sew the zipper to the lower front section (p. 65, 2a)

9. cut out the gusset pieces (both fabric and lining); cut the interfacing with no added seam allowance and fuse to the wrong side of the outer gusset fabric

10. with right sides together and matching edges, pin the gusset piece and the gusset lining together; sew around the edge leaving 8 cm [3⅛"] unstitched at the bottom for turning; turn right side out; press; blindstitch the opening closed`

11. with right sides together and matching top edges and sides, overcast stitch the bag back and front pieces to the gusset to complete the construction of the bag

8. line the bag back (p. 65, 8a)

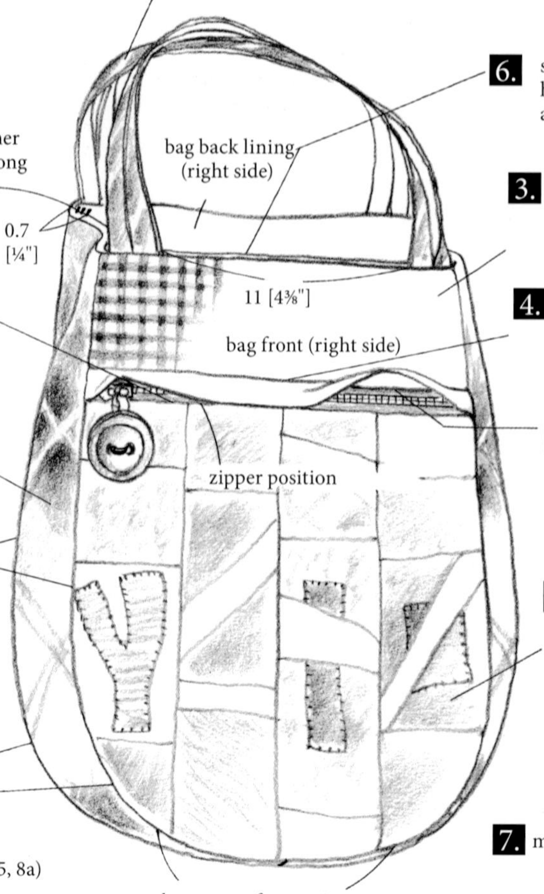

leave open for turning
8 [3⅛"]

6. sandwich the ends of the leather handles between the outer bag and the lining; sew in the lining

3. cut out the upper front section; cut the interfacing with no added seam allowance and fuse to the wrong side

4. sew the fabric for the zipper covering to the bottom edge of the upper section (this will cover the zipper (next step)

5. sew the zipper to the upper front section (p.65, 5a) making sure the zipper cover fabric hides the zipper (this makes the entire bag front

1. piece the front of the bag using assorted scraps of wool; cut to size using the pattern sheet as a guide; appliqué and embroider as desired; cut the interfacing with no added seam allowance and fuse to the wrong side of the pieced front

7. make the bag back (p. 65, 7a)

2a sew the zipper to the lower front sections

with right sides together, sew the zipper to the top of the lower front section

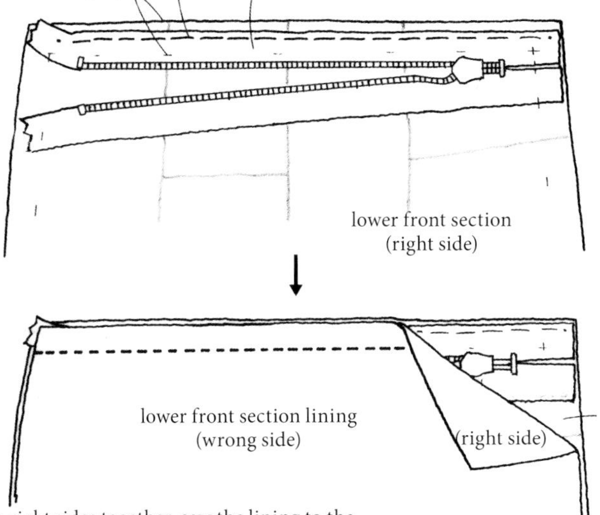

with right sides together, sew the lining to the lower front section

5a sew the zipper to the upper front section

stitch the zipper to the upper section using a continuous backstitch

iron the fusible interfacing to the wrong side of the upper front section

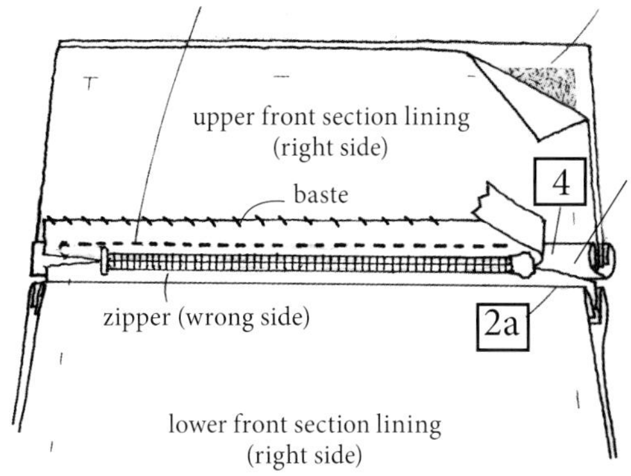

6a sew the lining

baste the edges of the handles down

with right sides together and matching edges, pin the lining and the front together; sew around the edge using the zipper opening to turn right side out; press

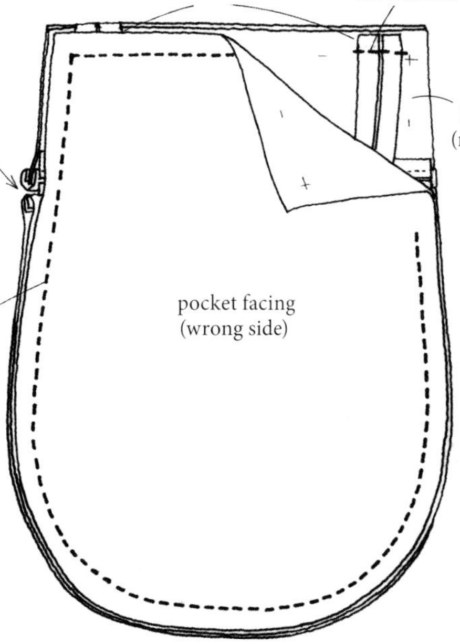

stitch the seams by machine

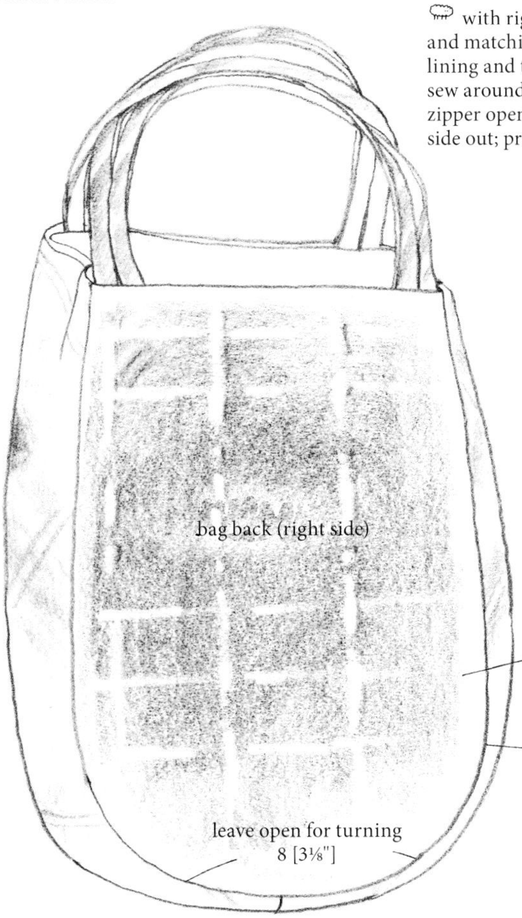

7a cut the bag back to size using the pattern sheet as a guide; cut the interfacing with no added seam allowance and fuse to the wrong side of the back

8a position the ends of the handles on the right side; baste in place (see #6a above); with right sides together and matching edges, pin the lining and the outer bag back together; sew around the edge leaving 8 cm [3⅛"] unstitched at the bottom for turning; turn right side out; press; blindstitch the opening closed.

8

Linus' Wall Quilt

⋯> page 16 - Pattern Sheet A & B (green)

Materials

Wool (quilt top background) - 155 × 155 cm [61" × 61"]
Assorted fat quarters and scraps of wool (for appliqué "picture" blocks)
Wool
  (lightweight for binding) - 25 × 165 cm [9¾" × 65"]
  (scallops, 126 pieces) - 80 × 100 cm [31½" × 39⅜"]
  (triangles inside scallops) - 60 × 100 cm [23⅝" × 39⅜"]
  (for appliqués inside blocks) - assorted scraps of wool
Wool (for edging around border) - 2.5 × 620 cm [1" × 244"]
  cut from a piece of 60 × 90 cm [23⅝" × 35⅜"]
Wool
  (lightweight for backing, sleeve) - 160 × 200 cm [63" × 78¾"]
  (scallops backing, 86 pieces) - 80 × 80 cm [31½" × 31½"]
Embroidery thread - beige
Perle cotton - lt beige

attaching the scallop border and border edging

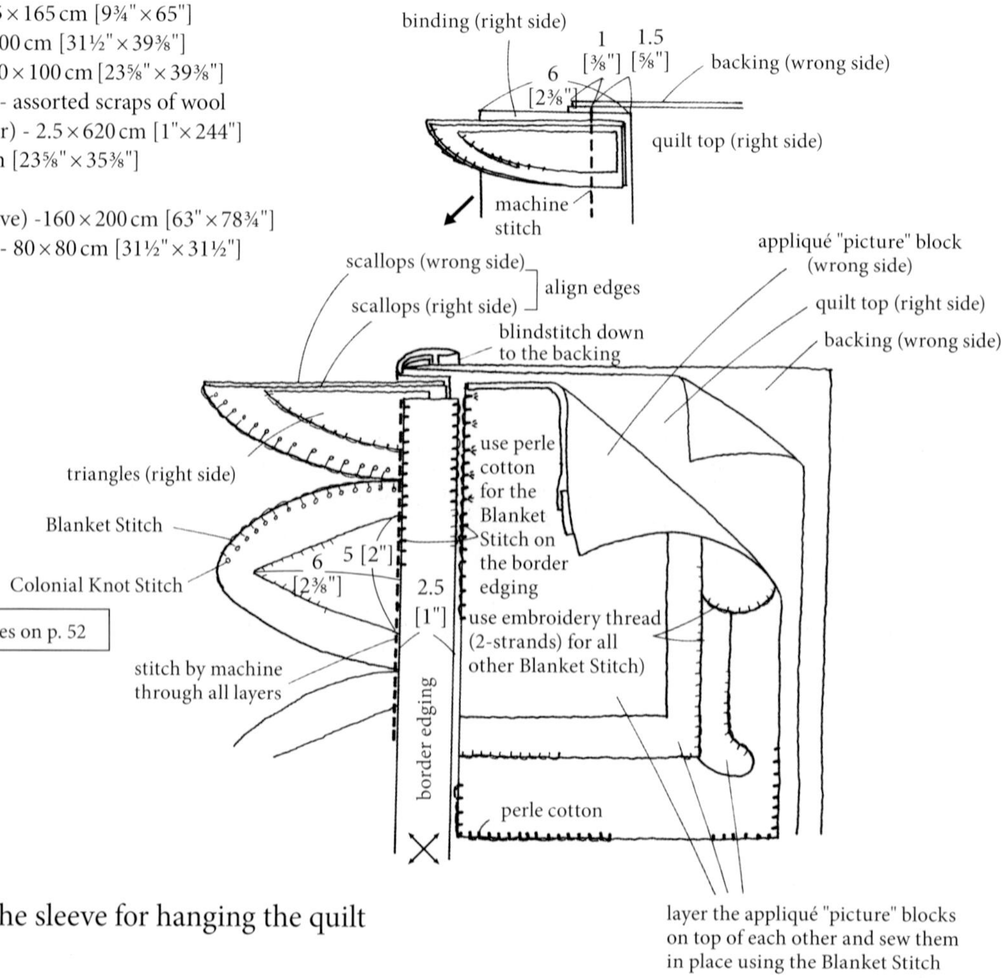

see embroidery stitches on p. 52

sewing on the sleeve for hanging the quilt

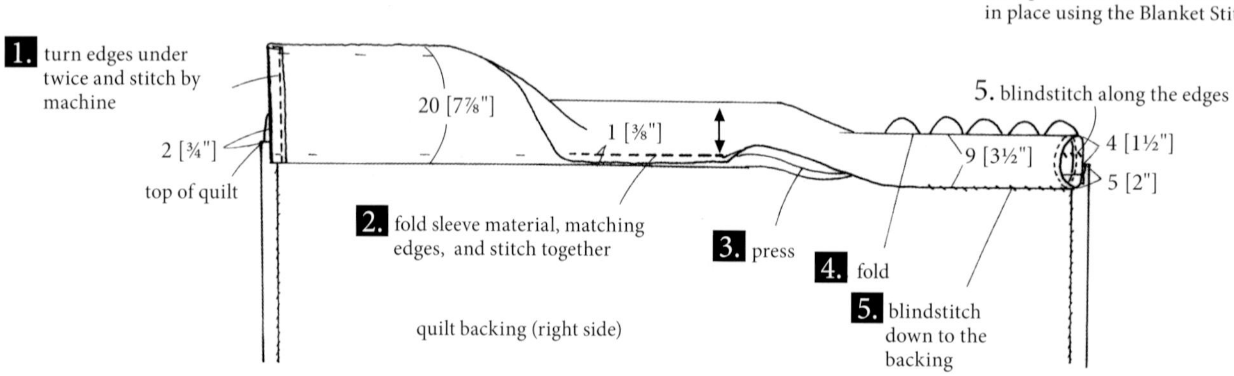

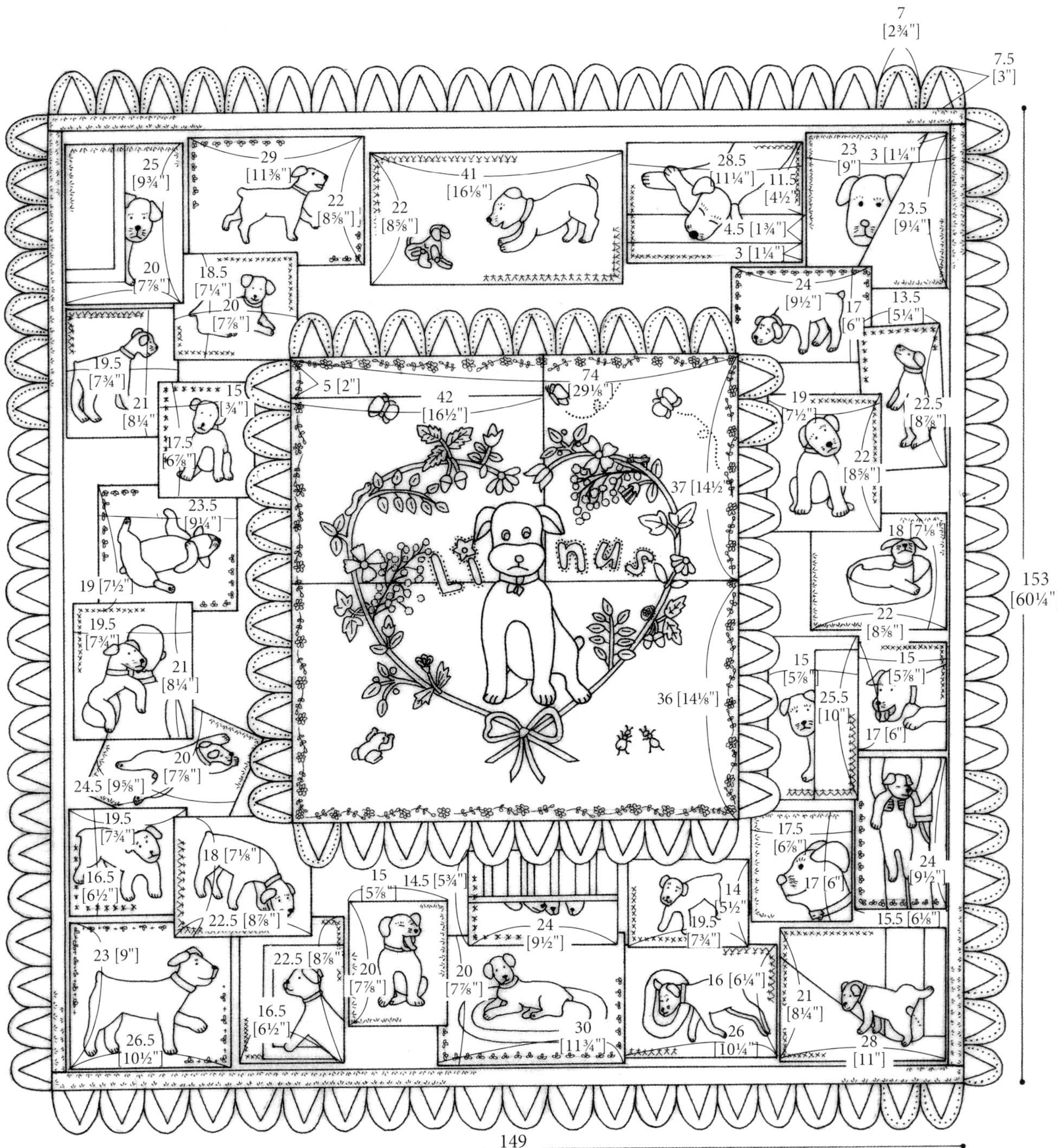

appliqué each individual picture block before stitching them to the quilt top; follow the pattern placement above or as desired

9 10

Warm Woolen Scarf & Pouch

→ page 18 - Pattern Sheet B (brown)

9 Materials (pouch)

Wool (bag body outer) - 25 × 30 cm [9¾" × 11¾"]
(bias strip for zipper opening, cut 2) - 3.5 × 25 cm [1⅜" × 9¾"]
cut from a piece of 30 × 25 cm [11¾" × 9¾"]
Assorted scraps of wool (appliqué and zipper tab)
Lightweight wool (lining) - 25 × 30 cm [9¾" × 11¾"]
Batting (lightweight) - 25 × 30 cm [9¾" × 11¾"]
1 Zipper (metal teeth) - 19 cm [7½"]
Narrow cord (zipper pull) - 15 cm [5⅞"]
Wooden beads - (zipper pull) - 2 @ 0.5 cm [¼"] ; 1 @ 1.5 cm [⅝"]
Embroidery thread - grey

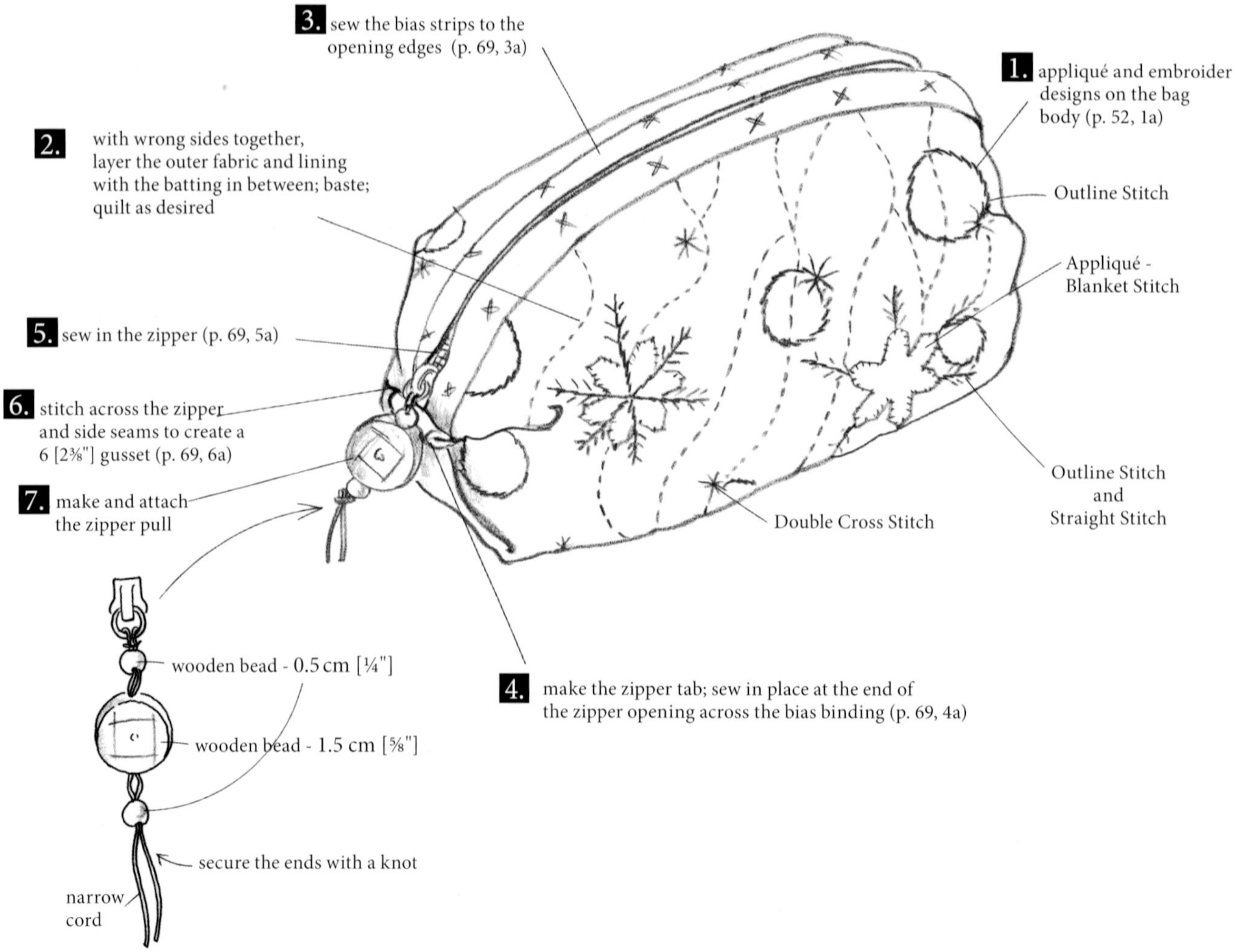

3a sew the bias binding to edges for the zipper opening

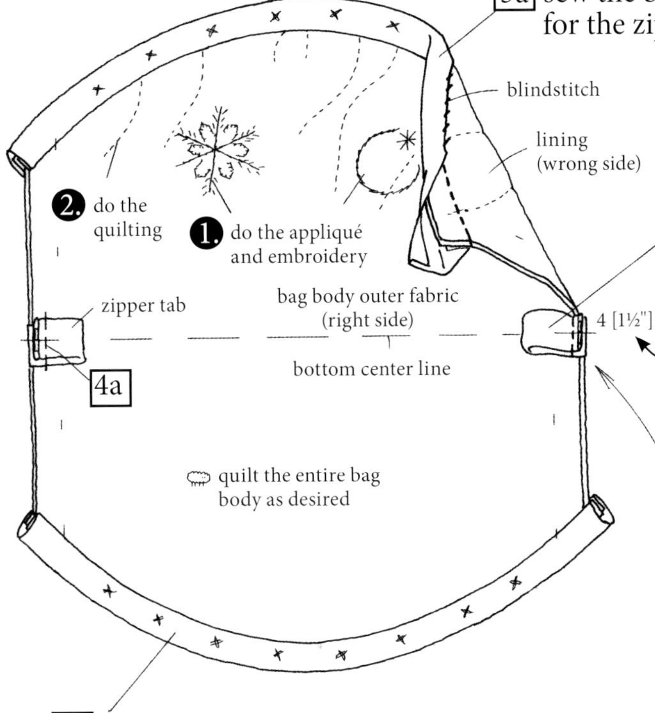

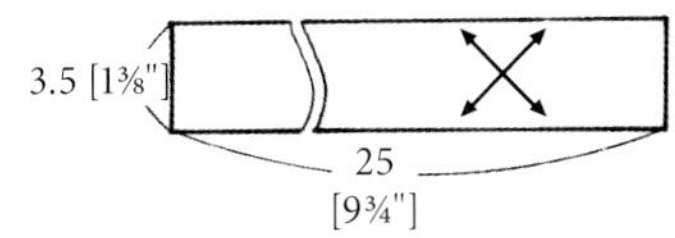

4a make the zipper tab

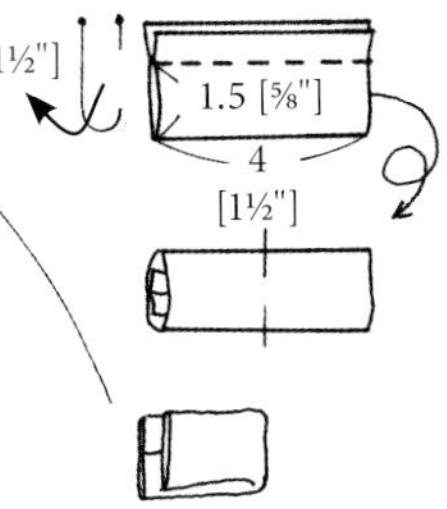

cut out a piece 4 × 4 [1½"]; fold in half, sew along the edge, turn right side out and press with the seam centered; baste in place on either end of the pouch as shown

6a stitch across the zipper to create gusset

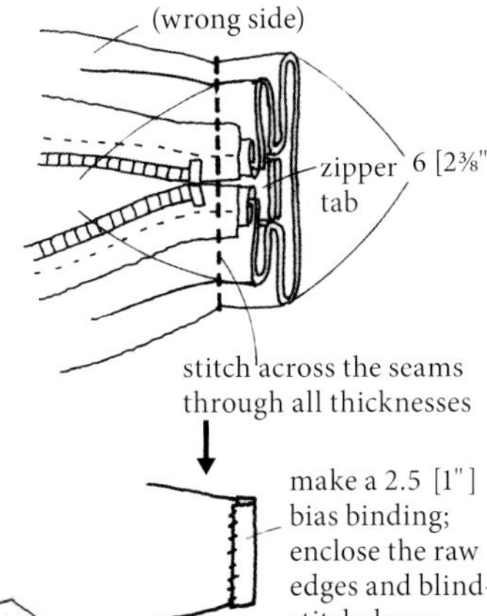

5a sew in the zipper

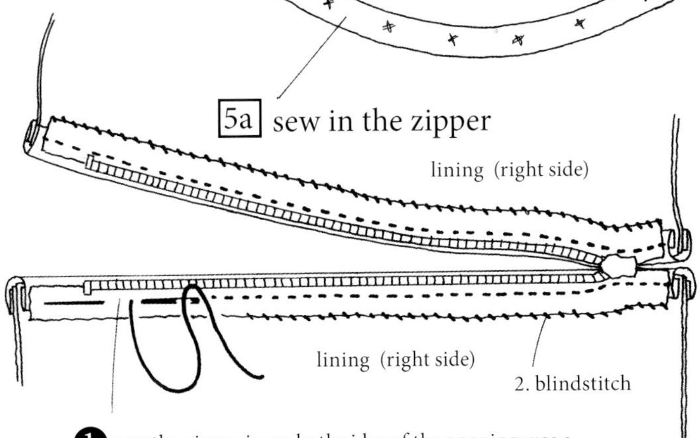

1. sew the zipper in on both sides of the opening; use a continuous backstitch, being careful to keep the zipper tape from puckering; blindstitch the zipper tape edges to the lining on each side

10 Materials (scarf)

Wool (the exact size of the scarf) - 21 × 157 cm [8¼" × 61¾"]
Wool - assorted scraps for the large snowflakes
Embroidery thread - grey

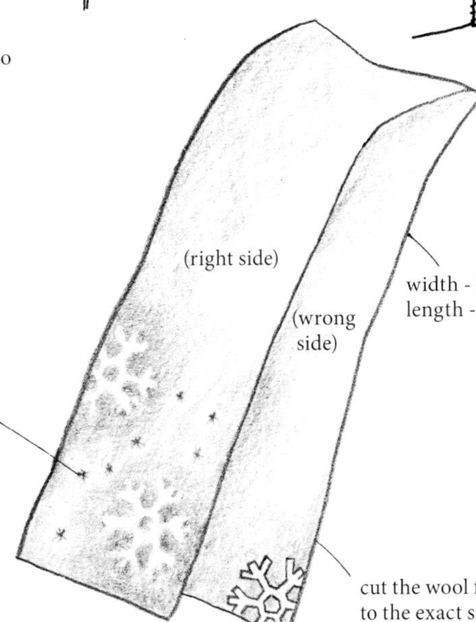

11 **12**

Needle-felted Scarves

⇢ page 21 - Pattern Sheet B (brown)

11 Materials

Wool tweed (exact size of the scarf) - 20 × 133 cm [7⅞" × 52⅜"]
Wool (appliqué) - assorted scraps

> to create the designs on the scarf, see the instructions for needle-felting on p. 19 using the needle punching tool

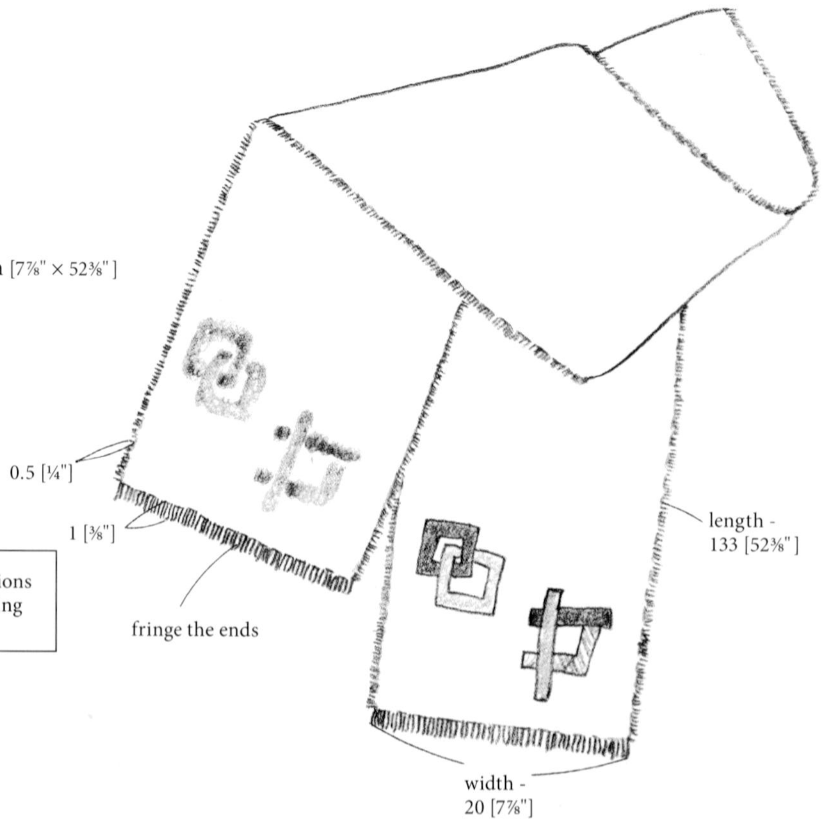

12 Materials

Wool plaid (exact size of the scarf) - 19 × 102 cm [7½" × 40⅛"]
Wool (appliqué) - assorted scraps
3 Metal buttons (for snowman) - 0.5 cm [¼"]
Perle cotton (carrot nose) - orange

> to create the designs on the scarf, see the instructions for needle-felting on p. 19 using the needle punching tool

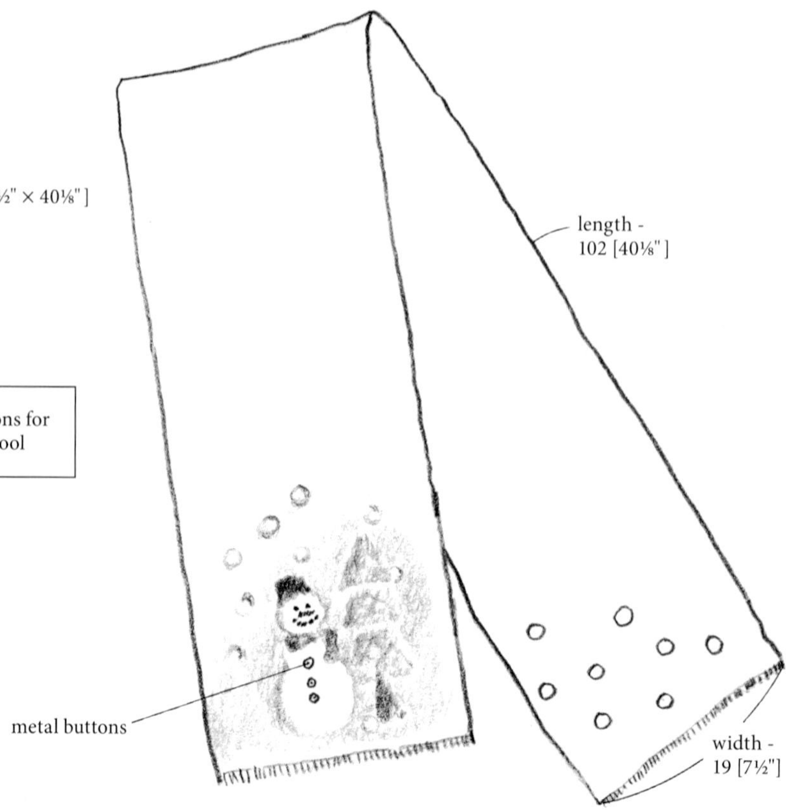

13 14 15 Woolen Bracelets

→ page 22 - Pattern Sheet B (brown)

cut out the felt or wool for the bracelet you are making; appliqué, embroider or needle-felt depending on the design; Blanket Stitch around the edges, adding a backing if called for in the directions

13 Materials

Felt (black) - 8 × 25 cm [3⅛" × 9¾"]
Homespun (assorted scraps for the appliqué)
1 Button (closure)- 1.4 cm [⅝"]
Embroidery thread - black
Perle Cotton - brown

14 Materials

Wool (dk moss green) - 4 × 25 cm [1½" × 9¾"]
Wool (assorted scraps for the needle-felted designs)
49 Seed beads (black)
1 Button - 1.5 cm [⅝"]
Embroidery thread - brown, dk moss green, red, blue
Perle Cotton - moss green

15 Materials

Felt (off-white) - 8 × 25 cm [3⅛" × 9¾"]
6 Buttons (assorted) - 1.2 cm [½"]
1 Button (closure)- 1.3 cm [½"]
Embroidery thread - green, dk brown
Perle Cotton - beige

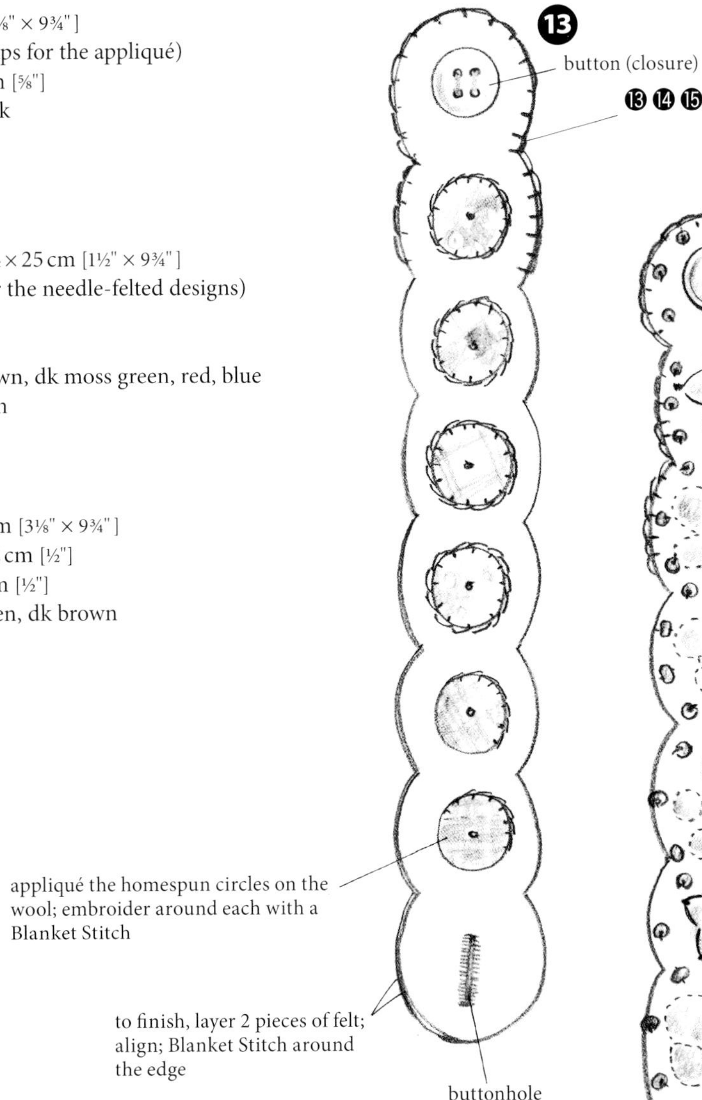

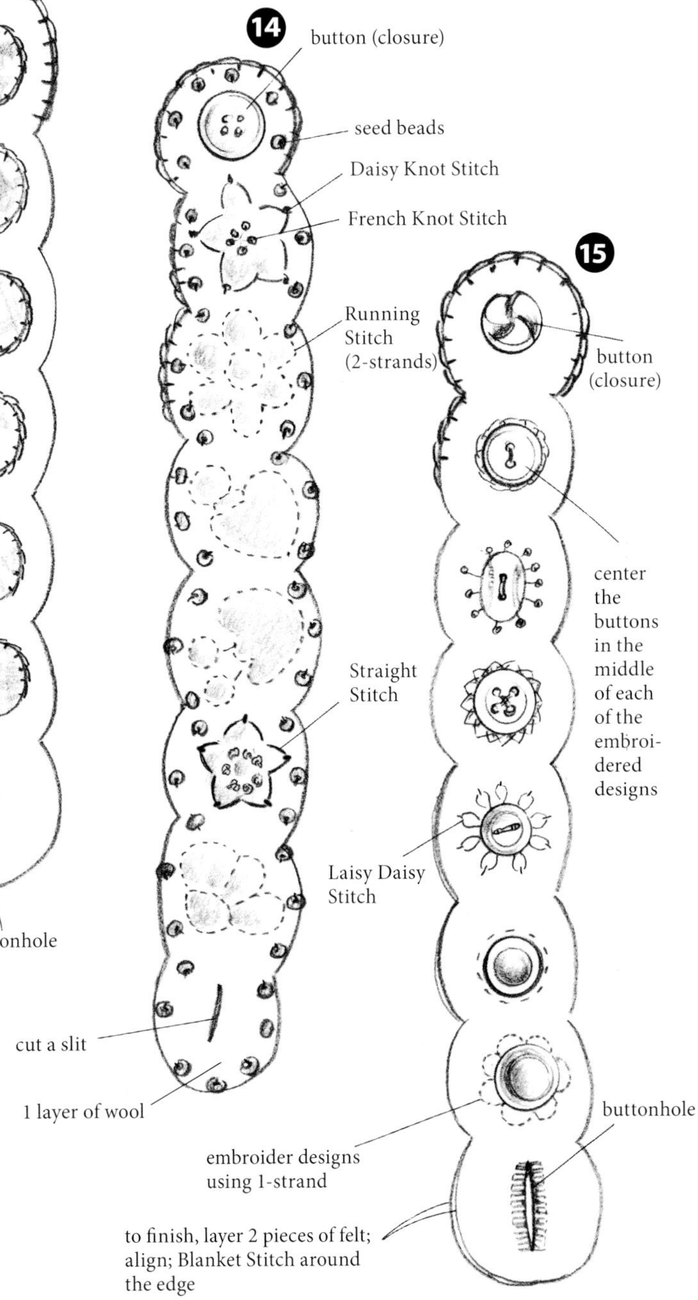

14 each design on this bracelet is needle-felted using the needle punching tool on p. 19

16

Plaid Button-Tab Bag

→ page 24 - Pattern Sheet B (brown)

Materials

Wool - plaid (bag front, bag back) - 80 × 35 cm [31½" × 13¾"]
Wool - houndstooth (bag opening) - 40 × 10 cm [15¾" × 4"]
Assorted scraps of wool (tab closures, pocket flap)
Assorted scraps of wool (pocket)
Lightweight wool (lining)
(bag front, bag back, pocket, bias binding) - 90 × 50 cm [35⅜" × 19¾"]
Assorted scraps of wool (tab closure backing, pocket flap backing)
Wool scrap (for the covered button)
Fusible interfacing (lightweight) - 80 × 70 cm [31½" × 27½"]
2 Leather straps (handles) - 2.5 × 36 cm [1" × 14⅛"]
Buttons (tab closures, 1 each) - 1.8 cm [⅝"], 2.1 cm [¾"]
Covered button - 2.1 cm [¾"]
1 Lg snap (pocket flap)

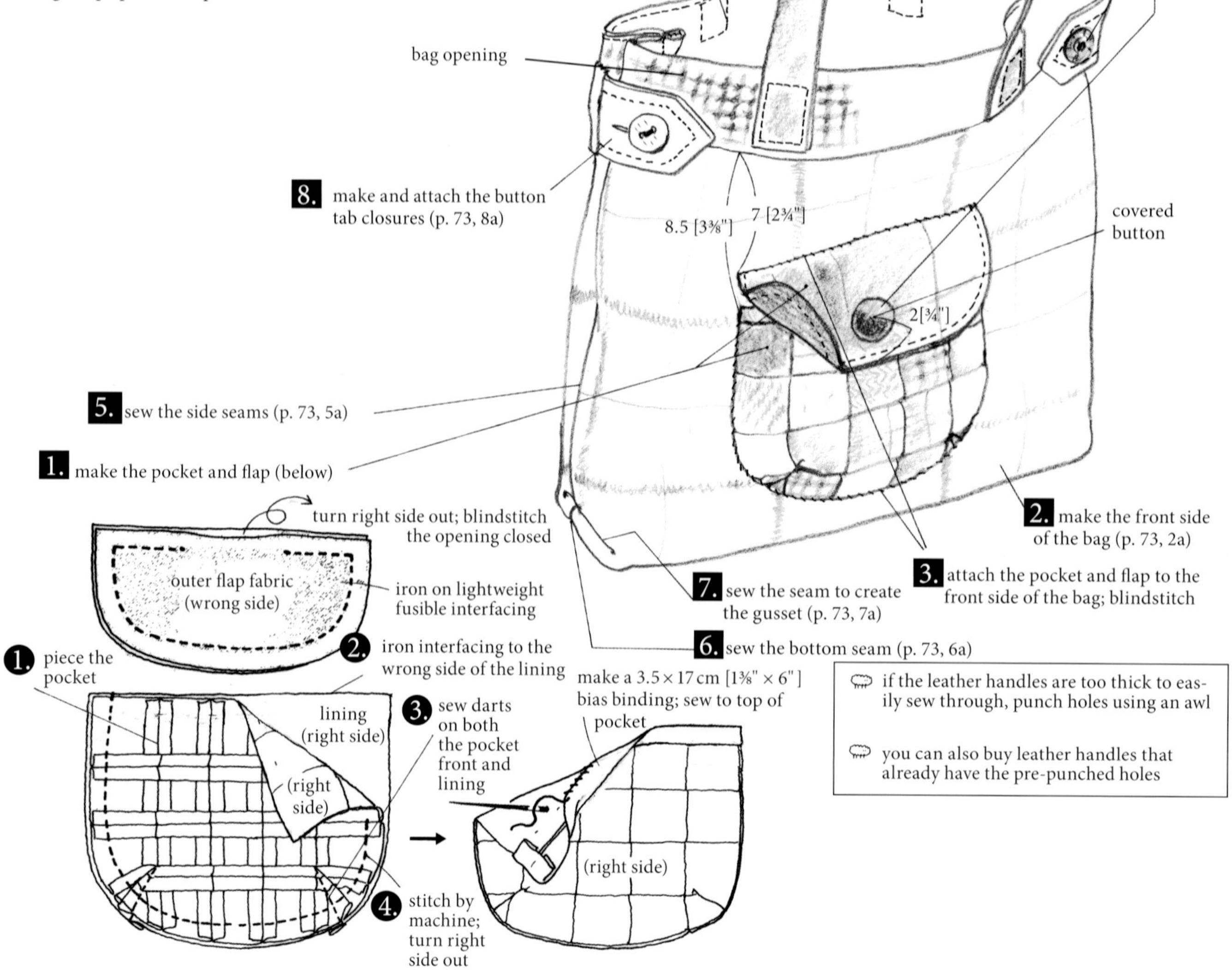

dimensional diagram

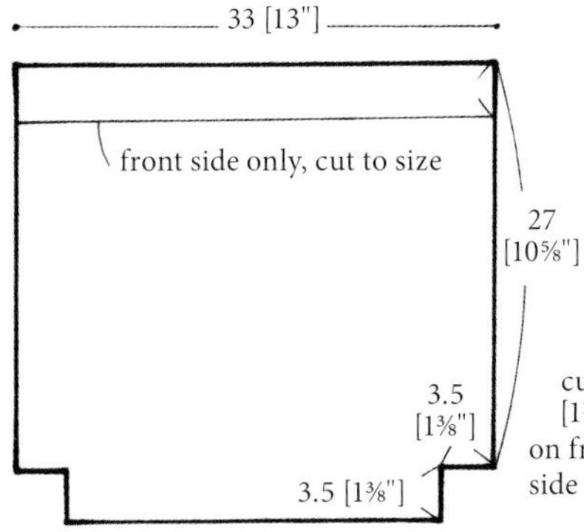

2a make the bag front

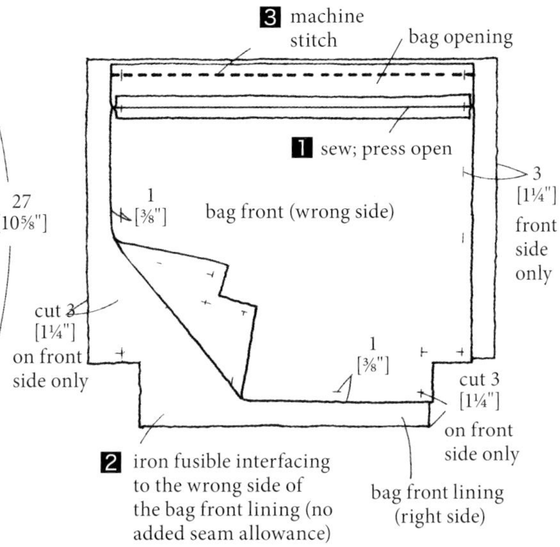

4a make the bag back

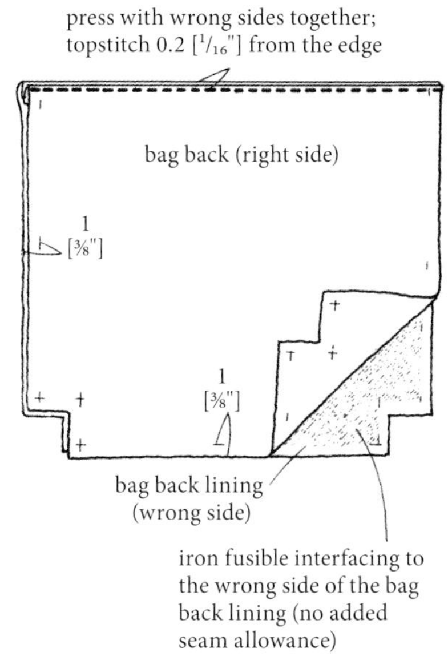

5a & 6a sew the side and bottom seams

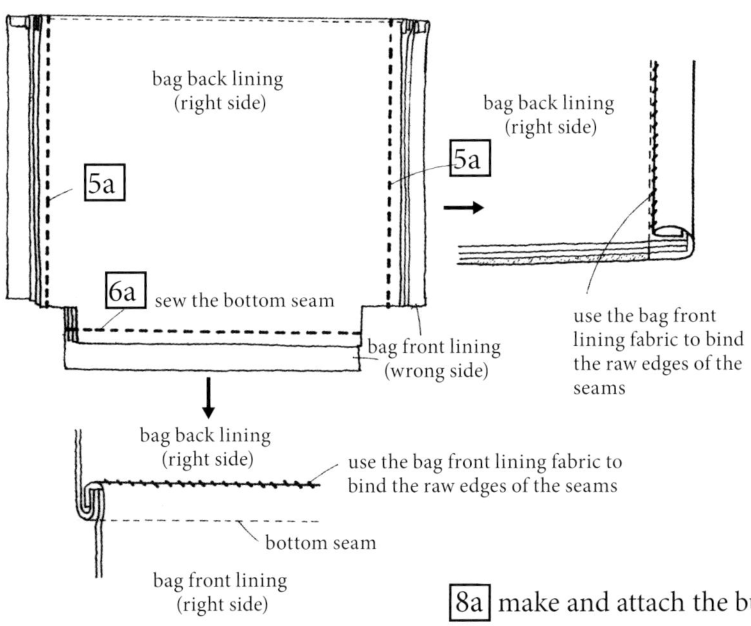

7a sew the gussets

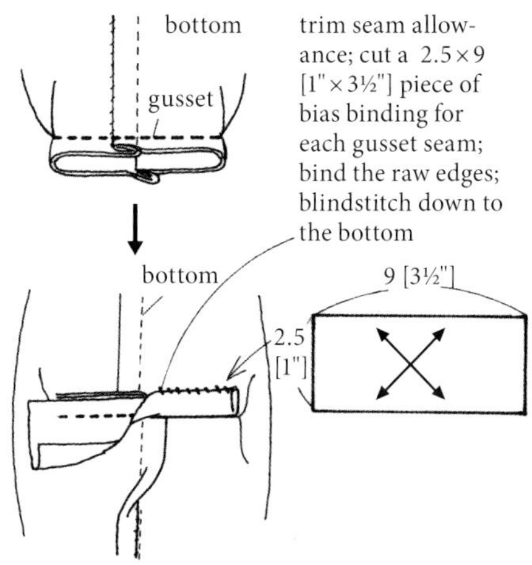

8a make and attach the button closure tabs

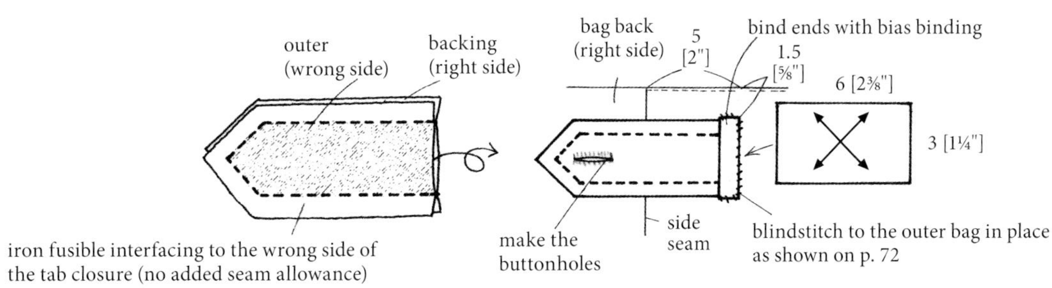

17 18

Cute Mini-Pouches

→ page 25 - Pattern Sheet B (brown)

17 Materials (Dog Pouch)

Wool
- (pouch back, gusset) - 50 × 25 cm [19¾" × 9¾"]
- (strap) - 20 × 5 cm [7⅞" × 2"]

4 Assorted scraps of wool (pieced pouch front)

Lightweight wool (lining)
- (pouch front, pouch back, gusset) - 50 × 25 cm [19¾" × 9¾"]
- (strap) - 20 × 5 cm [7⅞" × 2"]

Fusible interfacing (lightweight) - 35 × 25 cm [13¾" × 9¾"]

1 Zipper (metal teeth) - 12 cm [4¾"]

Narrow cord (zipper pull) - 10 cm [4"]

1 Zipper pull decoration

18 Materials (Cat Pouch)

Wool
- (pouch back) - 20 × 20 cm [7⅞" × 7⅞"]
- 4 Assorted scraps of wool (pieced pouch front)
- (strap) - 20 × 5 cm [7⅞" × 2"]

Wool (lining)
- (pouch front, pouch back) - 40 × 20 cm [15¾" × 7⅞"]
- (strap) - 20 × 5 cm [7⅞" × 2"]

Fusible interfacing (lightweight) - 30 × 20 cm [11¾" × 7⅞"]

1 Zipper (metal teeth) - 12 cm [4¾"]

Narrow cord (zipper pull) - 10 cm [4"]

1 Zipper pull decoration

complete each of the separate pieces for the pouch, A~E; then sew them all together to finish

17

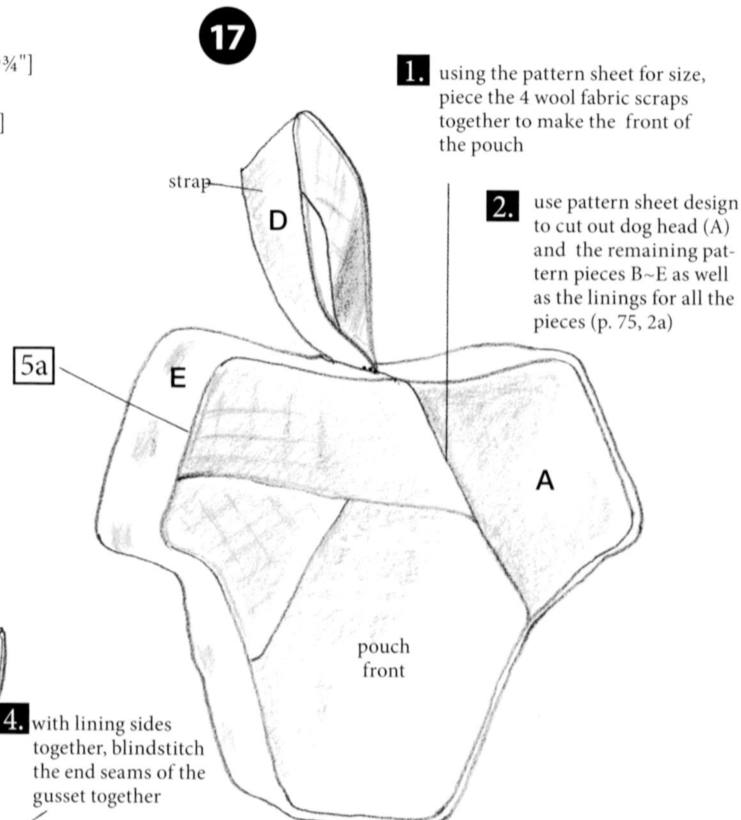

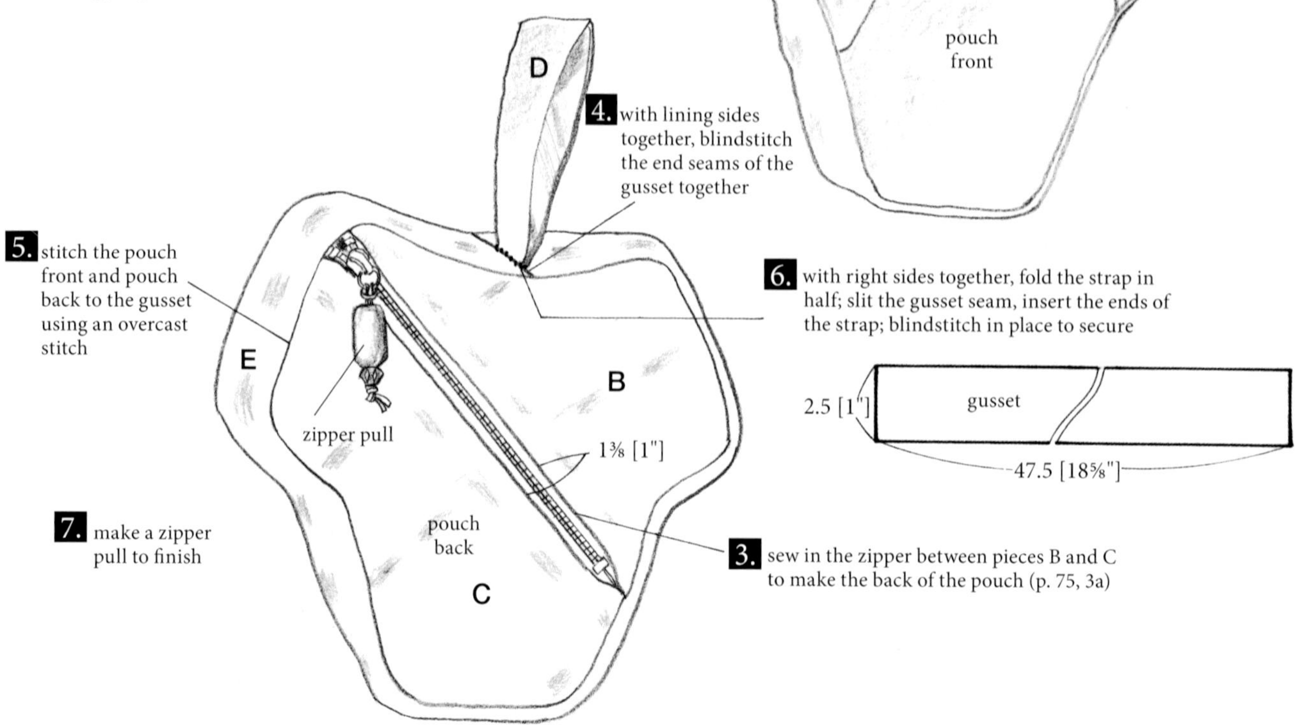

18

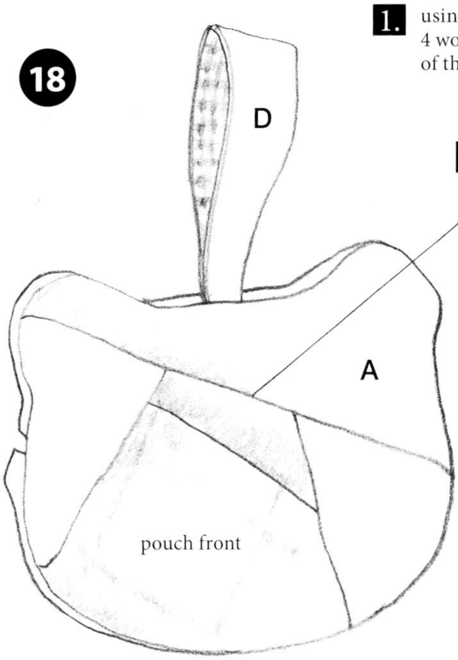

1. using the pattern sheet for size, piece the 4 wool fabric scraps together for the front of the pouch

2. use pattern sheet design to cut out cat head (A) and the remaining pattern pieces B~D; piece and line each piece (2a below)

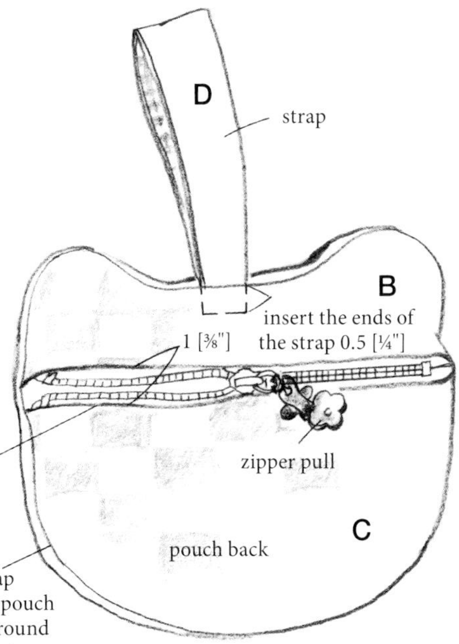

3. sew in the zipper between pieces B and C (3a below)

4. with right sides together and strap sandwiched in between, sew the pouch front and pouch back together around the edges with an overcast stitch; turn right side out to finish

2a lining pieces A~E

(piece A shown below, applies to all pieces for both pouches)

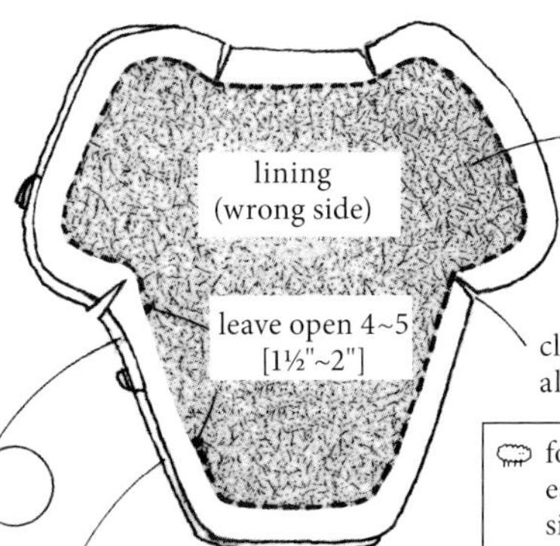

iron fusible interfacing to the wrong side of the lining (no added seam allowance)

clip into the seam allowances

turn right side out and blindstitch the opening closed so that each piece is fully lined and finished

> follow these directions for each piece A~E; with right sides together and matching edges; sew the pieces together to the matching lining pieces leaving 4~5 [1½"~2"] open for turning

3a sewing in the zipper

(applies to both pouches)

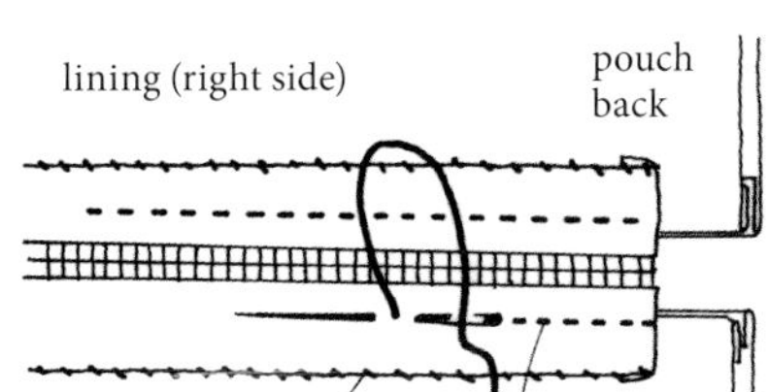

blindstitch the edge of the zipper tape down to the lining

sew the zipper tape to the front and back of the pouch with a continuous back-stitch; do not let the stitches show on the right side

19

Gathered Gusset Handbag

⋯> page 26 - Pattern Sheet B (brown)

Materials

Wool
- (bag front, bag back) - 70 × 25 cm [27½" × 9¾"]
- (gusset) - 80 × 15 cm [31½" × 5⅞"]

Lightweight wool (lining)
- (bag front, bag back, gusset, facing) - 80 × 40 cm [31½" × 15¾"]

Assorted scraps of wool (appliqué)
Corduroy (handle loops) - 6 × 22 cm [2⅜" × 8⅝"]
Fusible interfacing (heavyweight) - 35 × 45 cm [13¾" × 17¾"]
Fusible interfacing (medium weight) - 35 × 45 cm [13¾" × 17¾"]
Elastic (2 pieces) - 0.8 × 6 cm [⅜" × 2⅜"]
Handles - 1 pair
Embroidery thread - dk brown, green
Perle cotton - dk moss green

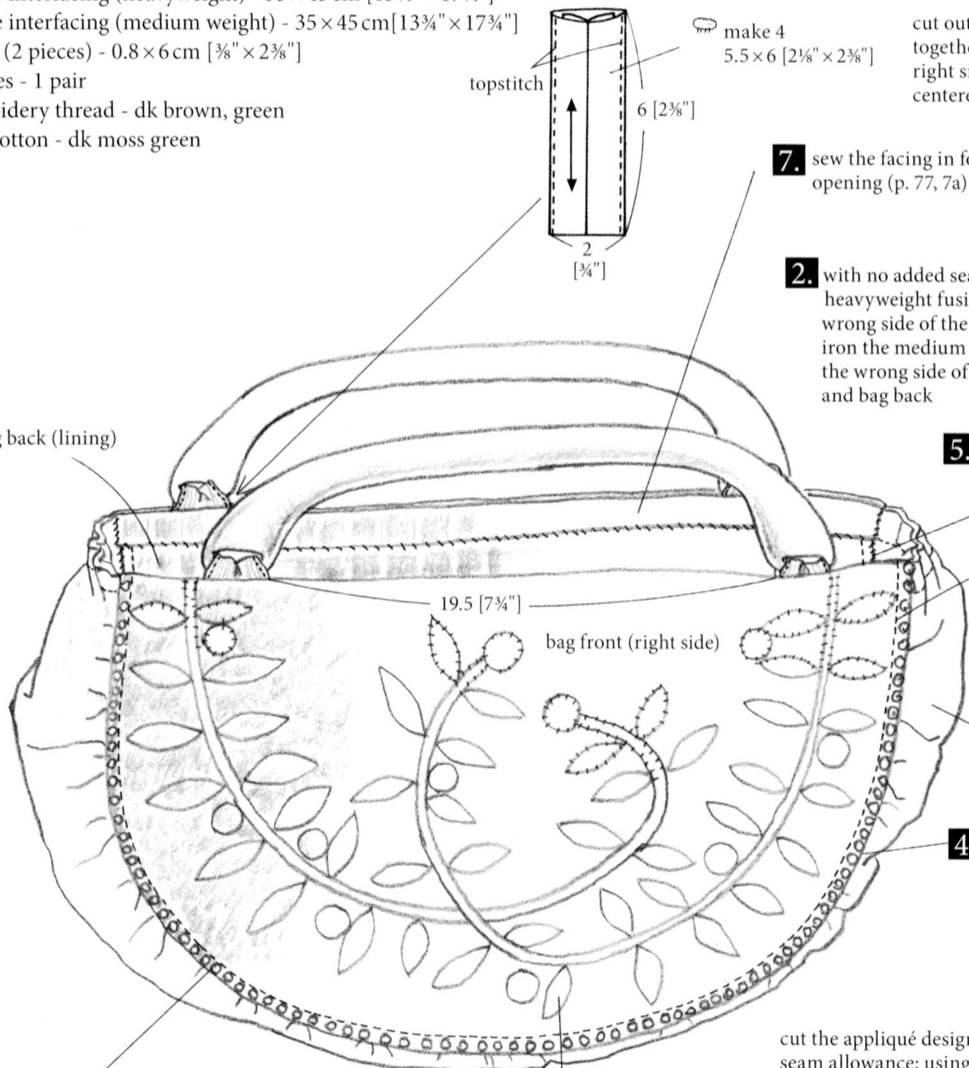

6. make the handle loops, insert through the handles; baste to the bag opening facing (p. 77, 6a)

make 4
5.5 × 6 [2⅛" × 2⅜"]

cut out 4 handle loops; with right sides together, sew seam along edge; turn right side out and press with the seam centered; topstitch on either edge

7. sew the facing in for the bag front opening (p. 77, 7a)

2. with no added seam allowance, iron the heavyweight fusible interfacing to the wrong side of the bag front and bag back; iron the medium weight fusible interfacing to the wrong side of the lining for the bag front and bag back

5. with wrong sides together, insert the lining into the bag, blindstitch it down (p. 77, 5a)

3. make the gusset (p. 77, 3a)

4. sew the bag front, bag back and gusset together (p. 77, 4a)

cut the appliqué designs out of the wool with no added seam allowance; using 2-strands of embroidery thread, Blanket Stitch around the design

1. using the pattern sheet, cut out, then appliqué the front

repeat the appliqué on the bag back as well

8. with 2-strands of perle cotton and 0.6 [¼"] apart, embroider Colonial Knot Stitches around the seam edge

3a make the gathered gusset

using the pattern sheet, cut out gusset pieces and gusset linings; add reference marks

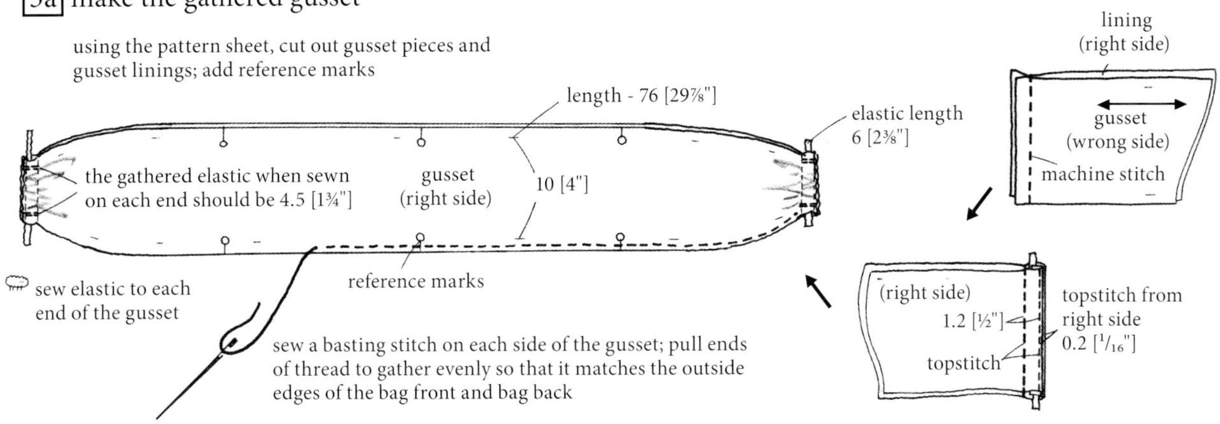

4a & 5a sew the gusset to the bag front and back; sew in the lining

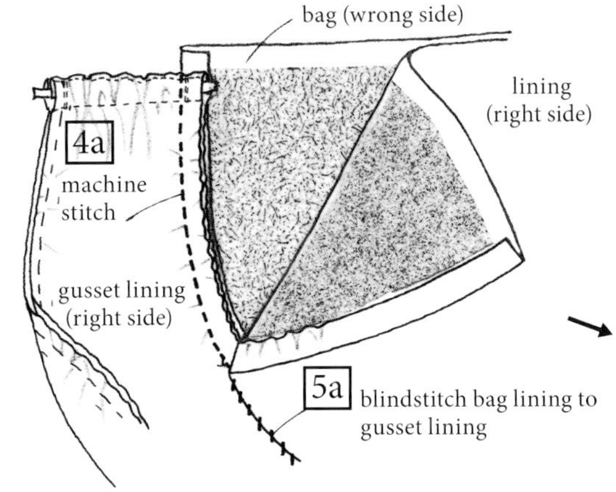

4a with right sides together and matching edges, machine stitch the bag front to one side of the gusset; repeat to sew the bag back to the gusset; with seam allowance folded under, blindstitch the lining in place to both the bag front and bag back, covering the raw edges

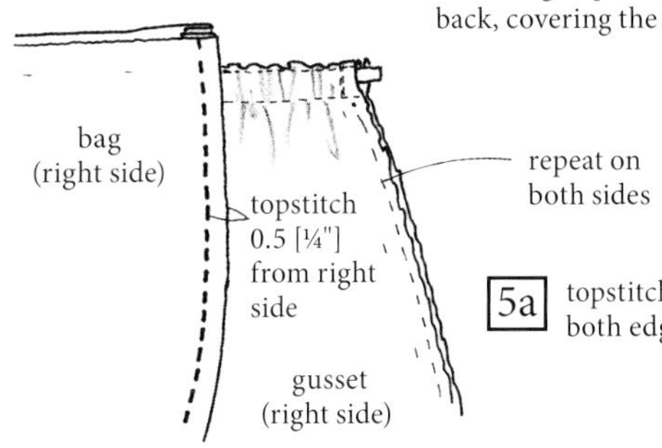

5a topstitch on the right side around both edges

6a & 7a attach the handles and sew in the facing

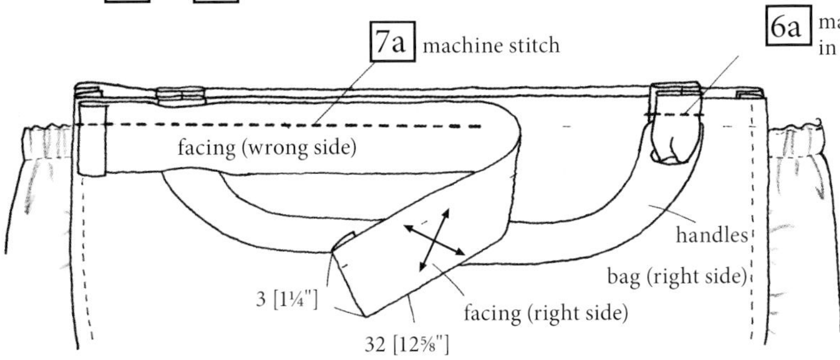

6a make the handle loops; insert through the handle; baste in place on the right side of the bag front and bag back

7a with right sides together, pin the facing to each side of the bag opening, folding in the edges to be even with the end of the bag; machine stitch end to end; turn facing to the inside, covering raw edges, and blindstitch down to the lining

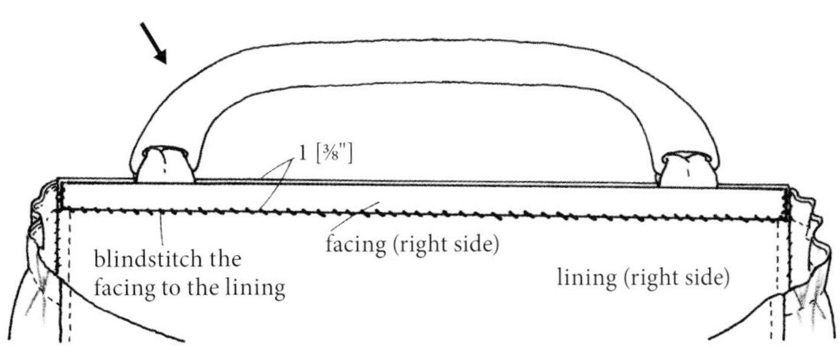

20

Floral Tea Cozy

→ page 28 - Pattern Sheet B (brown)

Materials

Wool (outer, cut on bias) - 60 × 50 cm [23⅝" × 19¾"]
Wool (lining) - 30 × 80 cm [11¾" × 31½"]
Wool (edging, cut on bias) - 30 × 30 cm [11¾" × 11¾"]
Assorted scraps of wool (appliqué)
Fusible interfacing (lightweight) - 25 × 80 cm [9¾" × 31½"]
Embroidery thread - dk green, green, beige, red, dk blue, grey-blue, lt pink

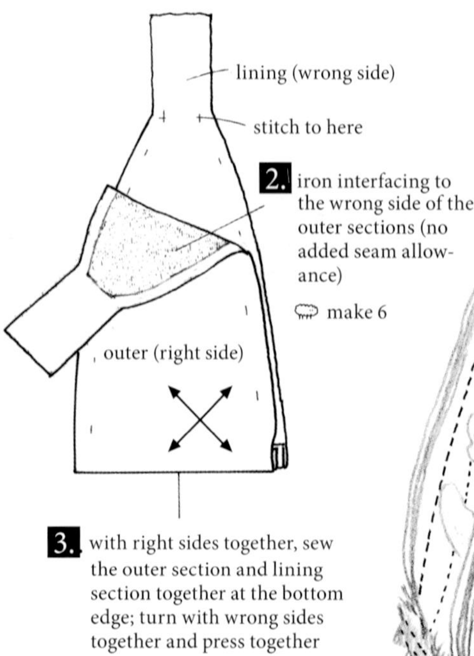

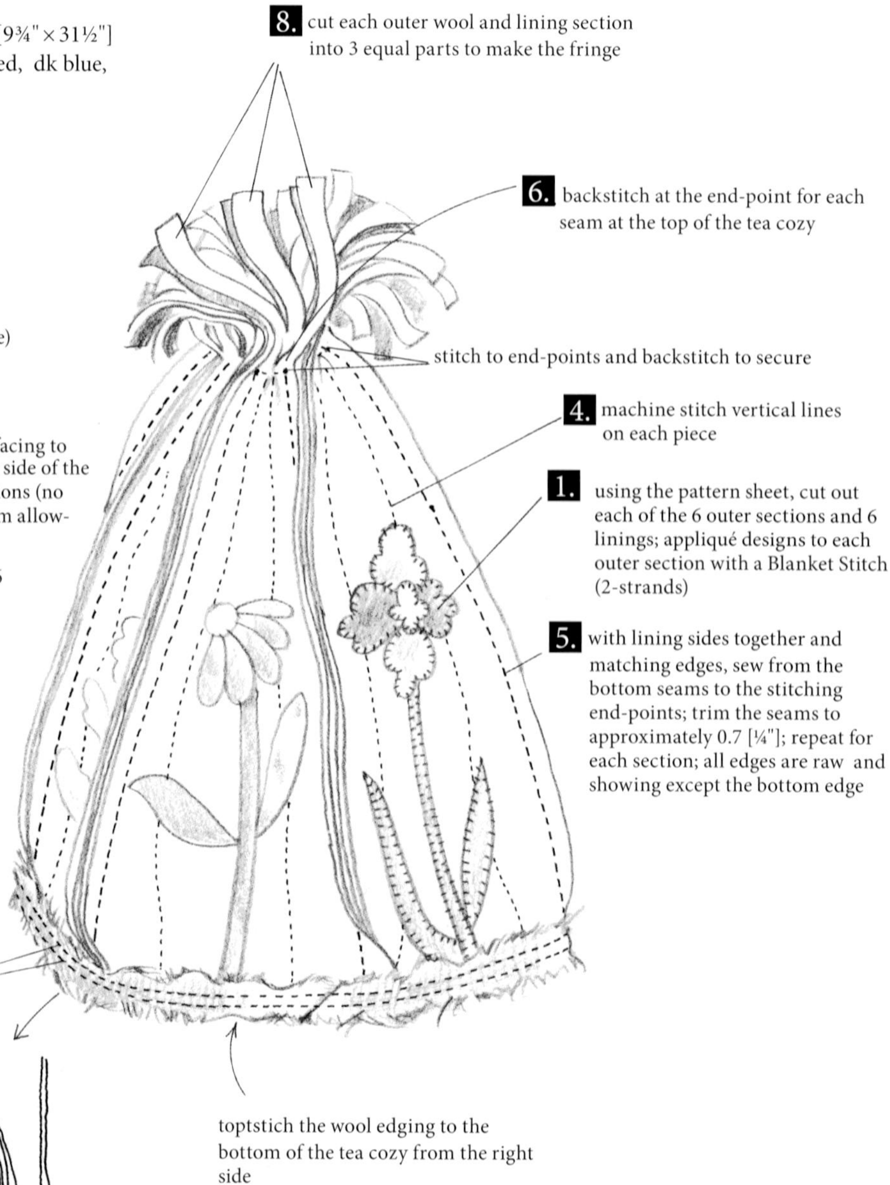

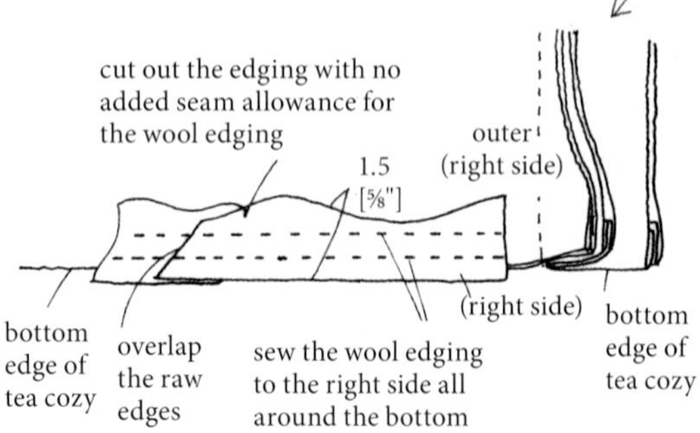

21

Hooked Rug Floor Mat

⋯⋯> page 30 - follow dimensions below

Materials

Wool (assorted colors for wool strips) - enough for the project*
Wool (backing for finishing) - 70 × 80 cm [27½" × 31½"]
Canvas or burlap (rug hooking base) - 90 × 90 cm [35⅜" × 35⅜"]
Fusible interfacing (heavyweight) - 70 × 80 cm [27½" × 31½"]

* She doesn't specify how much wool you will need for the strips you will use in each individual rectangle piece. It will all depend on how many different wool fabrics/colors you use, how wide you cut your strips, or if you make the exact same size rectangle pieces as shown below.
As a general guide, for a #8* cut wool strips (0.5~0.7 cm [¼"] wide), a $^1/_{16}$~⅛ of a yard (by the width of the bolt) will be more than enough for one rectangle piece below. Use either a wool cutter/stripper or cut the wool with your rotary cutter.

*the size of the cutting blade for a cutter/stripper

making the individual pieces

1. following the directions on p. 31, cut out each canvas or burlap base piece (32 if you are making the same size as below); rug hook each rectangle piece using the wool strips of your choice

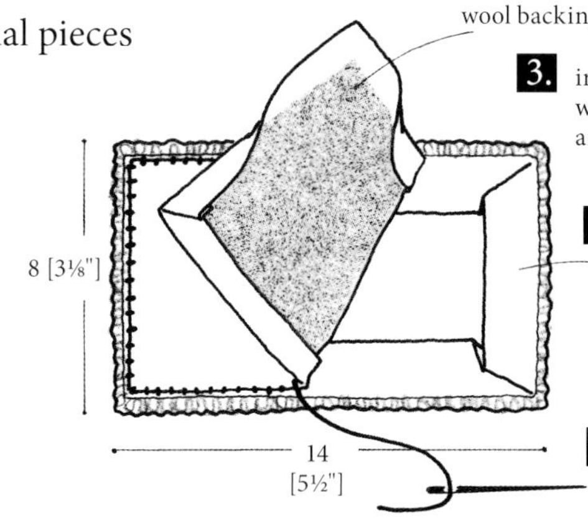

2. fold the canvas or burlap base to the inside so that it does not show at all on the right side

3. iron interfacing to the wrong side of wool backing (no added seam allowance)

4. with wrong sides together, lay the wool backing on the wrong side of each hooked piece; blindstitch around the edges

5. lay each finished piece with the backing side up in desired order; using strong thread, sew each piece to each other as shown to make the mat

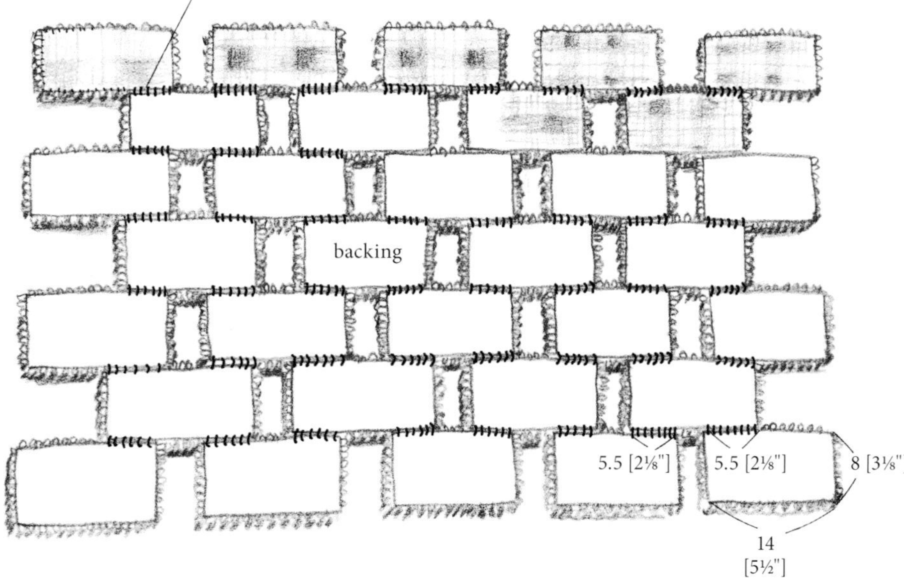

23 24

Dog & Cat Rag Dolls

⋯> page 34, 35 - Pattern Sheet C (brown)

23 Materials

Wool (plaid, for body) - 100 × 40 cm [39⅜" × 15¾"]
Polyester filling
Wool (assorted colors for wool strips for face)
Canvas or burlap (base) - 20 × 20 cm [7⅞" × 7⅞"]
Wool (lightweight)
  shirt - 50 × 50 cm [19¾" × 19¾"]
  collar - 3.5 × 22 cm [1⅜" × 8⅝"]
2 Buttons - 1.5 cm [⅝"]
2 Snaps
Wool (lightweight)
  overalls - 70 × 30 cm [27½" × 11¾"]
  shoulder straps - 10 × 20 cm [4" × 7⅞"]
Embroidery thread - white

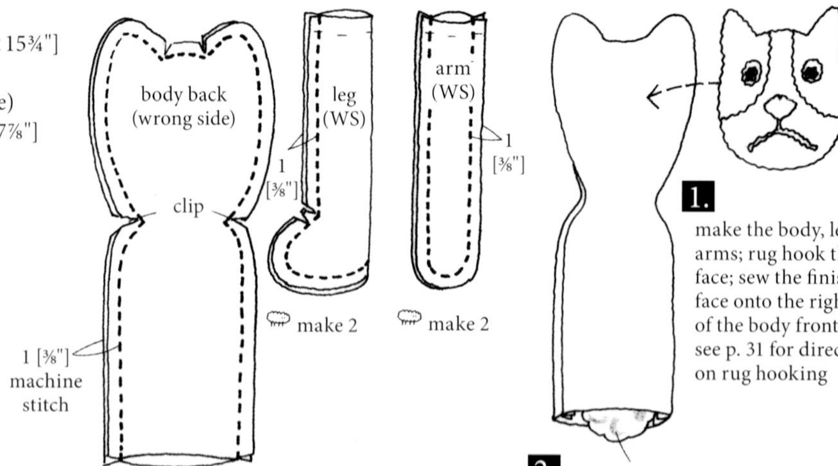

1. make the body, legs and arms; rug hook the dog face; sew the finished face onto the right side of the body front (face); see p. 31 for directions on rug hooking

2. fill with polyester filling

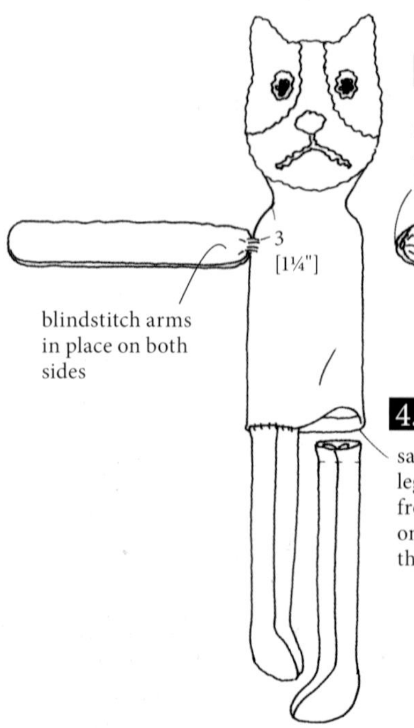

3. fill with polyester filling making sure the arms and legs are nicely rounded; baste the ends

4. sandwich the ends of the legs between the body front and back; blindstitch on both sides and close up the bottom of the body

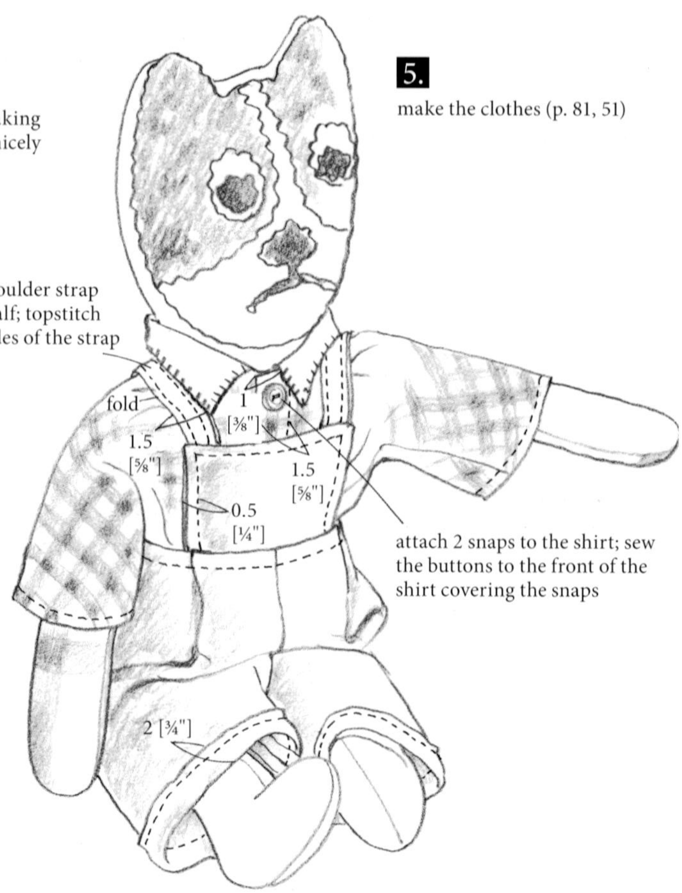

5. make the clothes (p. 81, 51)

5a making the overalls

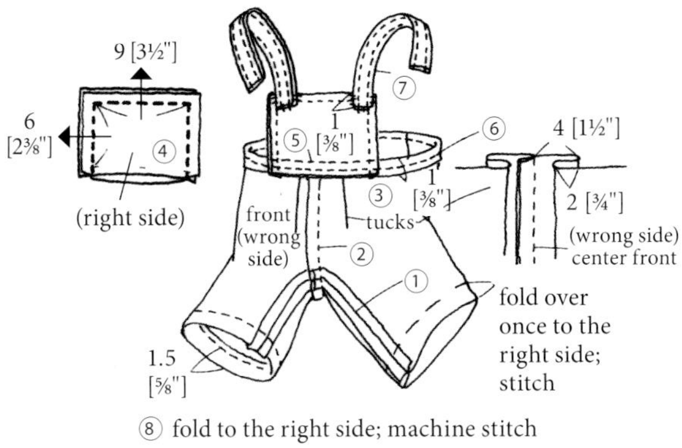

making the tail

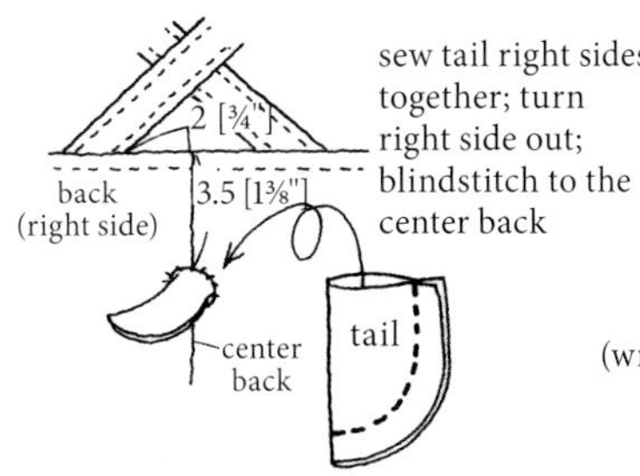

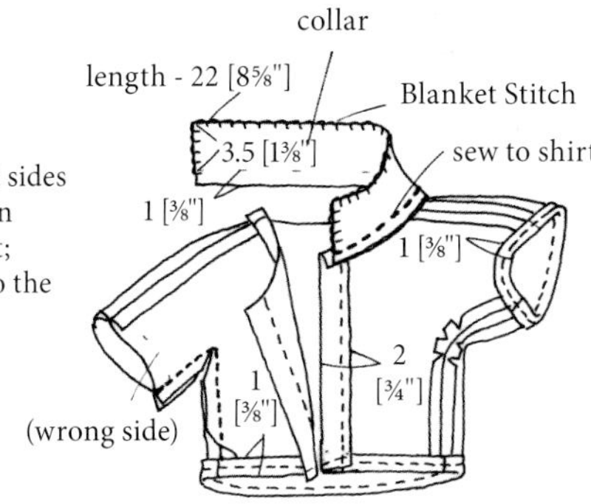

to finish the edges of the sleeves, front plackets and shirt bottom, fold under twice and machine stitch

cut out all pieces (see pattern sheet C and dimension given for the clothes illustrations); sew together the overalls and shirt; attach the tail to the back of the overalls

24 Materials

Wool (felt, for body) - 100 × 40 cm [39⅜" × 15¾"]
Wool (as needed for tail)
Polyester filling
Wool (assorted colors for wool strips for face)
Canvas or burlap (base) - 40 × 20 cm [15¾" × 7⅞"]
Wool (plaid, for coat) - 110 × 30 cm [43¼" × 11¾"]
2 Buttons - 1.8 cm [⅝"]
Wool (felt, for trousers) - 50 × 30 cm [19¾" × 11¾"]
Wool (scarf) - 6 × 45 cm [2⅜" × 17¾"]
Perle cotton - brown

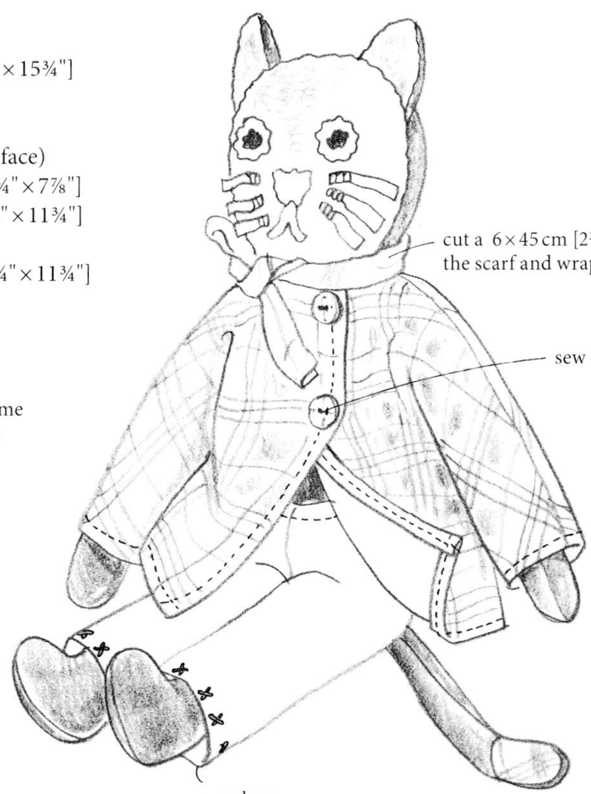

1. construct the cat doll following the same directions as for the dog, using the cat pattern pieces

2. cut out all pieces (see pattern sheet C and dimension given for the clothes illustrations); sew together the overalls and shirt; attach the tail to the back of the trousers

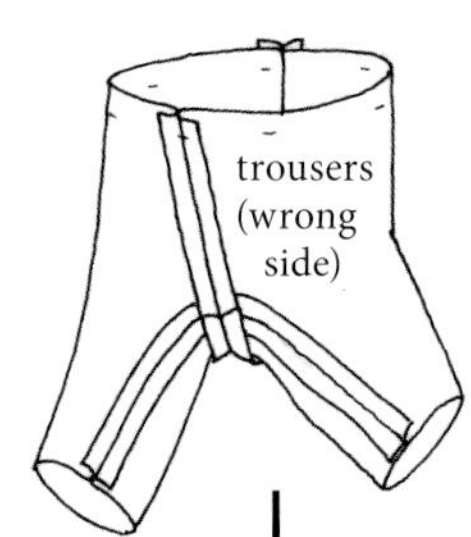

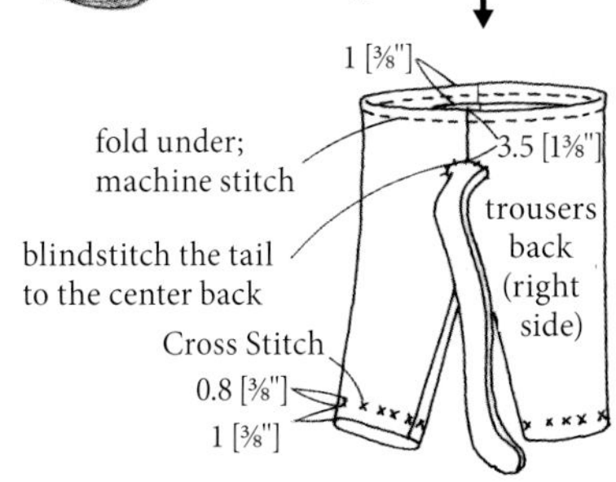

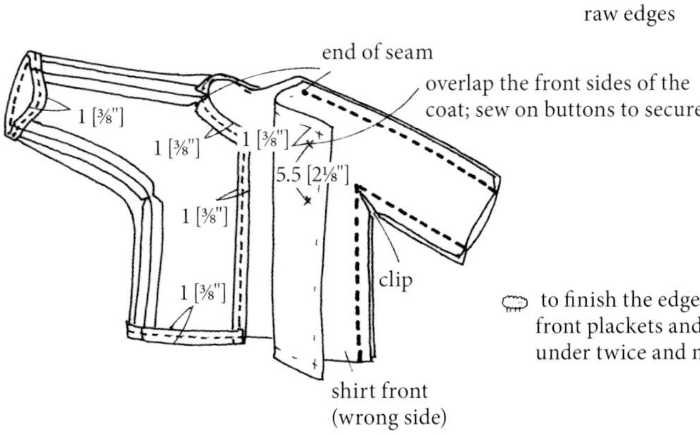

to finish the edges of the sleeves, front plackets and shirt bottom, fold under twice and machine stitch

25 **26**

Flag Cushions

⋯> page 37 - Pattern Sheet B (brown)

25 Materials

Wool (front, back, flange back) - 75 × 65 cm [29½"× 25⅜"]
Wool (flange front) - 50 × 20 cm [19¾"×7⅞"]
Assorted scraps of wool (stars and stripes)
1 Zipper (nylon) - 35 cm [13¾"]
Embroidery thread - black
Perle cotton - black
Cushion insert - 30 × 40 cm [11¾"× 15¾"]

1. use dimension diagram on p. 83, 1a; note that the back is 2 pieces with a zipper in between; cut out the pieces for the cushion front and back; cut out the stars and stripes; appliqué them to the front using the Blanket Stitch (2-strands)

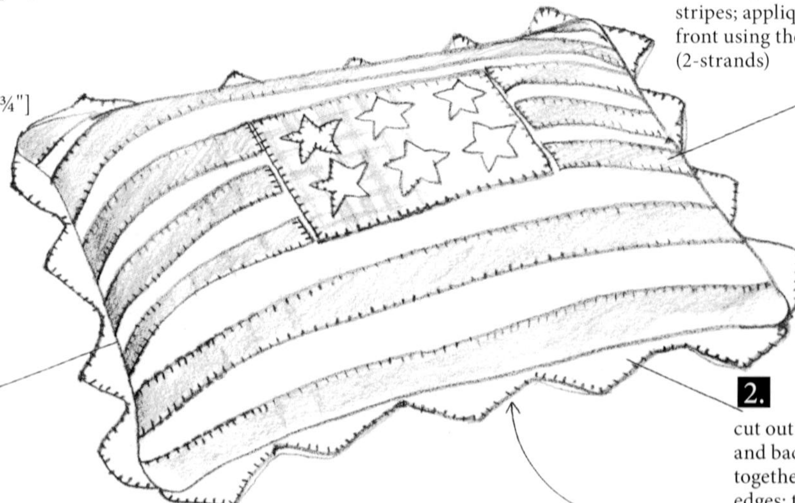

2. cut out the flange (front and back); with right sides together sew around the edges; turn right side out; Blanket Stitch around the edges with the perle cotton (see p. 83, 2a)

3. insert the zipper on the cushion back (p. 83, 3a)

4. with right sides together, sandwich the flange between the cushion front/back and sew around the edge (p. 83, 4a)

leave the zipper slightly unzipped so that you can turn the cushion cover right side out

5. finish the cushion (p. 83, 5a)

26 Materials

Wool (front, back, flange backing) - 70 × 50 cm [27½"× 19¾"]
Wool (flange front) - 40 × 20 cm [15¾"×7⅞"]
Assorted scraps of wool (stars and stripes)
1 Zipper (nylon) - 32 cm [12⅝"]
Embroidery thread - black
Perle cotton - black
Pillow insert - 25 × 35 cm [9¾"× 13¾"]

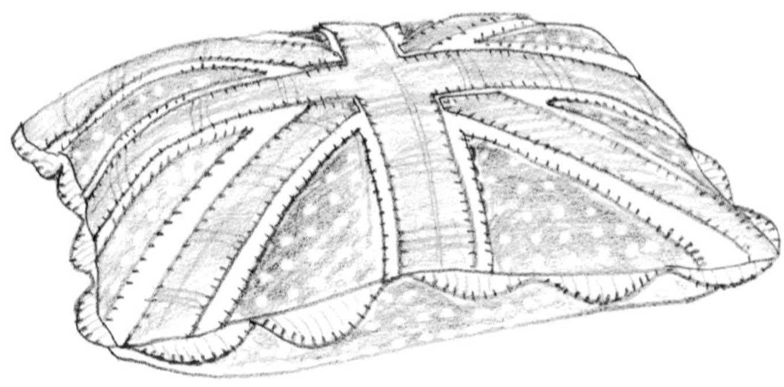

follow the same general directions, as above, to make this cushion

1a

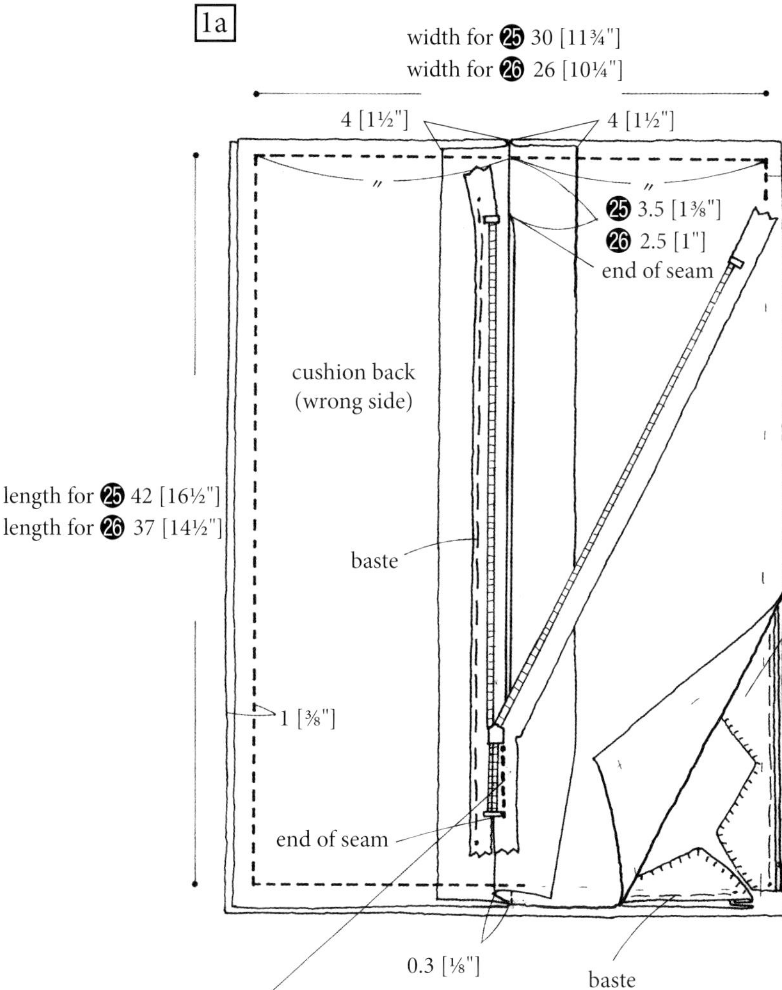

for the cusion back, cut out 2 pieces (size = L × W), depending on which cushion you are making; turn the inner (zipper) side under 4 [1½"]; sew the zipper on each side (3a below)

4a sew in the flange

sandwich between the front/back and baste in place aligning edges; sew around the entire edge of the cushion; turn right side out

leave the zipper slightly unzipped

2a make the flange

flange from cushion ㉕ shown

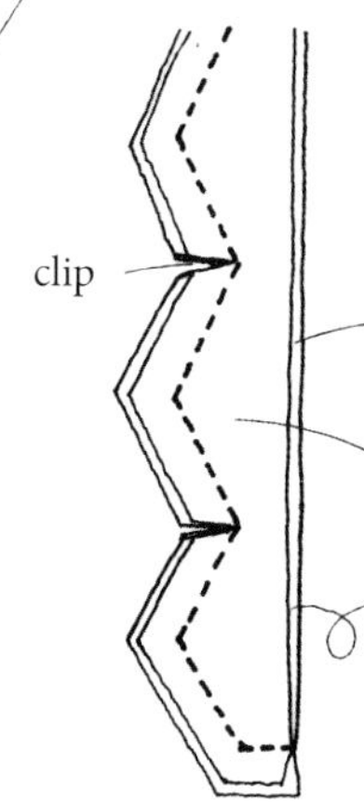

stitch with right sides together; clip into the "v"; turn right side out

3a insert the zipper

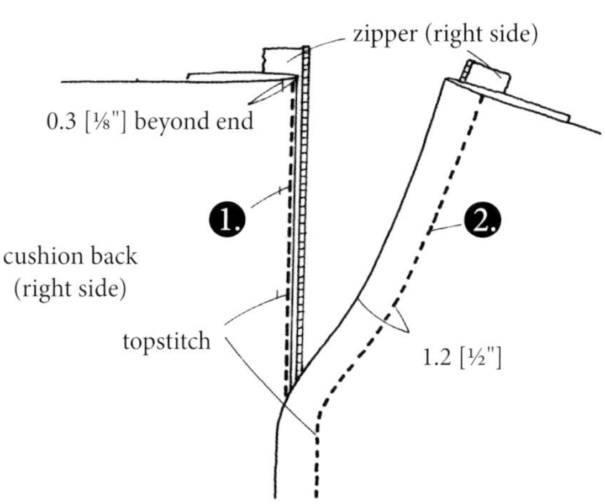

place zipper, right side up, with folded wool back against the teeth; topstitch in place; lay the second back piece on top of the zipper and stitch 1.2 [½"] away from the folded edge, catching the zipper tape to create the zipper opening in the back of the cusion cover

completed cushion
(back view)

flange from cushion ㉖ shown

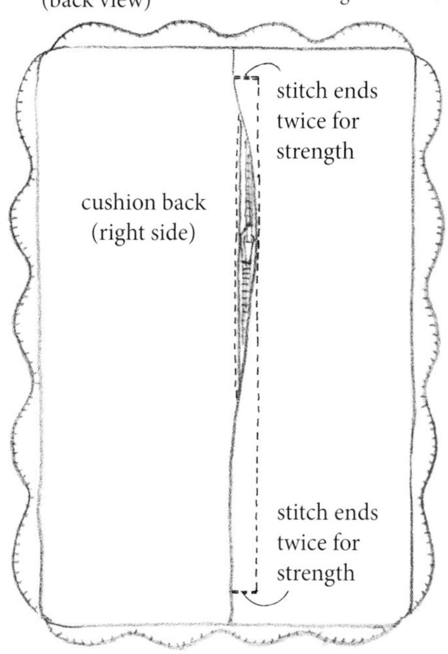

5a turn cushion cover right side out; stitch over the ends of the zipper, being careful not to sew through to the other side; insert cushion to finish

27

Seasonal Quilt

⋯> page 40 - Pattern Sheets C & D (green)

Materials

Wool
(center block, cut 1) - 45 × 45 cm [17¾" × 17¾"]
(surrounding blocks, cut 8) - 30 × 30 cm [11¾" × 11¾"]
(borders, cut 2 of each) - 15 × 120 cm [5⅞" × 47¼"]; 15 × 95 cm [5⅞" × 37⅜"]
(binding) - 4 × 500 cm [1½" × 197"] cut from a piece of 25 × 100 cm [9¾" × 39⅜"]
(backing) - 120 × 120 cm [47¼" × 47¼"]
Assorted scraps of wool (appliqué)
Wool (strips for rug-hooked vine) - enough for the project
Embroidery thread
Perle cotton

cut out each block; following the designs, appliqué, rug hook and embroider each block; sew the center block and surrounding blocks together; add borders; appliqué, rug hook and embroider the border; make the backing; with wrong sides together, lay the quilt top on top of the backing (no batting); stitch in the ditch to secure the top to the quilt backing; baste along the edges; bind the quilt to finish

binding the quilt

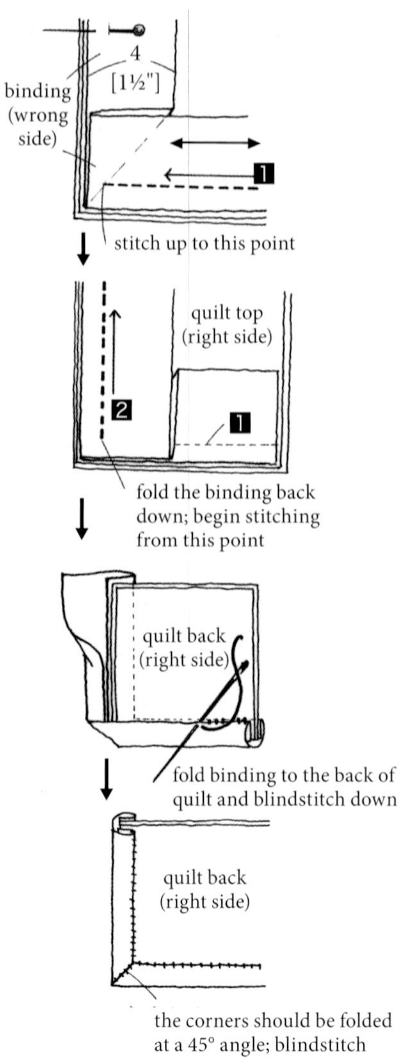

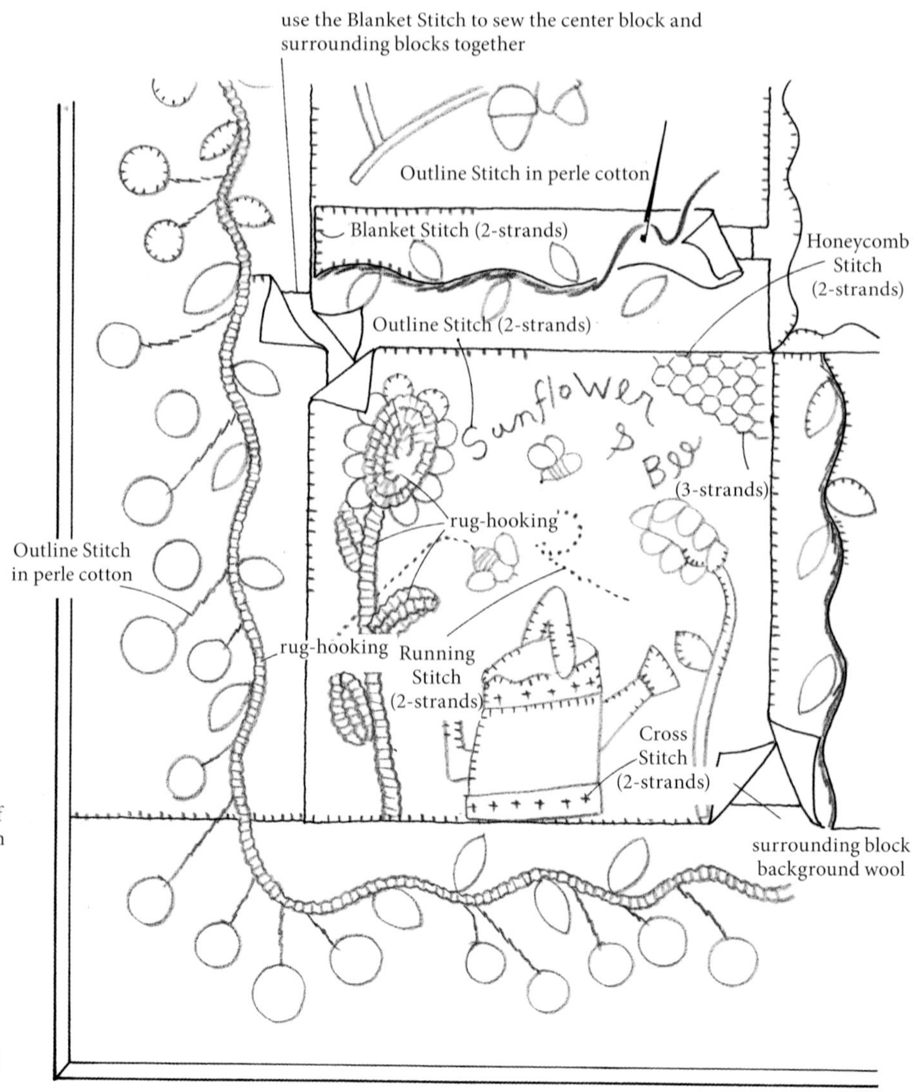

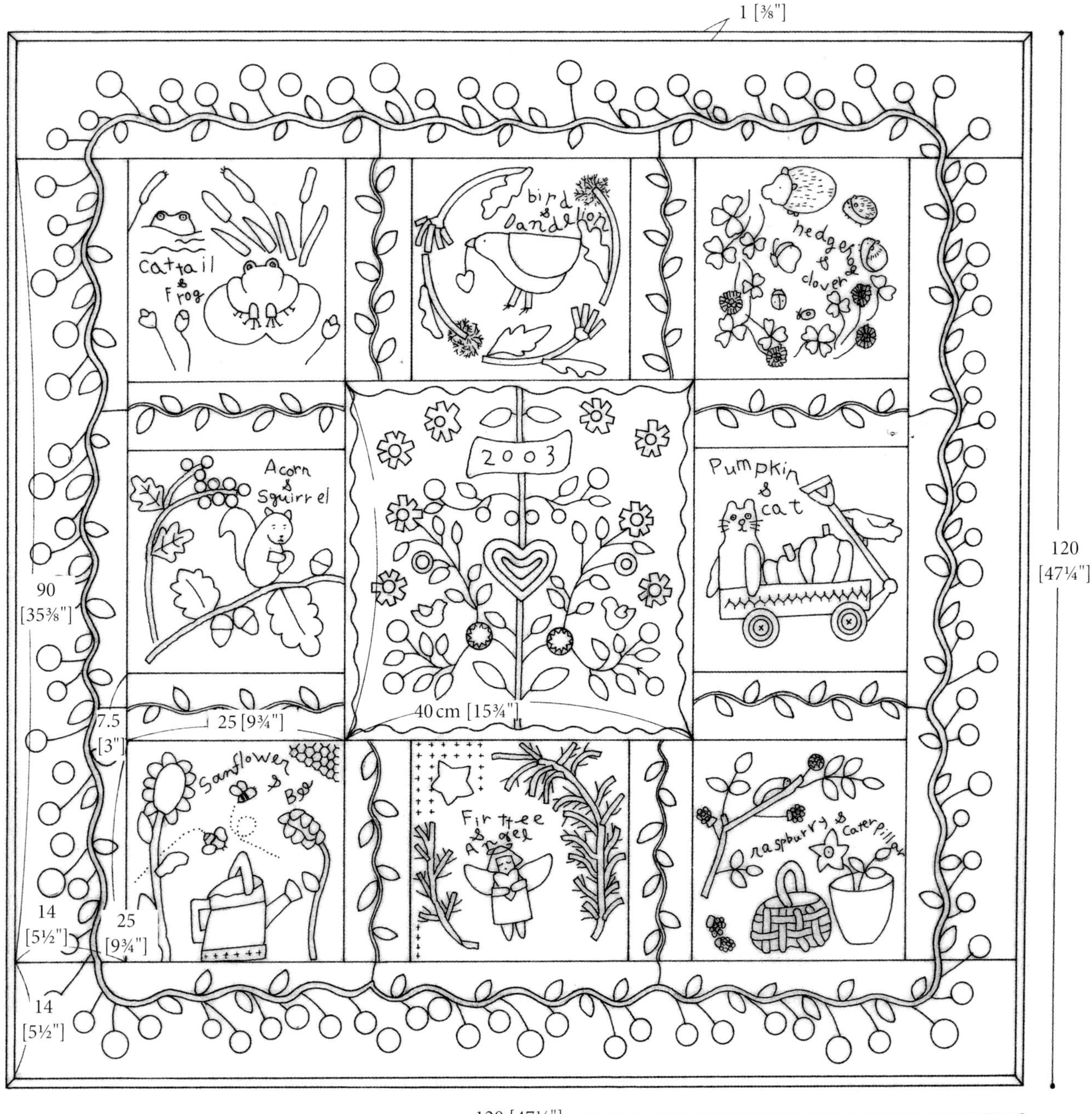
1 [3/8"]
120 [47¼"]
120 [47¼"]
90 [35⅜"]
7.5 [3"]
25 [9¾"]
40cm [15¾"]
25 [9¾"]
14 [5½"]
14 [5½"]
cattail & Frog
bird & Dandelion
hedgeg & clover
Acorn & Squirrel
2003
Pumpkin & cat
Sunflower & Bee
Fir tree & Angel
raspburry & caterpillar

28

Shoulder Bag

⇢ page 42 - Pattern Sheet C (brown)

Materials

Wool
(bag front, bag back, gusset) - 45 × 65 cm [17¾" × 25⅝"]
(pocket C) - 30 × 15 cm [11¾" × 5⅞"]
Assorted scraps of wool (piecing, appliqué)
Assorted scraps of wool (zipper tab, strap joint, pocket C closure band)
Lightweight wool
(lining for bag front, bag back, gusset, inner bias binding) - 45 × 110 cm [17¾" × 43¼"]
(lining for pockets A, B, C, pocket A facing) - 40 × 40 cm [15¾" × 15¾"]
Assorted scraps of wool (3 different for bias binding)
Fusible interfacing (heavyweight) - 30 × 60 cm [11¾" × 23⅝"]
Fusible interfacing (lightweight) - 15 × 60 cm [5⅞" × 23⅝"]
Batting (low loft, dense) - 2 × 10 cm [¾" × 4"]
1 Zipper (metal teeth) - 24 cm [9½"]
1 Zipper (metal teeth) - 17cm [6"]
Heavy woven cotton webbing (strap) - 4 × 85 cm [1½" × 33½"]
Hook and loop tape - 1.5 cm × 1.2 cm [⅝" × ½"]
Metal hardware (rectangle ring, double ring, 1 each) - width of the webbing (shoulder strap)
Decorative items (zipper pulls)
Narrow cord (zipper pull) - 10 cm [4"]
Embroidery thread - dk brown, brown

1. do the appliqué and piecing for the bag front and pockets

2. iron the fusible interfacing to the wrong side of the following pieces
- (heavyweight) - bag front lining, bag back lining, pocket lining
- (lightweight) - gusset lining

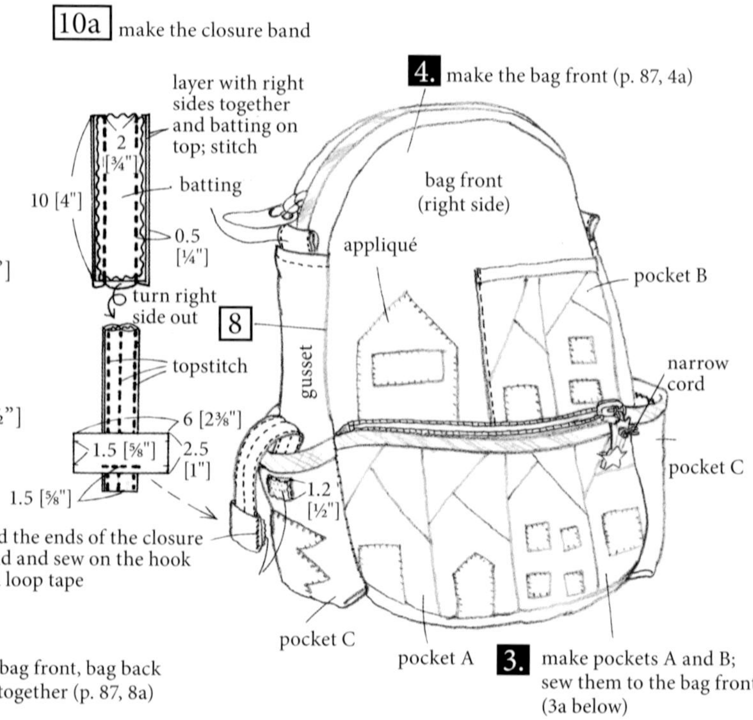

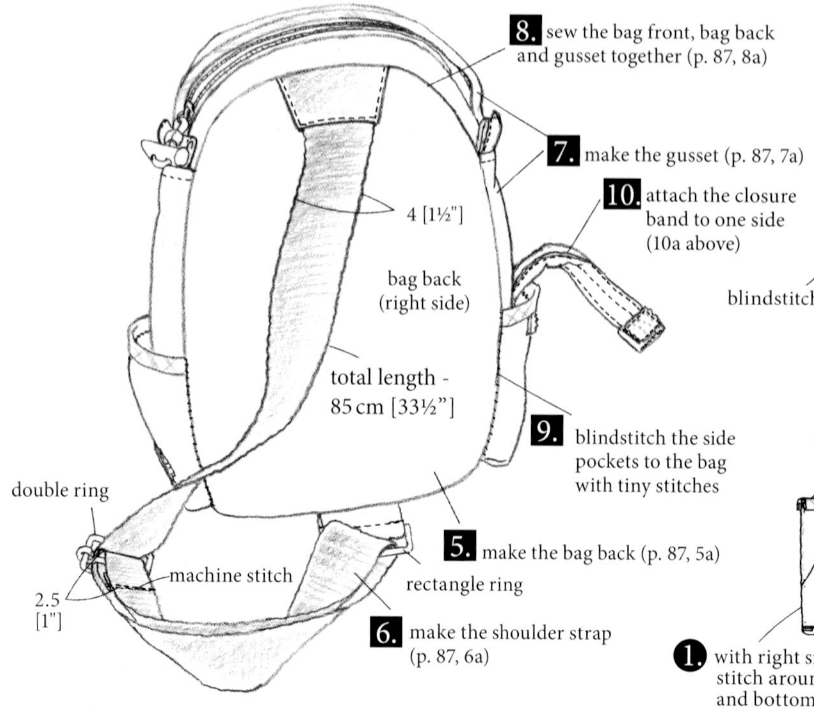

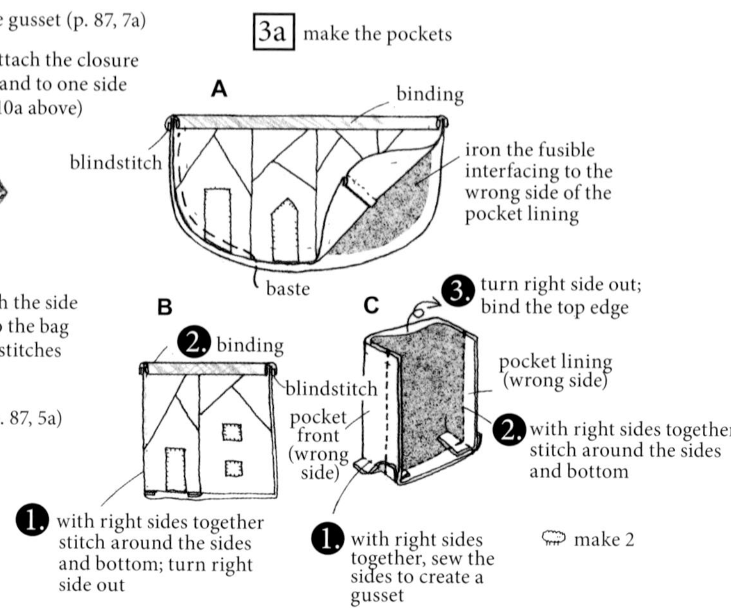

4a make the bag front

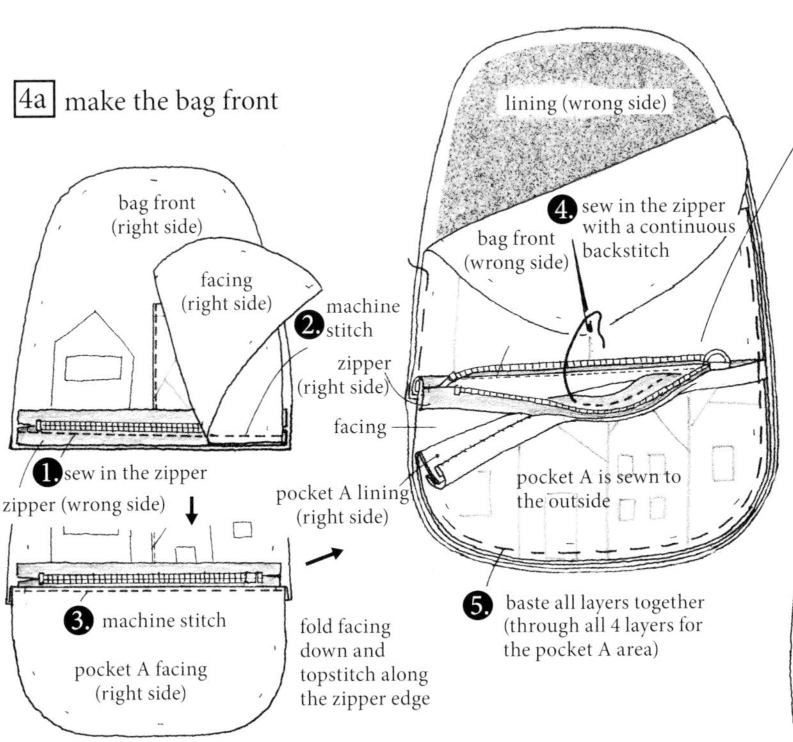

5a make the bag back

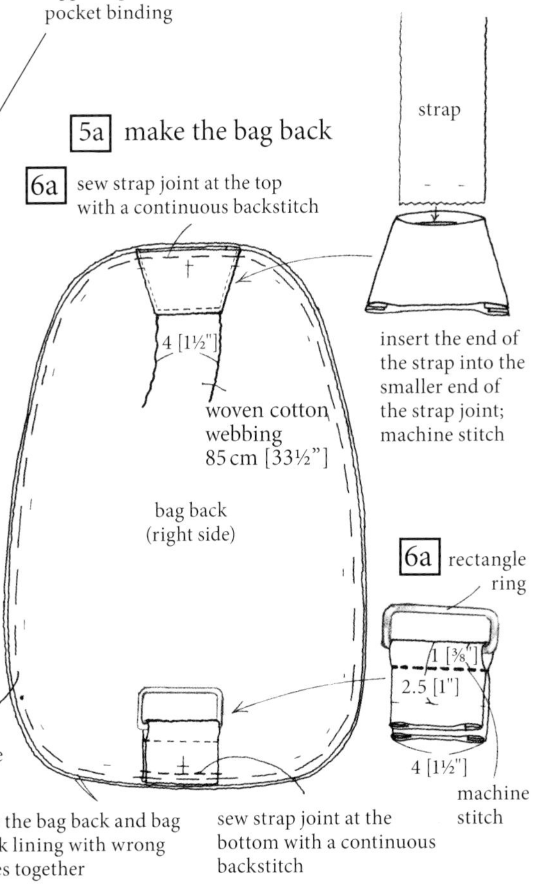

7a make the gusset zipper opening

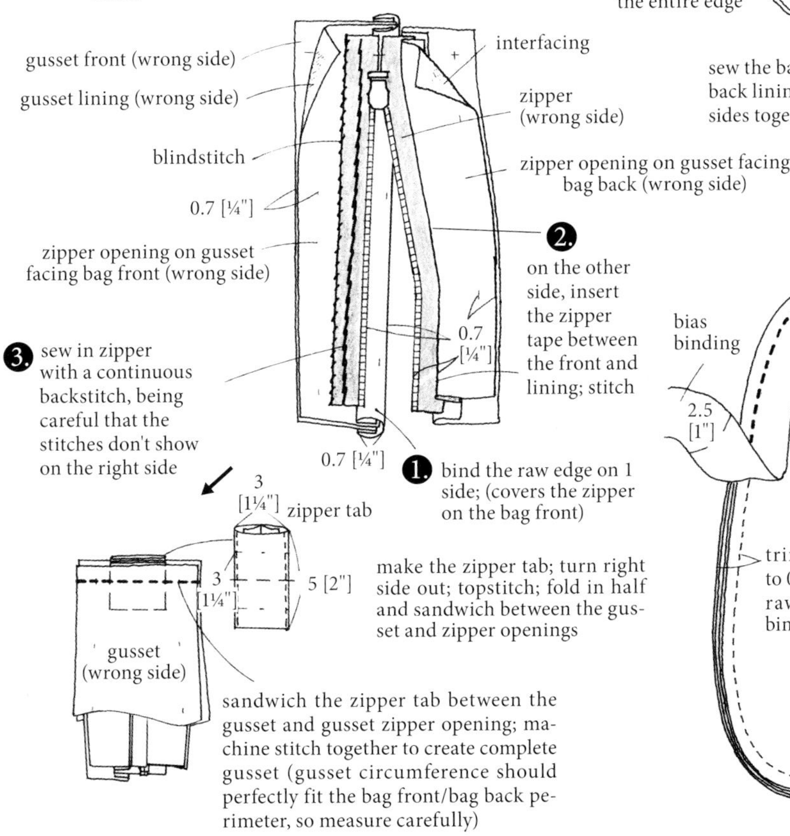

8a sew the bag together

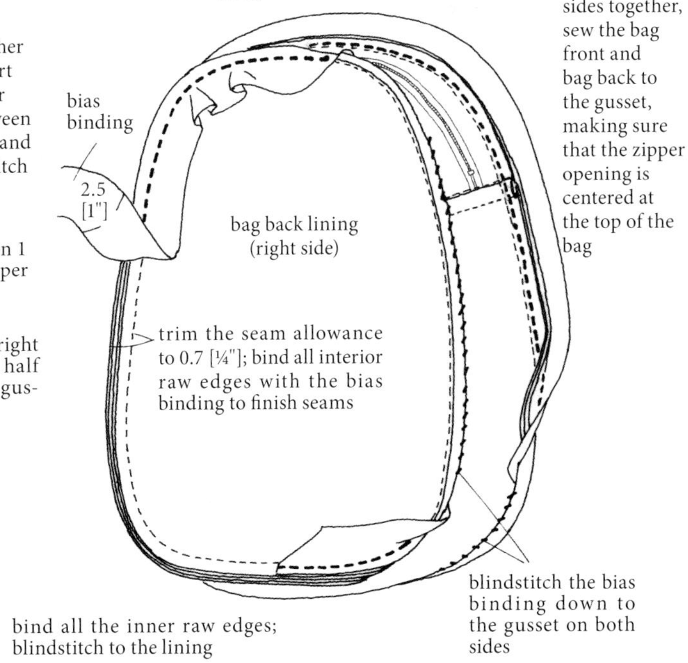

22

Turtle Pincushion

⋯⋯> page 33 - Pattern Sheet B (brown)

Materials

Wool (hands, feet, head, body backing) - 25 × 20 cm [9¾" × 7⅞"]
Assorted scraps of wool (piecing for the shell)
Homespun (tail, 3 pieces) - 1 × 6 cm [⅜" × 2⅜"]
2 Buttons - 1.3 cm [½"]
Polyester filling

1. using the pattern sheet as a guide, piece the turtle shell; use 3 [1¼"] finished Grandmother's Flower Garden template if desired

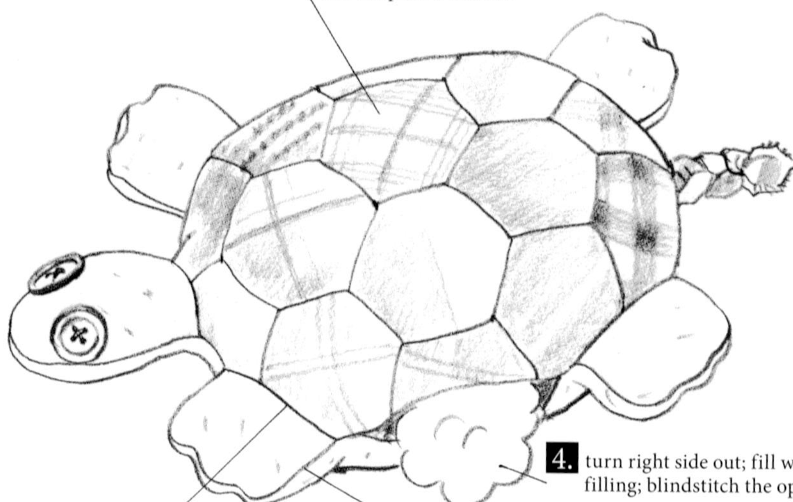

4. turn right side out; fill with polyester filling; blindstitch the opening closed

3. cut out the bottom backing of the turtle; with right sides together and matching edges, pin the top and bottom of the turtle body together; stitch around the edge, leaving an opening for turning (3a below)

2. with right sides together, sew the head, hands and feet to the shell at the appropriate areas

3a sew the turtle together

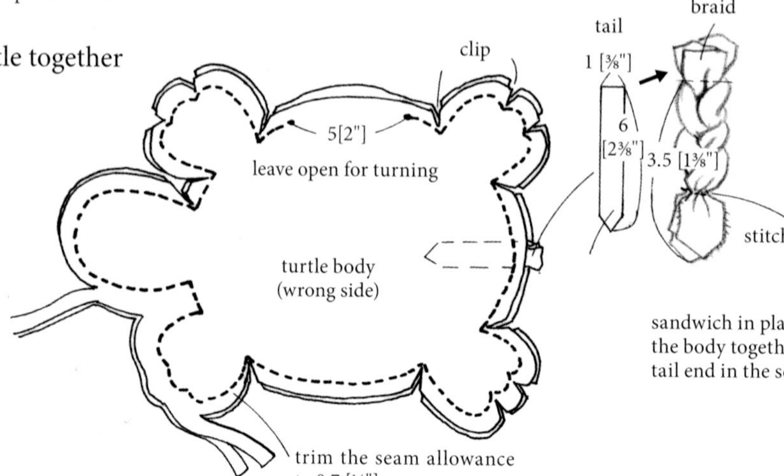

make the tail by cutting 3 pieces of homespun fabric; cut to size; braid

sandwich in place before sewing the body together, catching the tail end in the seam

29

Mini Peanut Pouch

⋯➢ page 43 - Pattern Sheet D (brown)

Materials

Wool (pouch front) - 50 × 35 cm [19¾" × 13¾"]
Lightweight wool (lining) - 50 × 35 cm [19¾" × 13¾"]
Wool (appliqué) - 30 × 20 cm [11¾" × 7⅞"]
Flannel - 50 × 35 cm [19¾" × 13¾"]
1 Zipper - 19 cm [7½"]
Narrow cord (zipper pull) - 10 cm [4"]
1 Zipper pull decoration
Braided cotton cord (strap) - 0.6 × 25 cm [¼" × 9¾"]
1 Metal grommet - 1 cm [⅜"]
Perle cotton - beige
Polyester filling (strap decoration)

2a making each peanut section

with right sides together lay the pouch front and pouch lining on top of the flannel; stitch around the edges as shown; trim the flannel 0.1 [1/16"] from the stitching

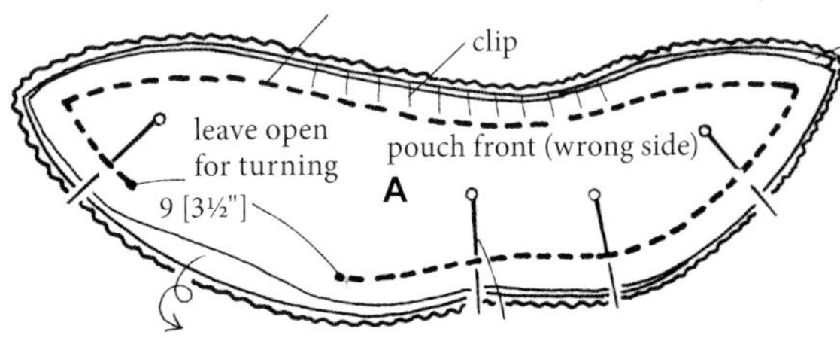

turn right side out; blindstitch closed

align edges and markings; stitch

5. bringing A and A' together, sew the zipper to each side using a continuous backstitch from the lining side so the stitches don't show through to the front

7. finish the top of the pouch; attach the strap (7a below)

8. finish the bottom of the pouch (8a below)

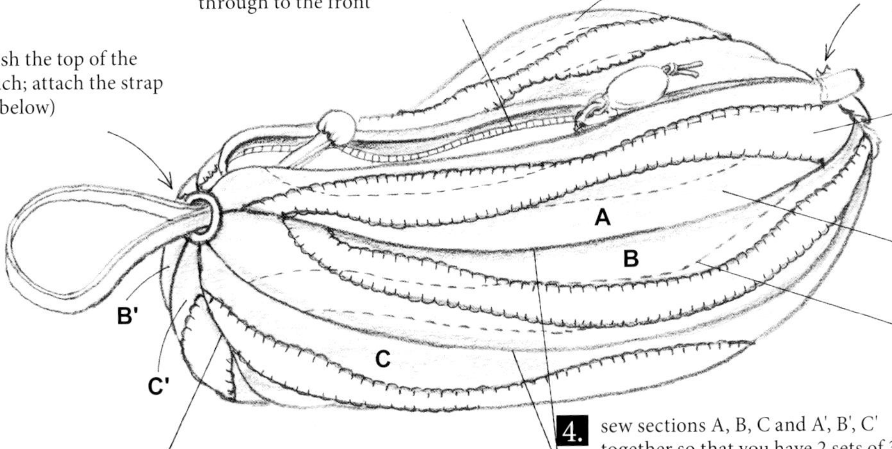

1. cut out the 6 sections for the pouch front (A, B, C and A', B', C'); stitch the appliqués to each of the pouch front sections using the perle cotton and a Blanket Stitch

2. cut out the 6 linings and flannel; make each of the peanut sections (A, B, C, A', B', C') (2a above)

3. machine quilt each section as desired

4. sew sections A, B, C and A', B', C' together so that you have 2 sets of 3 sections each (2 halves of the pouch)

6. leaving the zipper slightly open for turning, bring C and C' together and blindstitch together

to sew the pouch together, align each of the sections; pin carefully and blindstitch with tiny stitches

8a finishing the bottom

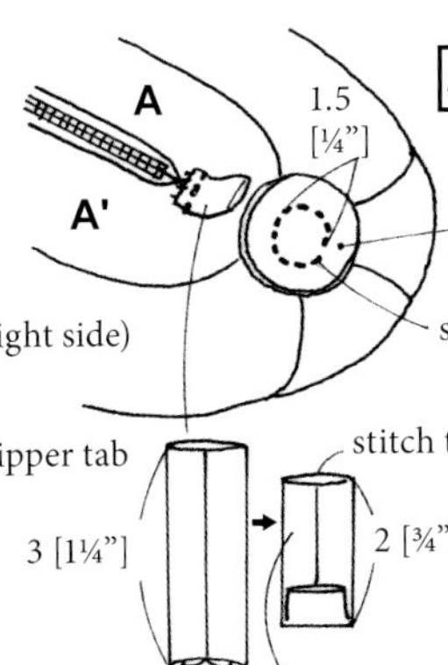

cut 2 wool discs, 3 [1¼"] in diameter

stack and stitch to the center bottom

stitch to base of zipper

fold up and blindstitch

make a zipper tab and stitch on the outside just below the end of the zipper stop

7a attaching the strap

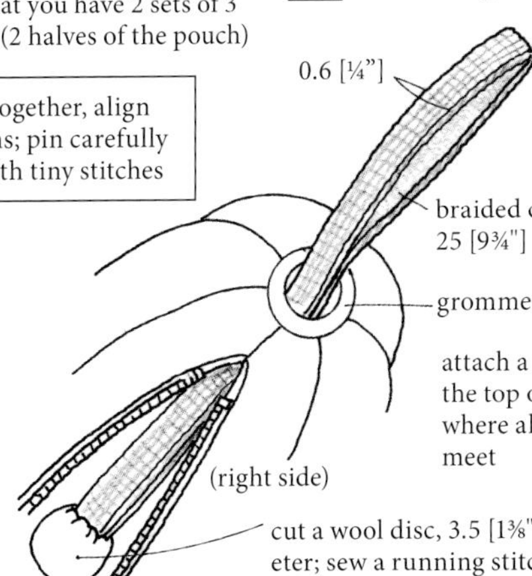

attach a grommet to the top of the peanut where all 6 sections meet

cut a wool disc, 3.5 [1⅜"] in diameter; sew a running stitch around the edge; fill with a tiny bit of stuffing; pull threads up to create a ball; stitch to the end of the strap

30

Childhood Memories Quilt

→ page 44 - Pattern Sheets C & D (green)

Materials

Wool
(quilt top background) - 140 × 150 cm [55⅛" × 59"]
(borders) - 40 × 160 cm [15¾" × 63"]
Wool
(lightweight for backing, sleeve) -110 × 270 cm [43¼" × 106¼"]
Assorted fat quarters and scraps of wool (for appliquéd blocks)
Embroidery thread - white, assorted shades of brown
Perle cotton - white, assorted shades of brown

cut out each block; following the designs, appliqué, rug hook and embroider each block; sew the center block and surrounding blocks together; add borders; quilt around each block to secure the quilt top to the backing (no batting); Blanket Stitch around the border edges instead of using binding; make and attach the sleeve for hanging (if desired)

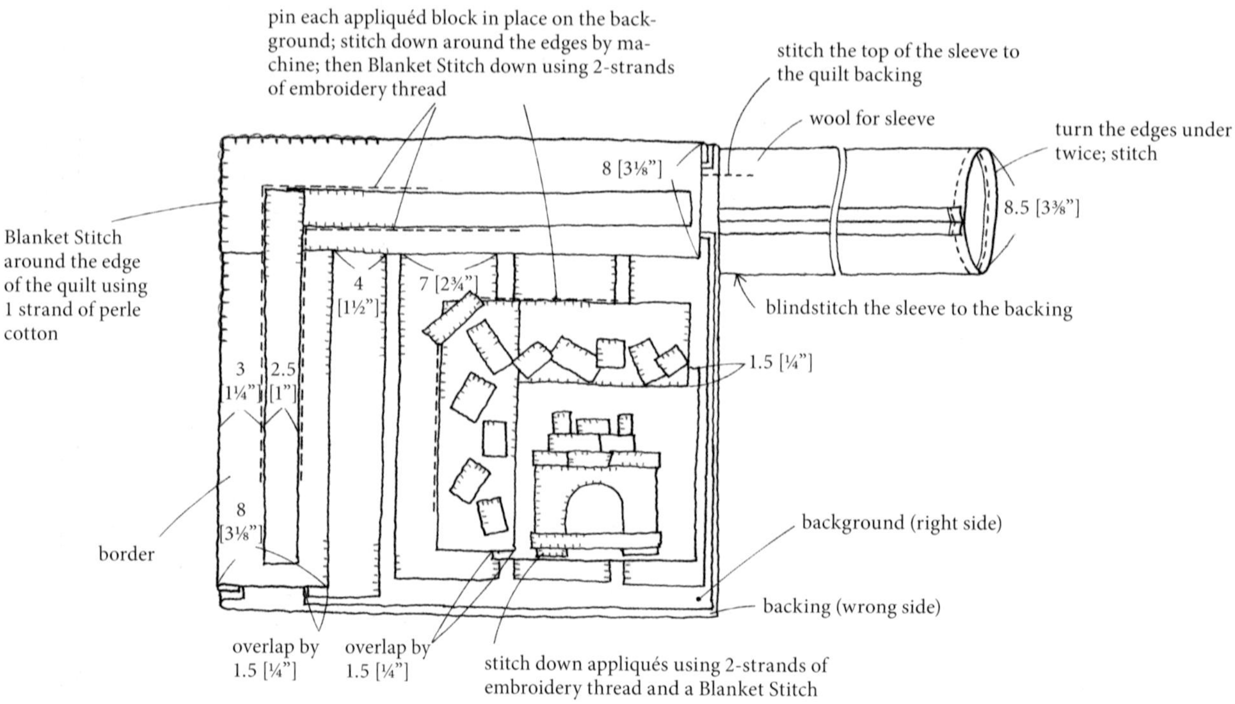

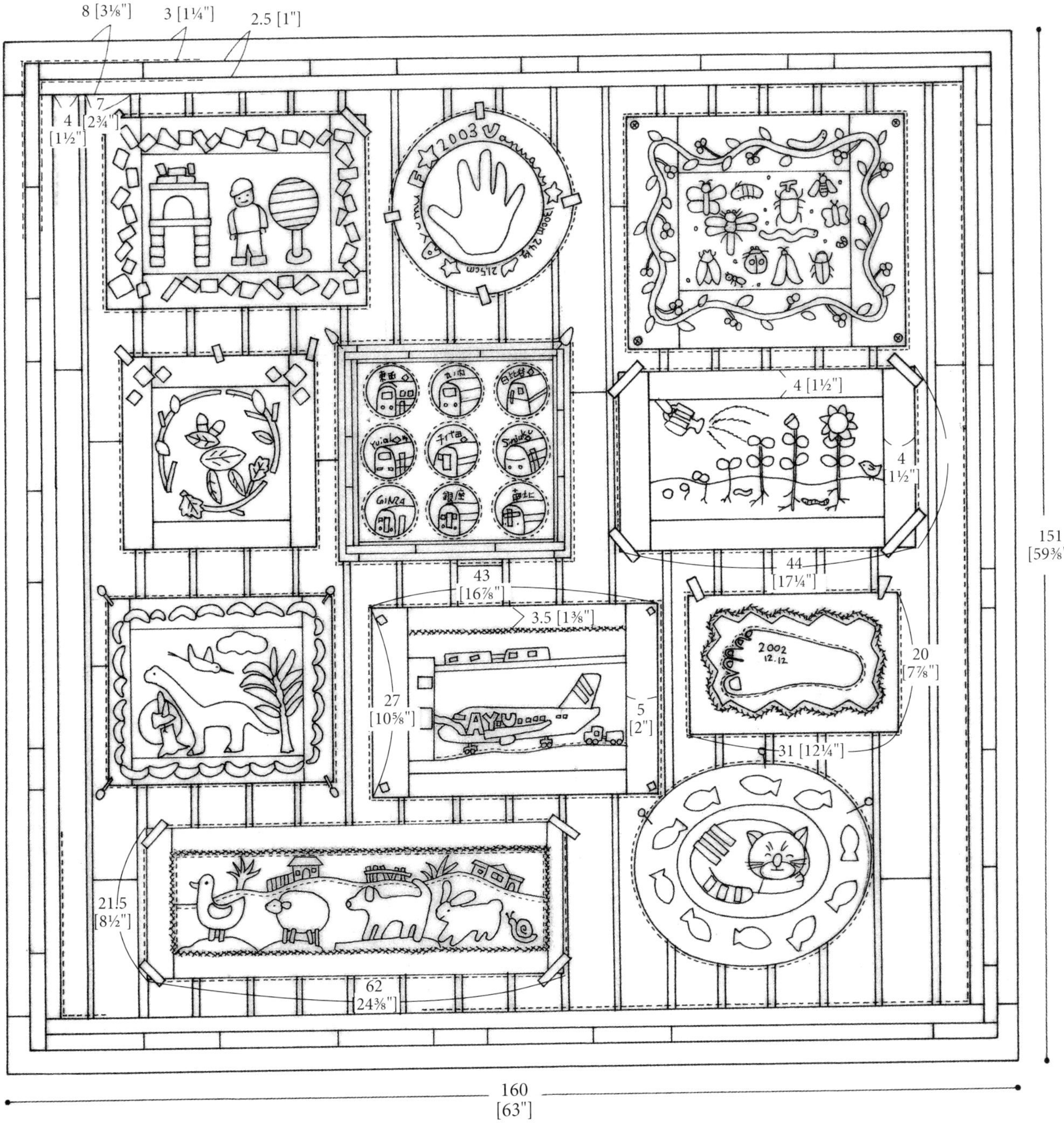
8 [3⅛"]
3 [1¼"]
2.5 [1"]
7 [2¾"]
4 [1½"]
4 [1½"]
4 [1½"]
44 [17¼"]
43 [16⅞"]
3.5 [1⅜"]
20 [7⅞"]
27 [10⅝"]
5 [2"]
31 [12¼"]
21.5 [8½"]
62 [24⅜"]
151 [59⅜"]
160 [63"]

31

Autumn Foliage Placemat

page 46 - Pattern Sheet D (brown)

Materials

Wool
(top) - 35 × 25 cm [13¾" × 9¾"]
(backing) - 35 × 25 cm [13¾" × 9¾"]
(border, follow pattern sheet) - 10 × 60 cm [4" × 23⅝"]
Wool
(lightweight for vine, cut on bias) - 35 × 35 cm [13¾" × 13¾"]
Assorted scraps of wool (for appliqués)
Embroidery thread - dk brown, green, moss green

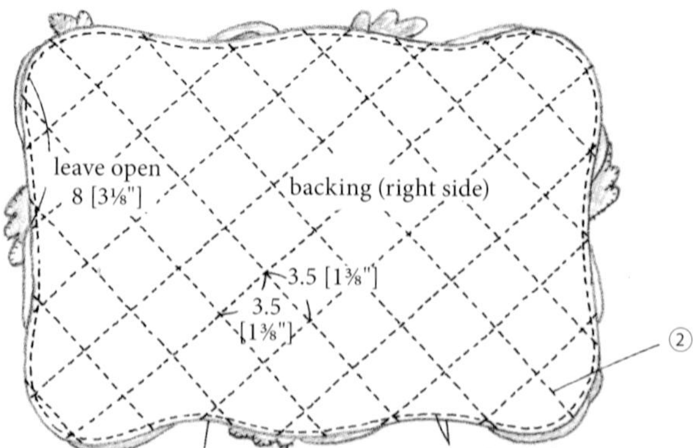

1. with right sides together sew the top and backing together; turn right side out; blindstitch opening closed; topstitch around edge

2. machine quilt in a 3.5 [1⅜"] grid using 2-strand embroidery weight thread for the top thread (p. 51, #17)

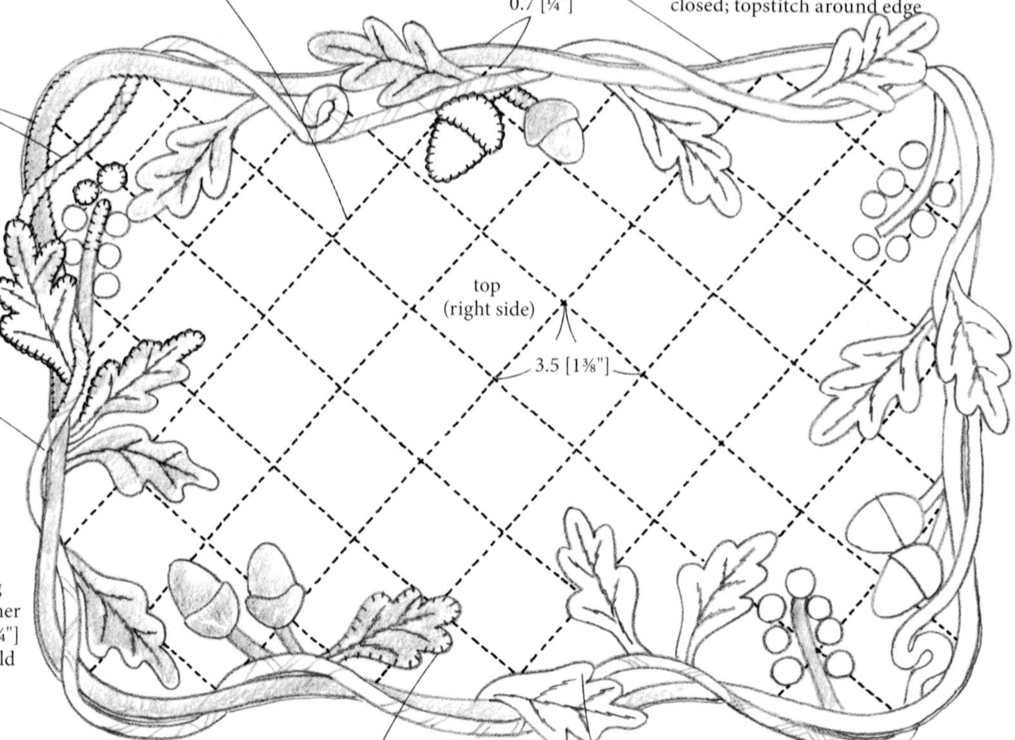

3. appliqué the leaves, acorns and berries to the placemat using a Blanket Stitch (2-strands)

make sure not to completely stitch down the appliqués that will overlap the border or vines; these will be stitched down at the very end

4. make the fabric tubes for the vines out of the bias binding

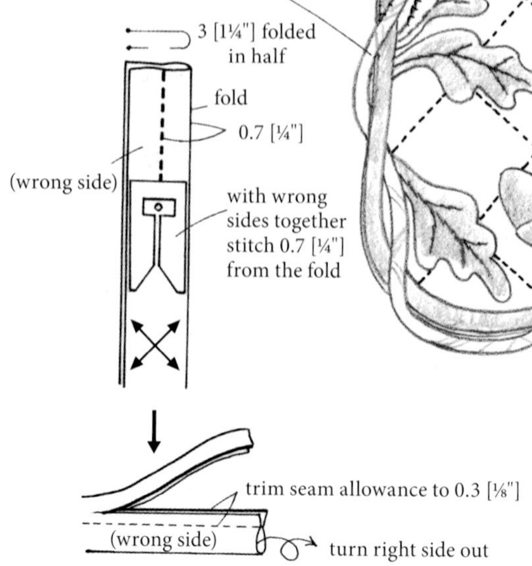

pin the vines in place, but don't appliqué down until after step 5

5. cut strips 0.7 [¼"] wide for the border; use the pattern sheet to follow curves; joined ends should be hidden under appliquéd vines or leaves; pin in place; when all the appliqués are where you want them, stitch down to the top of the placemat on both inner and outer edges

32 **33**

Teddy Bears

⋯> page 47 - Pattern Sheet D (brown)

Materials

Wool (head, body, arms, legs) - 60 × 60 cm [23⅝" × 23⅝"]
Small scraps of wool (paw and foot pads)
2 Buttons (eyes) - 1.3 cm [½"]
Polyester filling
Plastic pellets
Embroidery thread - black
Perle cotton - black

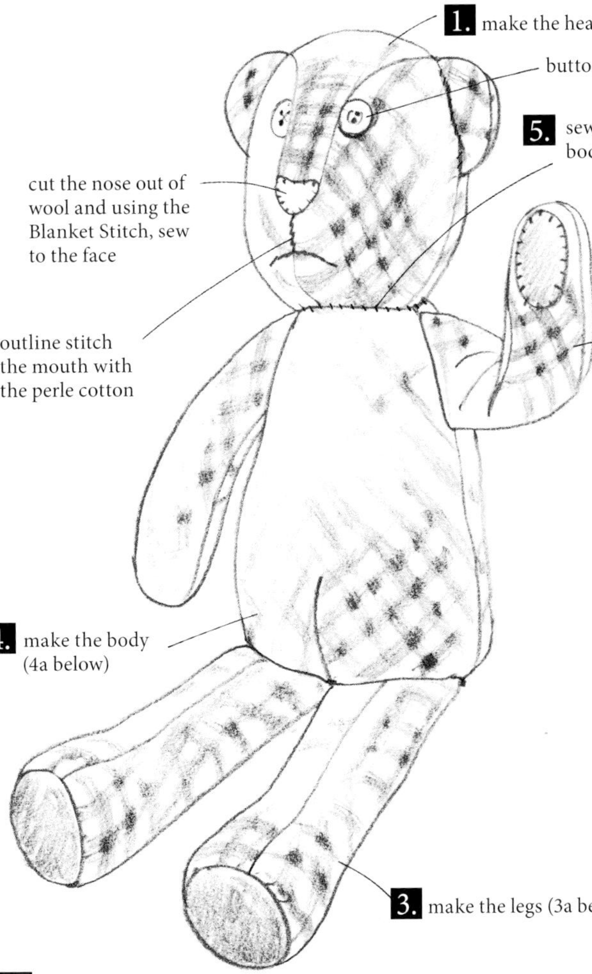

1a sewing the head together

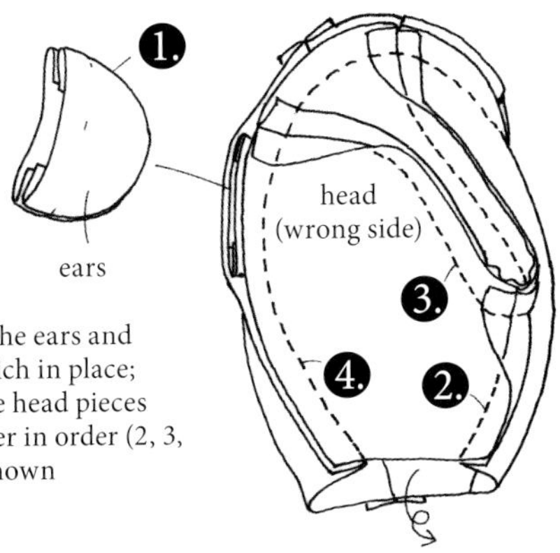

make the ears and sandwich in place; sew the head pieces together in order (2, 3, 4) as shown

5. turn right side out; stuff firmly with the polyester filling

2a make the arms

with right sides together, sew arm pieces together to make 2 arms; turn right side out; stuff bottom ⅓ of the arms with plastic pellets and top with polyester filling

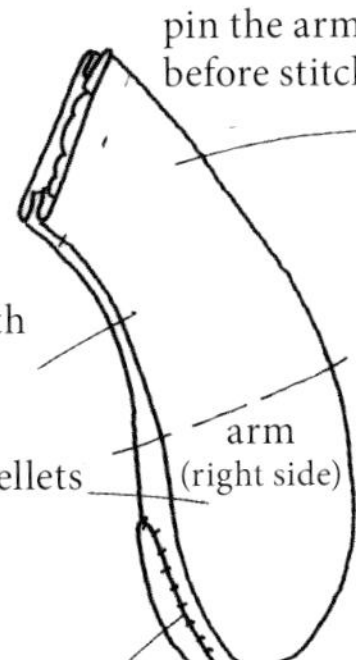

4a make the body

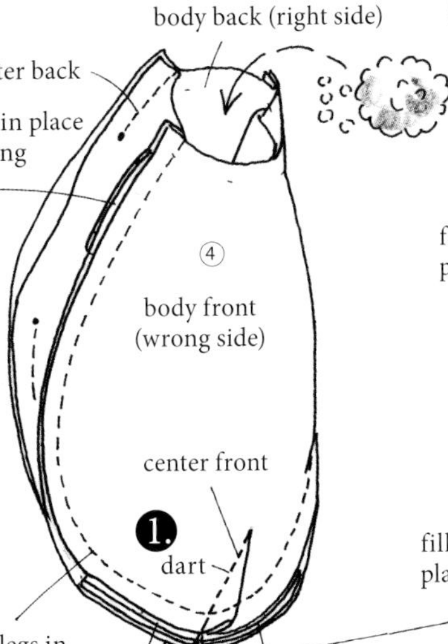

4. turn right side out; fill the bottom ⅓ of the body with plastic pellets; fill to the top with polyester filling

3. sandwich the filled arms and legs in between the body pieces (right sides together); machine stitch

3a make the legs

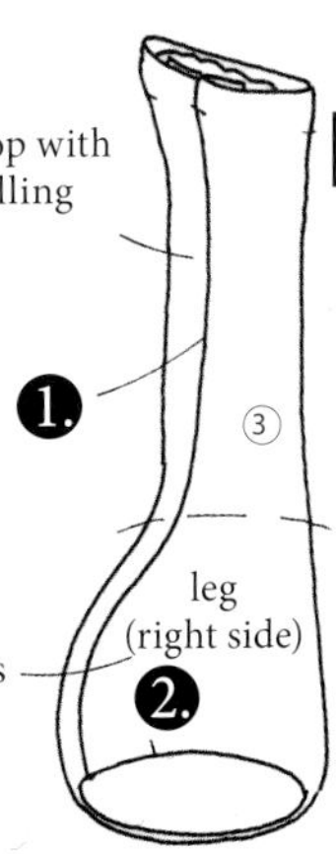

34

Sewing Notions Wall Quilt

⇢ page 48 - Pattern Sheets C & D (brown)

Materials

Assorted fat quarters and scraps of wool, homespun fabrics (piecing and appliqué)
Wool (backing, sleeve) - 120 × 160 cm [47¼" x 63"]
Thin-wale corduroy (bias binding) - 4 × 500 cm [1½" x 197"] cut from a piece of 80×80cm [31½" x 31½"]
Batting - 120 × 140 cm [47¼" x 55⅛"]
6 Buttons (embellishments) - 1.3 ~ 1.5 cm [½"~⅝"]
Embroidery thread - black, brown, orange, grey, beige, blue, green
Perle cotton - black, grey

cut out 42 squares; appliqué and embroider with the notions designs; make the blocks with half square triangles on each point for a total of 42 blocks; make the backing; layer the backing and quilt top, wrong sides together with the batting in between, baste; quilt and bind to finish

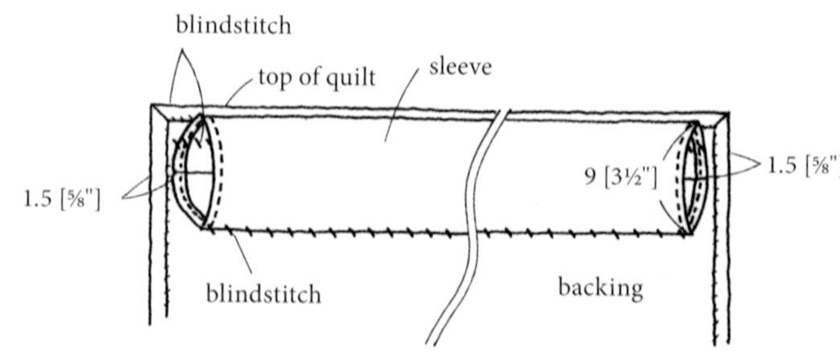

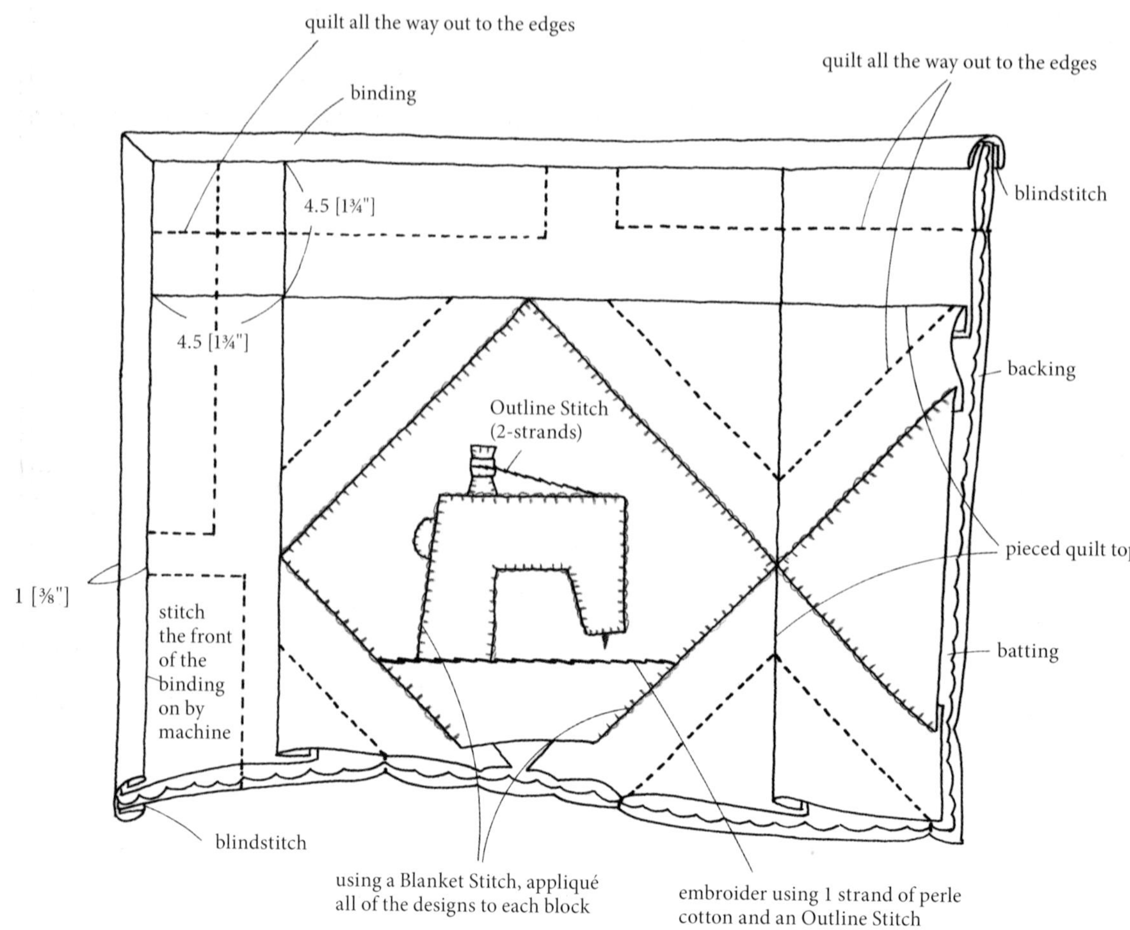

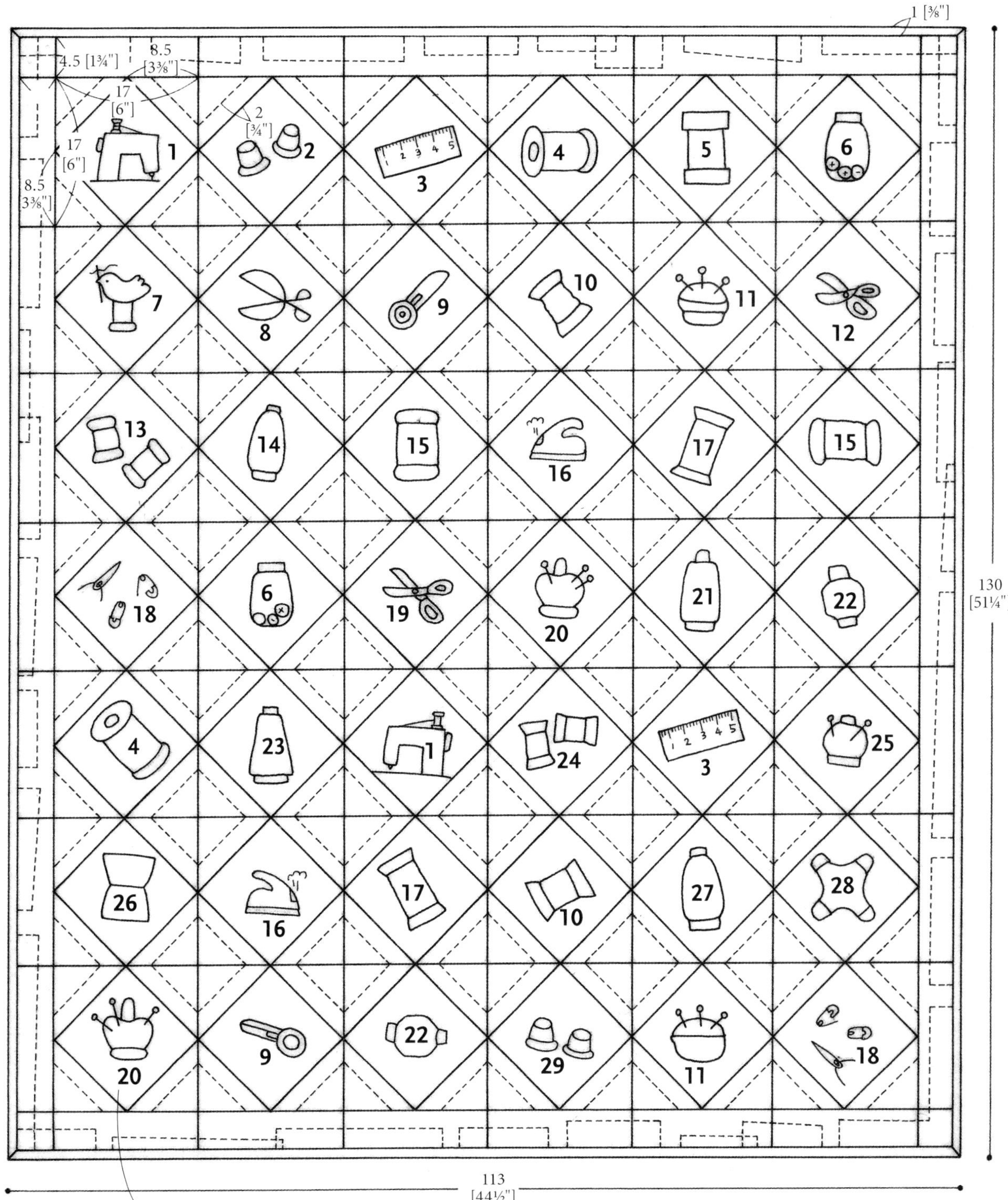

all of the appliqué designs (actual size) can be found on pattern sheets C and D

Yoko Saito, a prominent quilt artist in Japan, is known for her unique color sense and designs. She teaches extensively. Her work and teaching have been showcased on television in addition to numerous publications. Her creative works include books, block-of-the-month series in magazines and other designs sold in her shop and school, Quilt Party, which she owns and runs. Additionally, she teaches at the NHK Culture Center, acts as the educational chief at Nihon Vogue Correspondence School and is an active member of Needlework Japan.

Quilt Party Co., Ltd.
Active Ichikawa 2-3F
1-23-2, Ichikawa, Ichikawa-shi,
Chiba-Ken, Japan 272-034

http://www.quilt.co.jp (Japanese)
http://shop.quilt.co.jp/en/index.htm (English)

Embroidery Floss/Thread: LECIEN CO. Art Hobby Division Cosmo Dept.
7F Yotsubashi Grand Square
1-28-3 Shinmachi Nishi-ku
Osaka, Japan 550-0013

Production Assistants: Satomi Funamoto, Kazuko Yamada, Hiromi Yokota, Kazuko Matsumoto, Yoneko Kusumoto

Original Title: Saito Yoko no Woolwork
Author: Yoko Saito

First Edition: Originally published in Japan in 2004

Published by: EDUCATIONAL FOUNDATION BUNKA GAKUEN
BUNKA PUBLISHING BUREAU
3-22-1 Yoyogi, Shibuya-Ku
Tokyo, Japan 151-8524
http://www.books.bunka.ac.jp

Staff
Book Design: Kayoko Wakayama, Miki Wakayama, L'espace
Photography: Yoshikatsu Watanabe
Illustrations: Shikanoroom
Editor: Norie Hirai (BUNKA PUBLISHISHING BUREAU)
Publisher: Sunao Onuma

Translation: ©2013 Stitch Publications, LLC
English Translation Rights: arranged with Stitch Publications, LLC through Tuttle-Mori Agency, Inc.
Published by: Stitch Publications, LLC
P.O. Box 16694
Seattle, WA 98116
http://www.stitchpublications.com
Printed & Bound: KHL Printing, Singapore
ISBN: 978-0-9859746-3-3
PCN: Library of Congress Control Number: 2013940275

This English edition is published by arrangement with the Educational Foundation Bunka Gakuen Bunka Publishing Bureau (Tokyo) and in care of Tuttle-Mori Agency, Inc. (Tokyo).